Prophecy's Edge

by Michelle LaVigne-Wedel
and
Paul Wedel

Sweetgrass Press
P.O. Box 1862
Merrimack, NH

Library of Congress Card Number: 00-191445
Michelle LaVigne-Wedel. 1962-
Paul Wedel. 1959-

Prophecy's Edge / Michelle LaVigne-Wedel, Paul Wedel

ISBN 0-9702630-0-7

COVER DESIGN: The Electric Wigwam

Printed in the United States of America

Address all inquiries:
Sweetgrass Press
P.O. Box 1862
Merrimack, NH 03054-1862
www.sweetgrasspress.com

Foreword

Some people have unusual lives. Some people's are more so than others. My life, well, my life has been more unusual than even I could imagine it could be. I'm sure I'm not wrong to say the same applies to my husband, Paul.

The book you hold in your hands is not just a telling of our strange lives and the unusual way we found each other as we had promised we would when we were children running around ET space craft playing Batman and Robin, but also of the incredible things that began to happen to us when we did find each other.

We both knew the year of 1998 was going to be a special year as we stood in the sub-zero weather, on New Years day, watching the last bits of our ceremonial thank you fire burn out.   Still, we had no idea that afternoon that not only a new year had begun for the calendar, but also a new life had begun for Paul and me. It would be a life full of magic and wonder. A life where things I only thought were fairy tales or superstitions would prove to be true. A life where "we create our own reality" would become our theme song and war cry. A life where not only is anything possible but where the improbable, and I dare say the impossible, happens.

Before we decided to write all this down and share it with you we both thought long and hard about what we were doing. Paul is a quiet professional computer person who has no outward connections to anything unusual. I have been in the public eye for some time and many people in the UFO field find me on the "fringe". I knew what I had to say was bound to cause more raised eyebrows. Though to my own credit I have to mention that many of the things I spoke about in my first book, *The Alien Abduction Survival Guide* such as ET run schools and balls that convey knowledge when held, have become common knowledge and well spoken about in the UFO genre media since then.

Paul and I talked about the possibility that we were jeopardizing our security and jobs. We also thought about how this could alienate his family. Then we talked about the power of our experiences, the truths we have uncovered and the people out there just like us who are meeting their true soul mates and do not know what to do about it. Then we realized that the community was more important than any individual. Our struggle, our victory over adversity and our amazing discoveries once we were done could be an inspiration to others who are struggling to believe there is hope.

So as you read through these pages, pay special attention to the personal growth and progress of the soul that Paul and I become. Notice how the struggles that were so insurmountable when we first found themdid not hold up to the forces of our will, our love and our need to be on mission. Know that there is nothing in your life so terrible or so damning that you cannot overcome it if you keep your eyes on the light and your heart strong.

When you read about Rovere, Alex, the little people, Wannalancette, or any of the other amazing beings we have come in contact with as we joined together and continued in our work, please keep an open mind and open heart. We know these things are amazing and difficult to believe at times. We know because we have felt the same way even as it was happening to us. Yet we found ourselves realizing that it didn't matter because the messages and lessons these individuals have taught us, and we share with you are very real and very important.

Peace, Michelle & Paul

<u>MICHELLE</u>
Andy

The summer of 1969 was for me at seven years old, an endless time of excitement and games. That year, like the four before it, my whole family packed up the camper and headed out to spend the summer in a small campground in Tyngsboro, Massachusetts called Constantine Park.

We had our usual corner lot. My grandparents had the lot next to us and occasionally an uncle would occupy the one next to them. My dad would set out a wooden platform and the screen house, and we knew we were set for the summer.

From a child's eyes the summers were perfect. It didn't matter to us that we were only a few miles from home and only a short drive from the city of Lowell. We were 'camping'.

We swam, we played, we sang round the campfire. We re-discovered our summer season friends and made friends with some weekend trippers and passing visitors. Just as it was since my birth, the passing visitors included little gray people with big black eyes.

When I was home during the rest of the year, it seemed these little visitors came mostly at night, but here in the woods they came anytime. I never knew when I would see one standing in the brush or see a shining silver object through the trees. But it didn't seem to matter. They didn't frighten me and I just assumed that they lived in the woods.

My parents were not lucky enough to have the entire summer off, so each morning they would get ready and go off to work, leaving my younger brother and me in the able care of my grandparents.

Many an afternoon my grandfather would break his boredom by taking me for long walks beyond the limits of the campground to pick berries. Since my brother was only five, he would usually stay home with my grandmother. These walks became special times between my grandfather and me. For hours we would walk through the woods. He would stop and show me different trees and plants and what they did. He would tell me stories about people who lived in the woods and taught me how to walk through the brush and not make any sound. It was a magical time for me.

My grandfather is an extremely intelligent man. His knowledge of life stems not only from his many years - he was ninety-eight and going strong at this writing - but also from his obvious love of things that grow. For as long as I can remember he has had a garden and has known more about plants than any human being I have ever come to know. Some of this knowledge comes from books and practical experience, I'm sure, but some of it comes from traditional and aboriginal ways.

You see, my grandfather is a Canadian born Native American. His father was from a tribe called the Shawnonese and his mother was a Wyandot (Huron) Indian.

He spoke little of his heritage and even less of his people. He never spoke a word of their belief systems. All he told me was about the plants and animals, and an occasional anecdote about his life when he was growing up. Just about all of the knowledge he passed on to me has long been forgotten.

In the summer of 1969 I knew all these things, and I knew one more thing that would come back and haunt me. It was something I would have to face in the journey to discover my soul. I learned that my grandfather felt a deep sense of shame at being an Indian. It was a shame that was drilled into him by the catholic nuns who ran the school he went to and reinforced by the society in which he grew up. It was a shame he impressed into the souls of all in our family. It was, for lack of a better word, the skeleton in our closet.

I am embarrassed to admit that in 1996 that shame became an issue in my life. Still, it was only 1969 and I was a seven year old with a much bigger skeleton in my closet. Never mind Indians, I had a secret life with aliens.

When I look back to that summer, I remember the hot days, my red and blue blow-up floating raft, the baby flying squirrel my brother Ray saved and my mysterious friend Andy.

A funny thing about Andy was that when I met him I already knew him but I didn't have a clue as to how or why. Another funny thing was that I only saw him at night. I just could not figure that out. Why did his parents let him out only at night? For that matter, why were my parents letting me out at night to play with him?

Most of my play times with Andy were the same. Sometimes they differed a little bit, but for the most part a few times a week during that summer we would get together and do our 'routine' of things as most kids do.

I remember one night really well. I was lying in my bed in the cab-over part of the 15 foot travel trailer. I heard a kid's voice outside calling, "Hey, can you come out?" I climbed over my sleeping brother, and through the rungs of the ladder that stopped us from falling out onto the table below which was converted each night into a bed my sister slept in. I was careful not to step on her. She would wake up for sure. Then I opened the door and sneaked out.

Andy was there. He was usually dressed in cotton Pjs. Once he even had on a Batman like cape of dark blue material. This time he just had on a red shirt with blue trim and blue pajama pants. He was older than I was. He was almost as old as my brother Ray. I kind of felt special that he wanted to play with me and not my older brother.

"Hi, what do you want to do?" he would always ask the same thing. "Hi, what do you want to do?"

"I don't know?" Was my standard reply.

"Okay." We walked off toward the water's edge.   The water was actually a small pond that was created when the owners of the campground damned up a stream, but to me at that age and size it looked like a big lake.

At the edge of the water there was a tall homemade swing set. It was probably only about 12 feet tall, but it seemed to tower stories above us. The seats of the swings were thick boards of hard wood. We both stood on adjacent swings and started to pump our legs until we were flying high in the sky. We never sat on the swings. That was the little kid's way of swinging.

To this day I wonder why it never occurred to me to question why it was never dark around the swing set or even in the woods as we walked to the water. When I went out to play with Andy, there seemed to always be a strong bluish hue of moonlight in the sky. It never occurred to me that no matter how much noise we made, no one ever came and shooed us away, told us to go back to our own campsites or called my parents.

Just like the nights before, that night we played Batman and Robin. I always had to be Robin because I was shorter and younger. I protested a lot, but didn't really mind much.

"Da da da da da da, BATMAN!" We sang out the TV show theme as we swung high up. "To the Bat-poles!" Andy shouted. We jumped off our swings and hurried to grab a leg of the swing set and pretended to slide down. Sometimes we would run around the playground area. Sometimes we would jump back on our swings, which were now magically transformed into the Batmobile by the power of our imaginations.

Once in a while the Batman game became The Green Hornet. I liked being Kato because I got to kick things. Sometimes we would just swing and sing songs. Other times we would talk. When I asked him why he only came to play at night I got a series of clever but wrong explanations which included everything from his parents were vampires and only lived at night, to that he had a rare disease that made him sunburn in any daylight. I believed them all. I believed everything he said. After all, he was Batman to my Robin. He was the Green Hornet to my Kato. He was Captain Kirk to my Mr. Spock.

Usually our playtimes ended when he would tell me he had to go home and he would walk me back to the front of my campsite. I would just go back inside, crawl into bed and go back to sleep for the remainder of the night. I never wondered where he went, nor did I ever try to follow him. But this night was different. I remember it well.

We were playing on the swings again. He was Batman and I was Robin. I didn't want to be Robin and I was complaining that I wanted to be Batman for a change.

"It's not fair. You always get to be Batman," I whined.

"That's because I'm bigger and Batman is bigger," he insisted.

"Why can't I be Batman for a little while?"

"No, you're Robin," he said flatly.

"Please, Andy. Can I be Batman today? You get to be Batman all the time. Please?" I begged.

"No," he said with his usual air of authority. "But you can be Alfred if you want."

"I could be Alfred," I thought. Aha, he was giving in. There was a crack in his resolve. "Please Andy. Please Andy. Andy, Andy, Andy please!" I whined.

My friend stopped swinging and looked me straight in the face. Even at ten years old he had sharp blue eyes that cut deep into me. "No. You can't. And stop calling me Andy. My name is ANDREW!" he insisted. The emphasis on Andrew was incredible.

I remember feeling a bit shook up and confused, but I was sure that with just a bit more whining he would break and let me be Batman. So I persisted a bit more. "Andy! Andy! Raggedy Andy!" I sang out.

"Stop it!" he snapped.

"Raggedy Andy! Raggedy Annie!" I teased. "Your name is Annie! You're a girl!"

"Well, You're Pissy Krissy!" he snapped back. "Pissy Krissy! Pissy Krissy!" he sang back in a mocking tone.

Krissy? My body froze for a moment. He knew my secret name. He knew the name that only the little gray people and my special family called me. How did he know that?

I started to cry and run back to my campsite.

"Hey come back," he called to me. But I didn't stop.

I turned the corner on the path to find myself face to face with Hetar. Hetar is one of the taller gray beings most people think of when they think of aliens.

"Are you angry?" he asked me.

"He called me names," I blurted out like I was tattling on my brother to my Mom.

Hetar put his hand on my forehead and the next thing I was aware of was seeing my camper from above as it came closer and closer in a haze of blue light. Oddly enough, I was thinking the air vent in the ceiling had a crack in it. Then I went blank again and remembered nothing until the next morning.

I saw Andrew several more times during the summer of 1969. I was very careful not to call him Andy anymore. When the summer was over I said goodbye to all my daytime friends, but I never said goodbye to Andrew. He didn't come back that last night.

It just didn't make sense to me that he didn't come back, after all we were best friends.   Though he didn't show up to play at my house like he did that summer in the campground, I knew I was still playing with him. Because just about every time I was with the little gray people and the tall human like people with the pretty eyes, Andrew was there. We ran around the curving white corridors in our Batman and Robin Capes, that an ET woman gave us as a gift, screaming the Batman theme at the tops of our voices. When I dared, I still called him Andy, then ran in the other direction.

In the summer of 1970 we didn't return to Constantine park, rather we took a drive up into Canada, trailer in tow, to see the area where my grandfather grew up. All the while I didn't know that that summer's jaunt would take me closer to Andrew's home than I had ever been before.

<u>*PAUL*</u>
Angels Descend

In September of 1967, just as I was beginning grade three, my family moved from North Vancouver to Prince George, British Columbia. My father was a bank manager who had been transferred. We moved into a large, white house on Laurier Crescent.

One cool morning on a non-school day I told my mother that I was going outside to play and ran out the back door. When I stepped outside I looked up to my left and at about a forty-five degree angle from the ground I saw a perfectly symmetrical, round, fluffy cloud sitting in the sky. It looked odd. The first thought that popped into my mind was, "Wouldn't it be funny if I saw Mary on that cloud?" This was a reference to Mary, the mother of Jesus from the New Testament. I was raised a rather strict Catholic and at the time was very religious. I dismissed the cloud and my odd thought from my head and went about my business for the day, which at eight years old involved playing and seeing friends.

The day was uneventful until about 3:00 PM that afternoon. Once again I called out to my mother to let her know I was leaving the house and headed out the back door. As I was opening the door of the house, I looked at the clock in the kitchen and took note of the time.

I stepped out into the backyard, took a few steps and stopped. For no reason that I can remember to this day, I twirled around one hundred and eighty degrees and fell on my knees. It was as if I was jumping back from a rock falling out of the sky in front of me.

As I fell to my knees, I simultaneously clenched my hands together the way one would at church in a state of prayer. My head was back and I was looking straight up in the sky directly above me. I was amazed to see the same perfectly symmetrical, round, fluffy cloud that I had seen earlier that morning in the sky above my head.

Almost instantly, this round, fluffy, little cloud started to get bigger and bigger. I realized it was descending toward me. As it grew in size I noticed there were three figures on the cloud looking down at me. My sense of awe and wonder was augmented by fear that grew with every millimeter the cloud grew in size.

Soon I was able to see the figures quite clearly. They were not quite human looking because where there should have been faces, all I saw was brilliant white light that did not hurt my eyes. Draping down from their heads were brilliant blue veils. They looked much like the blue veils that are often depicted adorning the Virgin Mary. The blue seemed to shimmer and have life or a feeling of its own. It was as though the colors of these beings and their clothing had an emotion attached to them. I could feel the colors I was seeing.

The cloud and the beings continued to come closer until I realized they were coming straight for me. I felt tremendous fear like I had never known before in my life. I threw my body to the ground and prayed to them, "I believe, I believe, I believe. God, please forgive me. I believe!"

Suddenly my fear disappeared. As I tried to get up, there was an odd blip or shift in my vision. I looked up and saw nothing. The blue veiled people were no longer there. Not even the little fluffy cloud remained. The sky was clear and blue. This all seemed to take place within the space of two minutes.

Feeling somewhat bewildered and in shock I went back into the house. As I stepped in through the door I noticed the time was now about 3:30 PM. It didn't make sense but I didn't really care about the time.

My mother called to me. She wanted to know where I had been. I told her I was just in the backyard for a few minutes and came right back in. She said that I had been gone for a while and that she had gone out and called for me but heard no reply. It didn't make any sense to me. As far as I remembered, only a few moments had passed and I was in the backyard the whole time.

She still wanted to know where I had been and didn't believe me. She kept pressing me for an explanation.

I looked at her and could feel my face drop. I remember staring straight into her eyes and saying, "I saw Mary on a cloud."

"What?" she asked.

I didn't say anything else, but turned and walked upstairs feeling shocked and odd.

My mother called out several times as I walked up the stairs with a dead pan look on my face, "Paul! Paul! Paul!" But I just kept on walking.

I went up to a bedroom and lay on the bed facing the wall, just staring for the longest time. After a while I felt a little more myself and got up and went about my day. For the next twenty-five years I would believe in my heart and mind that I had experienced a miraculous vision from God.

After this experience I had the memory of an amazingly clear and very strange event I believed was a dream. The dream started with me standing in a completely black place. There were people on my left and right side who were holding my arms. Without warning, a door that seemed like an elevator door, opened in front of me. Beyond the door was a room that was brightly lit. I saw a bunch of children's cradles arranged throughout the room. At the end of the room was a beautiful woman holding a small child wrapped in some type of cloth.

I was directed to step into the room and did. The doors closed behind me. When I walked into the room, the woman holding the child spoke to me, but did not move her lips. Somehow though, I could hear what she was saying. She was so beautiful. She had long blond hair and blue eyes. She said hello to me and I said hello back.

I looked over to my right and I saw a short, strange looking being that was picking up a child out of one of the cradles and holding it. The being looked over at me, nodded its head and said, "Hello." The being had a woman's voice. I could feel everything about her when she said hello. She was so nice. I felt good and wanted to speak to her some more. Despite her short body, big head, and her large all black eyes, I felt so comfortable with her after she said hello.

"Look at me!" I suddenly heard from the blond woman in front of me. I turned my head quickly. I was filled with a sense of fear.

"Why are you shouting at me?" I managed to ask her.

"I'm not shouting. We have to talk about something important and I need you to pay attention. Do you know why you are here?" she questioned.

I thought for a moment. I was beginning to feel very uncomfortable because I didn't know. Nevertheless, for some reason I nodded my head up and down like I did know why I was there.

"It's wrong to lie." She became very strict and stern. "You shouldn't lie!"

I looked down at the ground not knowing what to do. I felt bad. I was so confused about what she wanted from me. I just wanted her to like me because she was so beautiful.

"If you don't know something you should ask," she said.

"I'm sorry," I answered.

"Look at the babies," she said.

I looked at them. There was something not right with them but I could not quite make out what it was.   I leaned over one of the cradles and reached down to take a better look.

"Don't touch them!" the beautiful woman shouted.
I pulled back quickly and stepped back. "I wouldn't hurt them," I said.

She seemed to soften a bit and asked me, "Would you like to help the babies? It is a very, very important thing to do, if you choose."

I thought for a moment. I was still very confused, but I reasoned that if it was important, maybe she would like me if I said yes. So, I nodded my head in the affirmative.

"Do not say yes because you want me to like you," she said.

"You don't like me, do you?" I asked.

"I don't like it when you lie," she responded.

I tried to figure out what to say. I realized that it would take a long time to prove to her I can be liked and that I'm not a liar. "Will I see you again?" I asked her.

"Not for a very long time," she said.

I thought for a minute. I felt like this was all so very important. It was something that would affect many people. I didn't know why I felt that way, but I did. I told her I wanted to help anyway.

She stared at me for a minute. Her face was so stern and strict. I was afraid of her. It bothered me that she was not friendly like the other woman there; the funny looking big-eyed woman.

"Okay," she said. "There are some things that have to be done.

I didn't know who they were, yet inside me I felt like I understood what was going on, even though it didn't seem to make any sense whatsoever.

There was a strange quality to this dream when I awoke. It was vivid and very real as if it was something that really happened. The reason for this would not make sense until twenty-five years later. Only then I would realize it was not a dream. It was what happened between 3:00 PM and 3:30 PM that afternoon with the people on the cloud.

Months later, on a warm sunny day, I decided to go for a ride on my bicycle. I told my mother I was headed up to the school on my bike to see if I could find any friends to play with. It was just after lunch and the sun was high in the sky.

We lived only about a ten minute bike ride to the school. I rode my bike around the crescent, through a small field and along the long straight street up to my grade school. When I got there no one was around, so I rode in figure eights and circles around the school yard for a bit.

All of a sudden I noticed the ground around me had turned blue. It was a most beautiful color of blue. It lasted a few seconds then went away. I stopped and looked around. There was nothing unusual. I began to ride around in figure eights and circles again hoping to make the ground turn blue once more. It didn't happen.

It got shady around me very quickly, as though a thick cloud was blocking the sun. I stopped and looked up. There was something blocking the sun, but it wasn't a cloud. It moved slightly and the sunlight hit my eyes. I had to cover them partially with my hands to look and try and make out what it was.

It moved out of the line of sight between the sun and myself and I could see it clearly. It was a round disk shaped thing. It moved away from me and over the roof of my school until I could no longer see it. I rode out, away from the building side so I could see more of the sky to see if I could find it, but to no avail. I rode further over to an open-air ice rink that was dry now during the warm months hoping to get a better view. As I approached I suddenly felt very, very tired, very quickly.

Somehow I instinctively knew to get off my bicycle and sit down on the ground. In one sweeping motion I half fell off, half dismounted my bike and in a sort of controlled fall sat down with my back leaning against a pole that held a light over the ice rink. I closed my eyes and fell into a deep sleep.

The next thing I was aware of, I felt myself laying down with my eyes closed and I heard movement around me. Then I heard words to the effect of, "I'm going to wake him up now."

When I opened my eyes I was laying on a table. There was a big handsome man standing over me. He was slightly wrinkled around his eyes. His blond hair was curly and thick. His eyes were blue but something was wrong with them. Their pupils were oval. The room was dimly lit and I could see my bike in a corner of the room.

The man had his hand on my chest. I heard him say, "Hello Paul." He smiled. I felt good throughout my body. It was like a feeling of love everywhere

He looked away and started to work with some type of instruments to the right of my head. His face got very, very serious. All the good feelings in me disappeared when he took his hand off my chest. I looked down the length of my body and noticed a bunch of short people wearing black cloaks with hoods over their heads. I could not see their faces. They were lined down both sides of my body from my chest to my feet. They had their hands stretched out over the top of me with their fingers outstretched. Their hands looked odd. Their fingers were unusually long and they didn't appear to have any thumbs.

I looked back at the man and was confused and afraid. Even though he seemed to be in a hurry, he stopped what he was doing and put his hand back on my chest. I once again felt good for a second. When he took his hand away all the good feelings left as they had before.

"What happened? Was I in an accident? I was riding my bike and..." I broke off my questions.

I heard the man say, "Don't worry. We just want to run some tests. Afterwards it will all seem like a dream."

I looked down at the hooded people and asked who they were.

One of them responded, "We will help make it a dream."

I tried to speak and one of the hooded people said, "You don't have to speak here, we can hear what you think and you can hear us."

I tried to sit up to see what was going on.   As I did, one of the hooded people told me to relax and not move. They seemed a bit concerned with me moving. I did my best to try and relax as I was instructed to do. I laid back down and didn't move.

The hooded people removed my clothing and I heard some type of instruction from the man with the blond hair.

Suddenly my body started to tilt up onto the left side and something was put inside my anus. It was incredibly painful. It felt as though I was being split into two. I started to cry.

There was some type of commotion behind me. The man with the blond hair began to command in a forceful and almost excited tone, "Knock it out! Knock it out!"

I cried out, "Please make it a dream! Make it a dream!"

One of the hooded beings said in a calm voice, "We will make it a dream."

Still, it hurt. My body shook and I cried.

The hooded being said to me, "It will work better if you relax."

"I'm relaxing! I'm relaxing!" I cried. I tried really hard to relax and the pain started to go away. Then I began to feel like I was floating. Despite the situation, I started to feel good.

A being asked me something about 'remembering' and then something about 'later.' I drifted and everything went black.

I woke up after a little bit. It seemed to me to be only about ten minutes or so after I got off my bike. Something wasn't right though. The first thing I noticed was the sky was all cloudy and it was windy now. The sun wasn't shining anymore. I thought it must have clouded over really fast. Then I noticed that I was not sitting against the pole where I sat or fell, but was now leaning against the ice rink itself. Moreover, my bicycle had been moved and was further away from where I left it.

I wondered, "How long have I been asleep?" I remembered nothing. I wouldn't remember the blond man again until my mid-thirties when the memory would come back like a blow from a sledgehammer and I would wonder how I had ever forgotten.

I picked up my bike and, feeling confused, walked out of the school yard. When I got to the edge of the yard, I looked to my right and saw a black oval shaped object hovering silently in the sky. It appeared as though it was something circular that was sitting slightly at an angle so that it appeared oval in shape. I could make out no features accept a completely black bottom. When I looked at it, I felt complete and utter terror. I looked away quickly. Though I know one would think I would have run, I just walked past the corner of the school about ten feet away and stopped.

I thought that it just sounded too crazy to be real, so I decided to screw up my courage and walk back ten or so feet around the school and look at it again. When I got there it was gone. I saw it there just fifteen or twenty seconds before.

When I got home my mother was angry with me because she told me I was not supposed to be gone for so long. I told her I had been up at the school and laid down for a short sleep for about ten minutes or so and had only been gone about thirty to forty-five minutes.

She told me that several hours had passed since I left. I checked the clock and she was right. I had no explanation for her. She was more than a little upset.

During my balling out, the telephone rang and my mother answered it. She spoke for a few seconds and I heard her say, "What? Paul was up there. Let me ask him if he saw anything." She came back into the room and told me that "so and so" just called and said she saw a UFO up by the school. My mother asked me, in a cross and concerned tone, if I had seen anything while I was up there. Fearing I would get into trouble, I said, "No."

I never spoke to anyone about that day again until I was in my thirties. I put the UFO out of my mind and it became only a memory of the day I fell asleep for what seemed like a few minutes and turned out to be a few hours.

By the summer of 1996 my contact with the non-human ETs most people call grays but I have learned call themselves Rye-hun (pronounced with a lot of air in the H sound almost like a gasp) was a well know fact. My first book *'The Alien Abduction Survival Guide* was out in the stores and I was working for commercial UFO magazine as Editor.   My experiences were ongoing and I was learning a lot from helping others learn to help themselves in the puzzle of self-discovery.   Everyone I worked with thought I had it all together and was totally complete.   But the truth was that I was feeling rather empty and alone.   My marriage was going through some major issues. Some of which stemmed from my book and my work, but most of which were always there, I just refused to see them.   I told so many people that if their marriage was strong, sharing their experiences would likely make it stronger, and if it were weak, it could destroy it.   All the while I had a blind eye to the fact that my own marriage was already dead, just waiting for someone to bury it. Still, in June of 1996 I was married to George and he, my children and my parents decided to go camping.

Years had passed from the days of the 15 foot camper. My parents now had a lovely 28 foot trailer that seemed more like a vacation hotel than a camper. We set up our tent next to their camper and readied ourselves for a nice calming vacation.

The first two nights went without a hitch. Sara, who was fourteen years old, had met a nice boy and was spending all her time with him. Kelly and John were having lots of fun playing in the woods, and my dad and I went fishing a lot. My mom cooked and cooked and cooked. George just sat around the campsite and read.

On the third day, Sara left the site early to meet with her friend. She didn't come back for lunch, and by late afternoon she had missed supper too. The boy's family was worried about him also. Soon we were on a full search for the pair before the sun went down. All the while we searched I knew it wouldn't turn up a thing. All my senses were telling me they had gone into the woods without so much as a flashlight. George could not accept this and when I dared to bring it up, he became irrational. The feeling I had was very strong, and I insisted. I just knew they were in the wilderness away from the campground. He didn't want to believe that Sara could have done something so irresponsible. Rather than consider it, he became angry at me for suggesting it. His behavior became more and more unreasonable, I couldn't take it anymore, so I walked away down to the lake to look for the kids.

When I got there, I sat on the beach for a short while and watched the sun dancing off the water. It had a strange calming effect on me. I fell into a much-needed meditative state. After a few moments I thought about the kids out in the woods. I knew they were there. I just knew it and nothing could convince me otherwise. So I got up and headed into the woods in the direction I felt they were.

As I walked, I began to feel strange. I was starting to become more and more uneasy. Something was watching me. Was it the kids? Was it a bear? I had no idea, but whatever it was I knew it was looking right at me.

I turned around and saw a man standing there. He was a slim man with cutting ice blue eyes. Somehow I knew him. He was so familiar, but my mind was racing. Questions flew through my brain. "What is HE doing here? Of all people, why him?" I wasn't wondering what any man was doing there. I was wondering what that particular man was doing there.

Oddly enough, I never thought to ask him who he was, what he was doing standing in the woods and if he had seen the kids. Moreover, I never thought to wonder if he had done something with the kids. I just kept thinking, "What is he doing here?" Then my mind went blank. I stood for a long moment starring at him. He did nothing to threaten or frighten me. He just looked at me and said, "Are you ready? It's time." For some reason, his words terrified me. I became totally panicked. I ran out of the woods as fast as I could.

When I got back to the lake, I sat exactly where I had been before, and stared into the now setting sunlight reflecting off the water. Not long after, the kids came out of the woods.

Even before the motherly, "Where have you been? I've been worried sick," I asked, "Did you see the man in the woods?" They both answered no.

The rest of the trip was not much to relay. The children were chastised for taking off without telling anyone where they were going, and in the confusion of packing tents and children's gear, I totally dismissed the man in the woods from my mind. It wouldn't be for some time before I realized who he was.

<u>*PAUL*</u>
July 1996
The Temagami Trip

In late July I embarked on an eight day canoe trip in the Temagami region of Ontario, Canada. It is an area known for its old growth forests and lookouts and I was looking forward to the trip. There were seven of us on the trip. Three canoes with two people each, a fourth canoe captained solo by a man I liked to call "Stan, the wild accountant." It was a spectacular trip that took us through some beautiful wilderness.

On day seven of our journey we paddled through some blistering hot weather. The water was absolutely calm, like a huge mirror on the face of the Mother Earth. We paddled long and hard that day until we reached our campsite at the end of the day. It was a sandy beach with a clearing that pushed back into the forest where we set up our tents.

As dusk fell and the moon began to rise, we started a fire. I walked down the beach and looked out over the water. I felt the atmosphere around me change, a presence seemed to come near me, as though a doorway were opening in front of my eyes out over the lake. I could feel the presence of a woman.

My instincts rose in me and for reasons I could not understand I heard myself saying, "Are you ready? It's time."

"No, leave me alone," was the response I heard in my head. Then the presence disappeared and the strange doorway in front of me closed up again.

"How odd," I thought to myself. I went back to the fire to join my companions and enjoyed a can of beer. We talked and joked for a while until the bugs got the better of us, then we went to bed.

The next morning we got up and packed up our site. Before we started out on the days journey, I paddled out to pump some water from the lake with a portable water filter. As I pumped water I felt something behind me on a small ten foot ridge that ran along the lake's edge.

I paddled over and docked the canoe on shore and climbed up the steep, small hill. The presence was extremely strong, but very, very peaceful. I spoke to it and it seemed as if it spoke back.

"Are you ready?" the presence asked.

"Yes, I've been ready for a while. When is it going to begin?" I answered.

"Now," replied the presence.

I then felt this huge presence turn itself to the sky and cry out, "Let the unity begin!"

"What are you talking about?" I asked.

"You will see," was the response. Then the presence was gone.

I climbed back down to the canoe and paddled back to pick up my partner and our gear for the day's journey. I had experienced presences throughout my life, as had my mother. I was used to experiencing such things and took them with a grain of salt. I would not understand the depth of its meaning for many months to come.

<u>MICHELLE</u>
Summer 1996
The Morning Star that Dances Backwards Through the Night

In the summer of 1996 I was working on a special issue of a commercial magazine I edited that dealt with ET contact themes. This issue was devoted to a Native American themed commercial conference. I was having some concerns about the whole issue. Things about verification of sources and credibility of some of that month's contributors kept popping up. The magazine publisher's President, who knew about my Native American background, seemed to feel that I might have been a bit too picky about a particular issue and asked me to step back and re-assess if I had any emotional involvement. I considered that this might be true so I sat down and tried to get things straight in my head.

Yes, I did have some issues with the Native American culture. Growing up with my grandfather, it was hard not to wonder if there was really something to all this or if it was all primitive, uneducated, mumbo-jumbo as he always taught me, but that wasn't the part that was bothering me. It was something deeper. It was something that was unbearably and unexplainably painful to me.

It wasn't that I did not believe and have respect for the Native cultures of the Earth, it was that I had too much respect in many ways. I found myself feeling that the people I was editing for publication were selling something that every drop of my blood was telling me was sacred. I found myself feeling pain that something I felt on a very basic primitive level was beautiful was being sold at this conference.

During the production of the issue, the publisher and I talked a lot about the Natives who were contributing to it. I had strong feelings that some of the statements one author and medicine man made about how his words came straight from God and therefore could not be questioned should be removed from the article he wrote. After a debate about the validity of individual thought and right to question, the publisher agreed with me and the statements were removed from the final edit of the publication.

Later it came to my attention that the author of that particular piece was not pleased with my editing of his words, which, in my opinion, was why when the people from the publishing company returned from the conference they had all been given "official Indian names" by this person, yet I had not.

I really didn't think this bothered me at the time. I know this sounds childish, but one night in mid August of 1996 I was laying in bed trying to sleep. I was very restless. My mind drifted to my work, and I thought about the conference, the medicine man and the fact that I didn't get a name. Despite my best efforts, I felt hurt that I didn't get a name, and slighted by the medicine man who gave out the names. In a flash of immaturity brought on by stress, I started to stew on the idea that I was actually the only one of the lot of them that, to my knowledge, had any Native blood in them, yet I was not given a name. With this going through my mind, I became sleepy. I thought I drifted into a dream. I was wrong.

Between my thoughts I found myself standing in a misty place. The mist cleared and I was standing on what seemed like a glass floor. I could see through it. Below me was a large globe of the Earth. It was not the Earth itself, but a schoolroom globe with the oceans in baby blue and each individual country a different color, outlined in black with its name written across it in big letters. I remembered thinking, "Geeze, this is strange."

I thought I heard a rustling of feathers, I turned to find a very, very, large Native looking man facing me. He was at least 6 feet 6 inches tall or better. He looked very strong. His hair was black with white and gray streaks in it. It was long and braided on one side. He had 3 feathers hanging from the red leather strip that tied off his hair; one was black, one was gray and the last was pure white. He wore a white animal fur around his shoulders like a collar. His clothing was tan and probably leather. His eyes drew my attention. They were bright green. It was the same shade of green I had only seen in alien eyes before. They were green like spring grass in sunlight or a like a new crayon. They were not a human color green.

He looked at me and said, "You want an Indian name?"

I was sure I was dreaming. I wasn't through my pouting attitude and my mood was not as good as it would have been had I had any inkling that this fantastic thing that was happening to me could have possibly been real. "Yeah, it would be nice," I replied like I was talking to a casual friend.

"Why do you deserve a name from the Mother?" he asked with forceful, strong words.

"Because everyone else got one and I'm the only one who's really even a part Native. I should have gotten one too," I complained to this "dream Indian".

"Why?" He looked deep into my eyes.

"Because I'm really part Native. I should have a Native name but this guy didn't say anything about me and..." I started with the whole long story like I was blabbing to my girl friends on the phone.

"Stop!" he said. "Tell me all you know about your grandfather and his people. What tribe are they from? What clan are they from?"

I didn't know quite what to tell him. I started relaying the story of how my grandfather came to the United States when he was a child. It was during a flood of Irish immigrants, so they crossed the border at a point where many Irish were coming in. When they were asked what their sir name was, my grandfather's father said, "We don't have a sir name. We are Shawonese". The man wrote down Shaughnessy. So my grandfather's family pretended to be Irish after that. They didn't want anyone to know they were Natives because in those days, no one would hire a Native for work. Native children couldn't go to regular schools. Sometimes they were even taken away from their parents and sent to boarding schools. I told him how my grandfather told me that back then everyone thought all Natives were alcoholics and thieves, and how he was told if he told anyone he was aboriginal they would throw them out of their home and make them live on the street with the alley cats. I told him how my grandfather still believes this is the way it is today.

He didn't react. "What do you know about the ways of your grandfather's tribe? What do you know of your ancestry?" he said without obvious emotions.

"Nothing really," I answered. I was actually starting to get a bit annoyed with this dream. It seemed too long and rather involved. I kept wondering why I would dream something like this.

"What do you know about your ancestry? You must tell me before the Mother will give you a name," he insisted.

I was getting impatient and restless with the situation. I kept wondering why I would dream something like this. Why couldn't I turn the dream around as I had done with so many dreams I didn't like in the past?

"Why do you deserve an Indian name!" he questioned with force as though he was getting angry with me.

At this point I became truly frustrated with the questions. After all, I was convinced it was a dream. If it was, I was in control. I didn't have to take the third degree from a dream. "Never mind," I blurted out in my ignorance of the truth, "I don't want a stupid Indian name anyway. Besides you would probably only call me *Running Bra* or *Stays on Phone*!" I snapped back with sarcasm.

The man looked at me with fierce eyes. "Enough!" he shouted with an awesome power in his voice that made me tremble.

Then, like a shot, I was no longer standing there. I felt my whole being falling at incredible speed. In a second's time my mind fell back to my body. My whole body jerked and convulsed from the "snap back" of my soul. I was lying wide awake. Sweat broke out on my brow and I was shaking. "My God, was that real? Could it have been real? My God, it was real! It had to have been real," I mumbled.

I sat there stunned at the reality of the event. Then it hit me. If it was indeed real, which I had established I personally felt it was, then I had just insulted some supernatural being who came to me. I was flippant and arrogant to someone who went though a lot of trouble to help me.

I was stunned, shocked, then embarrassed. I resolved that I had to get back to this person. I had to let him know I was sorry and wanted to hear what he had to say in a more humble, open way.

To that end, I lie in bed and concentrated on re-creating the state of mind I was in before it happened the first time, this time without the bad attitude. I focused on the idea of reaching out to this being to talk to him again.

After some time, I must have drifted back into that state. The first thing I was aware of was looking down at the top of my own head and thinking the part in my hair wasn't straight. Strange, I know. Then I found myself in the mist again. This time, when it cleared, I did not find myself with the Native man standing over the globe of the Earth. Rather, this time I found myself standing in front of a shimmering silver curtain of what looked like flowing ribbons. I tried to push through it, but couldn't budge it even the slightest bit. I tried to reach between the ribbons, but the in between was as solid as the ribbons themselves. On the other side of the curtain I could see the man standing there. He had his back turned to me.

"Please!" I begged. "I'm sorry. I didn't know this was real. I thought I was dreaming."

He didn't turn.

"I would have never spoken to you like that if I knew. I was sure I was dreaming. I'm Sorry," I explained sincerely.

There was still no response.

"Please! Are you so far above humans that you don't remember what it's like to make mistakes? Feel my intentions. I'm truly sorry. I'm truly embarrassed by what I did. Please. I don't want anything from you. I just need to apologize," I pleaded. "I don't want anything but to say I'm sorry. I'm not a divine being. I'm not perfect. Please forgive me." I truly felt terrible for what I did and I resolved that there was going to be a punishment period for my actions. "I understand I was wrong. When I am ready, will you come again?"

The man turned to me and the curtain came down. "Come." He put out his arm.

I walked on the glass floor above the globe of the Earth, just as before. This time I was far more humble. I walked until I was at arms length from this man. He smiled at me and said, "The Earth knows you and she calls you, *The Morning Star that Dances Backwards Through the Night*."

I tried to say thank you, but I couldn't speak.

He put his right hand on my left shoulder, "Be strong. Be happy," he said. This phrase would be said to me many times in the next year by both humans and non-humans alike. When he spoke those words, a large white feather dropped out of the sky and gently floated down. It touched his shoulder and his body dissolved just like in one of those "morphing" scenes in a movie. First he melted into a very large white bear. Not a polar bear, but a big black bear with white fur. Then he melted into a large white wolf, then down into a big white bird, probably an eagle. All the animals had the same striking green eyes. The bird looked at me for a short second then spread its wings and flew off, leaving me standing on the glass floor above the globe of the Earth. I watched the bird until it was very small in the sky. All the while the name, *The Morning Star that Dances Backwards Through the Night*, rang like a song in my ears.

Without warning, I felt myself slowly falling. There was no violent jolting this time. Just a gentle falling feeling, then a few moments of seeing nothing but white, then I opened my eyes to find myself sitting up in bed, wide awake.

After such a powerful experience you would think I would be very elated. But for weeks after something haunted me. It was something I couldn't put my finger on. I kept trying to tell myself that the whole event was a dream, but I couldn't make myself believe it. Dream or no, there was more going on than just someone telling me what my "cool Native American name" was. If it were not a dream, then there was a much bigger reason why I would be visited by such a being. I knew in my heart it was not a dream, thus I knew it was true that there was a bigger reason, but I didn't know what it could possibly be. I experienced waves of intense feelings of responsibility, but had no idea what that responsibility was for. At times the pressure associated with the responsibility was so overwhelming I was on the verge of being emotionally crushed by it. The people I talked to about this event consistently told me it was a blessing. But frankly, at the time I really wished it never happened. I didn't know it was just the tip of an iceberg I have yet to find the limits of.

<u>PAUL</u>
Paul and Mason Paddle the Moon

In the summer of 1996, I traveled by myself to Massassauga Provincial Park and camped alone on a lake called Spider Lake. Nothing much happened and I found myself feeling lonely so I came back out early. I decided I was going to take my next trip with someone else for company.

I had been toying with the idea of going to the Moon River for some time with my nephew Warwick. He was busy the following weekend but I could take his younger brother Mason. I was hesitant because Mason suffered from asthma. He was a much quieter person than his older brother and I really didn't know how he would do camping out.

After some thought, I felt that a night out would be good for him. Besides, the more I thought about it, the more I wanted to get him out into nature to give him a break from the hustle and bustle of Toronto. Still, I was hesitant because of the emotional distance between us. After some more thought, I called him up and asked him to go with me. He responded in an excited and affirmative tone.

"Maybe it will be alright," I thought to myself. "If it does turn out to be a bust, it will only be for one night. How bad could it really be? Nonsense," I thought. "We'll have a fine time. It will be an adventure." Little did I know how much of an adventure it would be. It would, in fact, be a trip that would change my life forever.

Friday came and I picked up Mason from my sister's house in Toronto. We headed up to the town of Newmarket where I lived. We spent the evening going over our route and discussing some of the protocols of the trip. We would be going through Mohawk owned land, and though I had heard it was fine to canoe the river without permission from the Band Counsel, I was still a bit nervous. So we decided we would try to keep our voices down and travel quietly until we found a campsite. The next day we got up about 7:00 AM and headed out.

We had some trouble finding the Moon River. We stopped a couple of times to ask for directions. We had to back track once because we thought we'd passed it, but soon enough, we found the river. In a short bit we were off, paddling east toward the reserve. I had been told by a gentleman I met a few weeks earlier on a canoe trip about a huge camp site the size of a small park in the middle of the reserve. I figured we could reach it in a couple of hours.

The river narrowed and we found ourselves having to drag the canoe up through several small rapids.

"I hope there's not to many of these," my nephew said.

"Don't worry. If we start to loose our minds we'll just find a place to camp and stop. Let's not kill ourselves today. We're just exploring, remember?"

"Good," Mason replied.

We soon passed by a tent. Then we passed its occupant standing by the river's edge with a fishing pole. I called out, then we stopped and talked to him for a bit. He bragged about some of the fish he had caught and we told him where we were headed.

He pulled out his topographic map and showed us that just ahead was the boundary to the Wahta Mohawk Reserve. His map stopped after that so we had no idea how far or difficult the trip might be. Mason and I decided to base our trip on the amount of time we spent travelling. I knew that however long it took to travel up river, it would take no longer to return travelling with the current and down the rapids on our return.

We encountered several more rapids, some of which we had to portage, others we simply got out of the canoe and dragged it with the gear through the water.

We rounded a bend in the narrow river and it opened up into a beautiful peaceful stretch of one of the most unique, gorgeous rivers I had ever seen. We passed by a cottage or two that belonged to residents of the reservation. The occupants of one saw us paddle by. I nodded hello to one of them, but they seemed indifferent. I felt a little less intrusive and my anxiety eased somewhat. "Perhaps it will be okay," I thought to myself.

Mason and I spoke in quiet conversation along the way. We stopped at different points when we thought we heard animal noises, in the hopes of seeing a moose or a deer drinking by the river.

After a few hours we could not find the large campsite I had heard about. Ahead we saw another set of rapids. We didn't wish to travel further, so we decided if there was no campsite at these rapids we would make one. As we approached, we could see a very old cabin sitting in a grassy, marsh area. There was no dock and no visible pathway to it from the riverbank.

We docked on the right side of the river where there was a natural pathway on the rocks to traverse the rapids. As we walked up I heard Mason yell out, "Come up and check it out! It's perfect!"

He was right. Not only was it a nice site, it came complete with a fire pit, a nice flat area under the conifers to put the tent, and some large overhanging tree branches on the far side to hang the food that night. It didn't look like anybody had camped there in at least a year. There was no sign of any recent garbage. We also discovered that the spring thaw had deposited large piles of wood that had the bark stripped off from their trip down the river. All we had to do was grab an armful and drag it over to the fire pit.

Mason started the fire early and took it upon himself to tend to it through the afternoon. It was hot, but I didn't mind as it helped to deter the three-hundred and eighty million mosquitoes and black flies that descended upon us through the day. We used up to an ounce of deet each that day and night trying to scare them off.

Almost as soon as we arrived and started to set up camp and get the fire going I started to feel rather uneasy. I felt like I was trespassing or violating somebody else's space. I began to hear sounds and noises, and suspected the resonance of the rapids were playing tricks on my ears. My nephew mentioned the same thing. I suggested the possibility of the white noise from the rapids creating auditory hallucinations in us. It felt eerie and I tried to figure out a logical explanation for the increasing frequency of sounds and voices I was hearing. I continually heard the sound of children playing. I would hear it for a minute or so and then it would stop. I tried to attribute every noise, no matter how clearly human sounding to the sound of the water.

Mason and I were quiet and didn't talk much. He seemed not himself. I know that I was not completely at ease either. Finally after about ninety minutes he came over to me and said, "You know, this place is freaking me out. It feels so eerie. About thirty seconds ago I heard the sound of children playing over there on the rapids and then it just stopped about fifteen seconds ago." He pointed to the east end of the campsite.

My eyes opened wide and my adrenaline started to build, "So did I!" I exclaimed. It became obvious to us both we were hearing the same sounds at the same time.

"Mason we must be near a Native school or something. Here we are thinking we're in the middle of the bush and we're probably within a couple of hundred meters of a school. The water and the rocks might be acting as some type of amplifier." We both paused and looked up the riverbank, wondering if that was in fact what was happening. I got up and hiked up the riverbank about twenty-five meters. Once I reached the top, I saw nothing but bush for as far as the eye could see, just dense brush. It also became completely silent. Later I looked at a detailed map of the area and discovered there really was nothing but bush for many miles around.

I walked back down the steep riverbank. As I approached the campsite the voices started up again. Something odd was clearly going on. At one point, through the afternoon, I heard the sound of young men singing clear, non-English syllables. In retrospect, I regret not writing down the words I heard.

We continued to collect beautifully, naturally cleaned and marked wood. Some we burned. Some we made into a little pavilion. We were a bit spooked by now and wanted to show some respect for the site and any forces or spirits that may be there. We tried to draw on any intellectual, emotional and spiritual resources we could find. Though unnerving, the energy that surrounded us was strongly spiritual in nature and I somehow knew that this was more than just eerie sounds, it was something that touched my soul. We thought that in some way we might appease the spirits of the place. We found an old piece of burnt wood that looked like a large raven's head. We also found a cut log that we placed it on, along with some sticks we laid down for legs and wings. Plus an unusual piece of wood that looked like a long neck with a partially finished human type head at the end that we laid on the ground at the top of our little totem by the fire.

I had experienced some strange things before in my life, but never before had I experienced hearing voices like this. Constantly, minute to minute, hour to hour, we would hear things.

At one point I was tending to the fire and the wind shifted so that the smoke came up my body and enveloped my head. I was looking west down the river. It looked different. "There's something in the smoke," I thought to myself. It was odd, yet very haunting and mysterious. It was quite beautiful in a way. I was lost in thought and startled when I felt a hand on my right shoulder. I turned. It was Mason.

"What?" I asked.

"There was a ball of light over your head," he said. He pointed to a place about eight feet above me.

"Was it a spark from the fire?" I asked.

"I thought it was. But it just hovered there, then it flew sideways across the river and off into the forest," he explained.

I looked at him, then at the river, shook my head and thought, "Strange river, strange fire, strange smoke, strange voices, strange sparks. Never mind, we'll be out of here first thing in the morning." It was so overwhelming that I was working my way deeper and deeper into denial.

We collected some more wood for the fire, building up a good sweat as we went. I decided to take a picture of our fire as Mason approached with a bundle of wood. He dumped the wood just as I called out to him. He looked winded and somewhat pained from the size of the bundle he had just carried up to the site. I snapped a picture, looked over at him and smiled. Then I heard a voice in my head say, "That's the picture that will change your life."

I looked at the fire and saw what I thought was a large perfectly round spark hovering just above the flames. As if it knew it had been discovered, the spark started to move in a small spiral. It became obvious that it wasn't an ordinary spark. Gradually it started to move up the column of smoke. As it rose it left the smoke and continued to rise high into the sky.

"How odd that it isn't dissipating," I thought to myself. It continued to rise straight up into the air until it disappeared from sight. I had no explanation and put it in the back of my mind. I shook my head and walked across the campsite to take another picture of the fire.

After collecting wood, we decided to go swimming. My nephew got into his trunks first and went down to the base of the rapids where the water seemed deeper. I watched him stand there looking at the water from the shore for about five to ten minutes. I thought he was just getting up the nerve to jump in the cool water. He came back up bone dry so I kidded him about being a wimp. I told him he should just jump in and that I would be in shortly.

He told me the water was a bit cold but not too bad and that it was not the water temperature but an incredibly eerie feeling that prevented him from jumping in.

I should point out that my nephew grew up in downtown Toronto and had many friends, some of whom were "street kids". Both Mason and his brother, Warwick, had hard teenage lives and had been in their share of trouble. That was one of the reasons I would take them on trips, to show them there was more to life. Warwick was well on his way to creating a life for himself, but Mason was still working on it. Considering this, it would have taken a lot to scare him. His fear of an empty pool of water did not make any sense to me.

Still, there was something strange about the place, so we both agreed to swim at the upper portion of our campsite to the east. I heeded my nephew's feelings and did not want to venture down where he had been for some reason that I could not explain. The feeling at the upper end of the site was much friendlier. Maybe it was my imagination, maybe it wasn't. In either case we both felt more comfortable there. We swam for a bit, changed into our clothes and went back to tend the fire to warm up again.

Looking back, I do not think I have burned a fire for as long as we did at this place. From about 1:30 PM to about 11:00 PM that night we had a raging fire going. It was comforting. Still, almost constantly, we heard voices and sounds of varying kinds at intervals of between every thirty seconds to every couple of minutes. It got to be very nerve wracking by dinner time.

At one point during the afternoon I was standing by the fire and heard the clear, distinct sound of the telephone in the living room of my house ring. There was an unmistakable and rather annoying quality to the sound of its ring. It was about 4:00 PM. I found when I got home there was one message on my answering machine at the exact same time.

We settled down around 5:00 PM to make dinner, then relax. We talked for a bit and tried to keep our heads together. Still, the uneasy feeling continued. I kept my ax, "Betsy", especially close to us that evening.

We did some sky watching after sunset. The banks of the river didn't offer the panoramic view you would normally get when camped on a lake. The voices seemed to settle down more and more as darkness descended over the land and the fire burned down. I found that odd. One would think eerie events would increase the darker it got.

After a while, we got into the tent and settled in for the night. We were not in bed for ten minutes when we heard animal noises. At least that is what I thought at first. In my mind, I figured I was hearing raccoons pitter-patter about. But they were odd foot steps for raccoons. They were too fast like "pat pat pat pat pat pat pat" one after the other. I was refused to acknowledge they were the sounds of a bipedal creature walking quickly about the site, not a quadruped.

"Did you hear that?" asked Mason.

"Yeah, it's probably just raccoons or something," I assured him.

A few more minutes passed. Mason was restless.

"Man it sounds like there are little people or kids outside," Mason said again. His words woke me from my drifting sleep.

"What is it?" I asked.

"It sounds like there's people outside," Mason repeated.

"If it's bothering you just go out and see for yourself. Make sure and take Betsy with you," I suggested, referring to my ax.

He lay there for a few more minutes. The number of foot steps increased. I was content to let the raccoons clean up whatever little food stuffs they could find. I felt safe in drifting off to sleep. I knew from experience that any bears would only be interested in the food we had safely suspended fifteen feet off the ground on the edge of camp.

Soon his anxiety got the better him and Mason jumped out of his sleeping bag, threw on his shoes and grabbed the ax. He hurriedly opened the tent flap door and stepped outside. It was completely silent for a moment, then I heard Mason scream a loud terrorizing scream. "Aaaaaaaaaaahhhhhh!" he yelled.

I was now wide awake and smiled to myself. "What is it, raccoons?" I asked. I was sure a city kid like Mason was just startled by the sight of a raccoon coming out of the woods.

"No. It's a kid."

"A kid? What is he doing?" I asked.

"Get out here now!" Mason shouted.

"Why? Just ask him over," I said.

"You don't understand. You've gotta see this!"

"Why? What is it? What's wrong?" I asked again. I was tired and a bit overwhelmed by the strange events of the day. I did not want to deal with any other strangeness. I didn't bother to get up.

"He doesn't look right. He's got a big head and he's real skinny. Something's wrong with him. You've got to see!" Mason called back with excitement.

"Mason don't make fun of him." I imagined the kid would go get his big brother or something like that and we would really have some problems.

"Heeeeey!" I heard Mason yell again and run over to the bushes.

"Mason! Are you okay? Leave the kid alone and come back here!" I called out.

A few moments later I heard Mason approach the tent and come inside. Something was wrong with him. I rationalized that being out here alone, on top of all the voices we heard that day, had really started to get to him. I knew that it had gotten to me and I didn't want to deal with anything anymore. It was as if my mind was on overload and was shutting down. I just wanted to go to sleep and leave in the morning.

"Did you scare him off?" I asked.

"Yeah, he ran into the forest. Man, was that ever weird."

"What do you mean, it was just a kid. He probably lives nearby and was just out checking out our fire. I bet there's a house nearby that we don't know about." I tried to find an explanation.

"You don't understand. He didn't look right! He was really skinny and he had a big, big head, and he had on a real expensive looking shiny jogging suit or something."

"Well then he's not going to rip us off if he's got the money for an expensive piece of clothing is he?" I responded. I guessed that was Mason's concern.

"You don't understand, he wasn't normal. It wasn't human. I don't want to talk about it anymore." He rolled over and went to sleep.

"Thank God," I thought to myself, "now I can get some sleep." I reasoned that the darkness and weirdness of the day probably distorted his vision. We could talk about it tomorrow. If anybody came back in the meantime, I would just go out and speak to them in a civil tone and explain things.

I drifted off to sleep and was glad to go. I thought, "What a rare spiritual experience on Native land. Once we get through it, it will be something we will talk about the rest of our lives." Still, I just couldn't handle the idea of my nephew claiming to see some non-human thing. I had been spooked to my limit and was shutting down inside. I convinced myself there was some logical explanation. It was the best way I knew to deal with things at that point.

Sometime through the night something strange happened. I believed I started to dream. In that dream, I woke up in my tent and saw the tent door was open and light was coming in. I felt the cool dampness of the air. I looked up and saw three small beings crouched at the tent door. Their chins were pointed. They had little in the way of a nose or mouth. Their skin was shiny and their eyes were huge and black. They were a dark tan color that seemed to change shades at times. There was some kind of light coming from the east end of the campsite on the river.

"Wow, what a clear dream of aliens," I thought to myself. "Amazing what the mind can create." I put my head back down to go back to sleep. I sensed some type of consternation around me. Then I heard a voice in my head that was clear.

"No, we are real," the voice said.

"Yeah, sure," I responded and looked up again. There they were again. "Wow, this dream really is clear." I thought to myself, and put my head back down. I thought for a moment and considered the possibility that what I was dreaming might be real. "Why am I not waking up?" I wondered.

I looked up a third time and asked, "How do I know you are real and not just a dream?"

There was a momentary pause and then I heard, "You requested communication."

I remembered just two weeks earlier, when I was on a trip on the Pickerel river, I and a few companions saw a strange wobbly light in the sky. I remembered thinking it might have been a UFO. I "thought" to that light in the sky that I wanted some kind of communication or contact.

I sprang up in my sleeping bag. I pressed my hands together in a manner one would if one was praying. "I mean you no harm. I mean you no harm! Please don't go anywhere I need to speak with you! It's so good to finally meet you again!" I was hysterical. It was becoming more and more difficult to believe it was just a dream. Somewhere in the middle of all of this, and to this day I am still not sure of the sequence, I turned to wake up Mason.

"No, don't wake him up," one of them said.

"Are you kidding! This is one of the biggest things that could happen in a person's life. In the history of man!" I yelled.

I woke Mason up and promptly freaked right out. He jumped out of his sleeping bag and looked at me, then looked at them, then looked at me again. I tried to reassure him there was no danger, and that I had asked them to come. It didn't matter to him, he was wide eyed with terror. It was as if the shock to him was too great.

To the right of the three beings some arms and hands appeared. I could not make out their features, only that they appeared to be small. A horribly violent struggle ensued between Mason and the beings whose hands I saw. I pleaded with both parties not to hurt each other. They dragged Mason out of the tent like he was a sack of wild potatoes.

Mason was screaming horrible screams of utter terror. I begged and pleaded for it to stop. As quickly as I did there was complete silence. Then, a second later, I heard Mason say, in a low, monotone voice that was difficult for me to recognize as his, "I'm okay."

It was quiet now. Somehow I managed to settle inside and was only focused on the beings in front of me. I began to plead with them again when the one in the middle said in a clear, firm voice, "What do you want?"

"There are so many things. Where to begin? Something went wrong along the way. I need to heal, to understand. I need to wake up. Yes, if I could wake up it would solve many other things."

"I cannot do that!" responded the being in the middle. His tone seemed calm but surprised.

"No, no!" I said. "Not wake up in the normal sense. I mean become conscious, enlightened, a state of grace, whatever name you want to use. I need to wake up! It's very important that I wake up. I understand this is something that I must do for myself but can you help me? It is very important that I wake up. Can you please help me?" I was surprised at the speed that these words came out of my mind in this dream like state.

I stared into the eyes of the being in the middle. I knew from his voice he was a male. His eyes were magnificent. When I looked into them I felt like I was swimming in a large sea. He was standing so close to me, all I could see were his eyes. There was a long pause. It seemed like five seconds or so passed as I stared into the large magnificent eyes. Then I heard a long, slow response, "Yesssss." The sound of the 'S' was long. It was a haunting tone that carried a strong sense of thoughtfulness to it.

Part of me was really beginning to believe I was not having a dream. This was too weird. Still, I was elated. It took me a minute to digest his answer. I started to become more and more elated. In excitement, I pulled my hands apart and started to wave them up and down as though I scored a touch down at a football game. I reached over with my right hand to slap him on his left shoulder in gratefulness. Half way through the swing I heard him quickly say, "No, don't!" But it was too late. I hit him and he went straight down sideways. He banged his head on a rock and didn't move.

I recoiled in horror. "Oh my God, forgive me!" I cried. I felt I could not communicate my regret sufficiently. Here, a being was granting me my greatest wish and my first response was to smack him to the ground. I wanted to help but somehow knew not to move.

The other two beings moved quickly to examine him.

"Is he alright?" I asked in a desperate tone.

"His skull is crushed," I heard a voice in my head say.

I couldn't believe it. "Oh please, I'm so sorry."

Then next thing I remember, I was walking across the campsite in darkness. Now I was not with little, odd colored aliens. I was with children that looked to be between the ages of eight and ten. I couldn't understand what was going on. I didn't remember anything from a few moments ago. All I knew was these kids wanted me to go with them to their place. I saw two small children carrying a stretcher. It looked like a human arm from a larger person was hanging over the edge of it. Later, I wondered if it was the being I hit, or my nephew. I also wondered how some of them could be so strong as to pull my nephew out of the tent, while another one would be so weak that a simple slap sideways on the shoulder would knock him down. But for now, it didn't matter.

I looked east, down the river. There was a huge white object parked across the river on four legs. In my head I thought, "What's a water tower doing parked over the river?"

"Where are we going?" I asked the child in front of me.

"Over to our place," he responded. Somehow I got it into my head I was going to their parent's house for dinner. I felt so odd, so disoriented. I could feel the night air. I could feel myself walk. Why was I not waking up?

"Where is your place?" I asked.

"Over here," he said pointing at the large white object. It appeared to be well over ten meters across, and more than seven meters tall. The bottom of the object was at least six to eight meters above the river.

As I looked at the object, I thought, "What an odd looking water tower." I could not understand why it had a small door and a ladder that hung down like stairs to the ground. I saw a child halfway up one of the legs. He appeared to be working on some cables through a hatch in the leg.

"Is he safe up there on that tower leg?" I asked the young man in front of me.

He waved his hand in a reassuring gesture and said, "He knows what he's doing. Come on."

I felt concerned for the children's safety. I didn't feel it was a good idea for them to be climbing up such a tall object, not to mention I didn't really want to climb onto this thing myself. I said, "No, we can't go there without your parents permission. That's wrong. It's too dangerous."

"Okay. We'll go over to the house," the young boy said. He pointed across the river to the old unoccupied cabin. I felt this was okay, so I agreed.

The next thing I remember seeing in front of me was a house in the forest. It didn't really look like the cabin across the river. It had five or six concrete steps in front of it. The child I had been talking to climbed up in front of me. I followed after him.

He turned around, looked at me and said, "Be careful. The stairs are steep." They didn't look too steep to me. I started to climb.

It seemed to take forever, step after step after step. How could five or six steps go on like this. It was tiring and I could not figure out why I wasn't waking up. This was such a tiring dream. Why couldn't I just get back into my tent and dream there? I stopped for a moment and looked around.

After a few seconds I heard a voice from behind me. "We can carry you up if you wish."

"No, no. I'm not that old yet. It's just confusing. Do you understand?" I asked.

"Yes," a voice replied.

So I got up my energy and hurried up the stairs. There were no railings I could see but I could feel my hands holding some type of rail. Finally, I got to the top of the stairs and entered the house. I had to duck to get through the door, it was so small.

"They need to fix that," I thought to myself.

Inside, everything was white. The interior was huge. It was much larger than the small house I believed I had just climbed up the stairs to.

I was brought to a platform like a catwalk that ran around the circumference of the craft about halfway up to the ceiling. All the walls seemed to be rounded. Down below me, and in the middle of the area, I saw a huge coupling of some kind. Suspended in the middle of the coupling, as though floating, was my nephew, Mason.

"When are we going to eat?" I thought. "This is a weird dinner. What type of people are these who have dinners like this?"

The coupling moved back and forth. I cannot recall if it rotated all the way around. A voice from behind me on my right side said, "You will be next."

I watched some more then I heard the same voice say, "He will die soon." He was referring to Mason.

I felt awful. None of this made sense. Some part of me felt the truth in these words but how could that be? How would anyone know the future? When I recalled the conversation, my own questions confused me. It was not the reaction I thought I would have had. I realized that when I was standing there in that ship, I was more aware of things than when I recalled the event. Rather than demanding to know why, when or how, I asked, "Is there nothing that can be done?"

"No."

"Will he live until Christmas?" I asked.

"No," the voice responded.

"Is there anything that can be done to bring meaning to his life?"

"That has already been arranged," the voice answered.

None of this conversation made any sense to me.

"Is there anything you can do to extend his life?" I asked.

"We will see what we can do," the voice said.

I felt sad. What a horrible dream. I wanted to wake up now more than ever. Things blacked out again. The next thing I was aware of, I found myself floating. I knew I was in the huge coupling Mason had been in earlier.

I'm not sure why, but I was laughing. I couldn't remember what the being just told me about. All I was aware of was that exact moment. Something was hilarious.

What a sensation! My laughter trailed off and I said, "You have interesting dinners." I paused for a moment then said in a direct but not mean tone, "Liar!"

As soon as I said this, I heard several men and at least one woman laugh like they were having a good hearty joke about something. Soon things went black again.

Later I remember lying on a table. My nephew was lying next to me on my right side. Standing on my left side in front of me was a hazy figure that did not look human. Then I heard a male voice in my head again.

"You have a hernia. It will have to be fixed," he said.

"Ooh, no," I responded in a drawn out tone.

"You have a second one that is coming through. It will break through on a canoe trip."

"Oh no!" I said again, even more disappointed.

"There is a third one, but it is smaller. You will get it fixed when you get the second one fixed. The first one will be painful, but the second one will not be as bad."

"Oh, no. I don't believe it. Oh God. I have to get them fixed," I said. Meanwhile I was wondering what exactly a hernia was.

"Thank you for telling me. I know it's bad news but I'm glad you told me," were the best words I could articulate in my groggy state.

The next thing I remember is ever so vaguely walking back to the tent with Mason and the small children. I was tired. What a long dream.

The next morning we woke up. I had a bad headache. I felt groggy. I remembered having a weird dream the night before and the area of my back where my kidneys are had a dull ache.

"What was that dream about anyway?" I thought to myself. "All these voices and the haunted feeling of this place has gotten to me."

I got out of the tent and went to get our food. I couldn't hear anything other than the rushing water. After hearing voices and sounds for nine and half hours the day before I was only too glad to have an uneventful morning.

After a few minutes of clanging around I could hear Mason shuffling about and soon he too emerged from the tent. We didn't talk much, just idle chit chat while we ate breakfast, cleaned up, then packed up our gear and prepared to leave. The eerie feeling around the campsite had dissipated during the night.

We went over the whole campsite several times checking for and cleaning up garbage before we left. We took care of some of the biological necessities and soon we were in the canoe and paddling away. I looked back at the campsite and didn't know whether to say "good riddance" or "thank you" to the place.

As we paddled I talked to Mason. "Man I have a really weird headache," I said.

"Me too," replied Mason.

"I had this weird dream last night too. I dreamt I woke up in the tent and there were three aliens at the door flap of the tent. I woke you up and they ripped you out of there."

"Yeah, me too," replied Mason.

"What?" I exclaimed, "You're saying you had the same dream?" I asked in a tone of disbelief.

"Yeah," he replied. He didn't seem surprised at all.

"Oh man, that's too weird. We both hear voices all day. We both wake up with weird headaches. Then we both had the same dream." I became really uneasy. "I don't want to talk about this any more," I said. I'd reached my limit. The whole experience had pushed me beyond my paradigm's level of comprehension. I just wanted to paddle and relax and forget about things for a while. I wasn't going to degenerate what I felt was a rare spiritual experience on a Native reserve by bringing up any talk of aliens in connection with it.

Not that I didn't believe in aliens, I had experiences when I was younger. But they were a thing of the past. In my adult life, I had decided that any objects I saw in the past must have been planes. This included the one I saw just two weeks before when I asked for contact. I reacted to the whole experience the night before by going completely into denial. I tried to change the subject and redirect my memory of the night before.

"What about that kid you saw last night, eh?" I asked.

"Man, that was weird," Mason said.

"What do you mean? He probably lives in the area."

"You don't understand. It was weird," continued Mason. He shook his head from side to side. "It wasn't like anything I'd ever seen before. It wasn't human."

"Oh come on," I said, " all those voices got to you the way they got to me. It was dark and your perception was probably distorted."

Then Mason turned to his right and looked back at me and said in a quiet voice, "It was an alien."

"A what?" I asked.

"It was an alien," he said in a louder voice.

"Yeah, right. You saw an alien. Please, don't denigrate all this by talking about aliens."

Mason's demeanor changed quickly. I could see him take a deep breath. He turned to face me once again and yelled at the top of his lungs. "You don't know what the fuck you're talking about!"

I was taken back by his shouting. I remember thinking he could have used another cup of coffee or something. Besides, we vowed we would be quiet as we traveled along the river and this was clearly outside the boundaries of our agreed upon protocol for the trip. We had agreed that we didn't want to bring attention to ourselves and we both knew there was an occupied cottage just down the river.

I knew Mason was furious with me so I thought for a moment about what I should say. Finally I spoke. "You say you saw an alien. Fine, you saw an alien. I wish I'd seen an alien."

As soon as I said this Mason started to shake his head from side to side, then turned to me once again. Still shaking his head, he said in a sarcastic tone of resignation, "You don't believe me." He turned back around and we paddled. I could feel the waves of anger and disappointment coming off of him. I decided not to say anything for a while. So in silence, we just paddled.

Then something else happened. As we paddled along I looked at the shore to my right, admiring the view. As I paddled I saw flowers, grass, reeds, trees, flowers, little man, flowers, grass, reeds. LITTLE MAN?! I swung my head back to look. I saw what looked like a blur rush from a stump into the tall grass along the river. It moved so fast, it could not have been an animal. I was in shock. I shook my head and looked at the stump. "It must have been the stump," I tried to rationalize to myself.

No matter how I tried, I couldn't make myself believe it was the stump. I did not see a stump. What I had seen was a small man, approximately six to eight inches in height. He looked European and had thick, bushy, red hair. He also had a very thick mustache and beard. When I paddled by I looked directly into his eyes. He looked back, directly into mine. His eyes were very, very intense. As he crossed my line of vision he nodded his head slowly up and down. As we moved along the shoreline, he moved out of my line of vision. When I looked back, he darted off.

"My Lord, Mason! I thought I just saw a little man! I turned around to look back and saw a blur. It must have been a small animal or something. Man, this place is really getting to me. First we hear voices all day, then dream about aliens, now I'm seeing little people. Let's get out of here," I said, breaking the silence.

As soon as I said this, we both heard a loud snicker, like someone plugging their nose trying not to laugh. I turned around and looked at the forest in shock. I stared with a glare that would have caused a moose to shudder. Then I heard the same snicker type sound, only it was slightly different and had an underlying whistle sound that wasn't there before that made me wonder if it was not just a bird.

"Thank God," I thought to myself. I turned around and paddled on.

We began to talk again. We talked some more and eventually we were friends again. For some reason we both seemed to forget our conversation from earlier. When I look back, I realize it was really strange how we seemed to be forgetting the night before so quickly as the day proceeded.

We came up to the largest set of rapids we figured we could safely traverse and got out to spot them. They went in a straight line at about a ten degree angle for fifty feet, then we would have to make a sharp left turn and go down a horseshoe shaped waterfall. It would be close. The canoe would barely fit into it. The water was not too deep and being the daring wild Canadians we were that morning I said, "Let's do it!" So we did. We didn't dunk either. We flew through those puppies like professionals. We were both insufferably pleased with ourselves. We both wore a grin from ear to ear. I screamed a mighty war cry as we completed the run. "What an amazing day this is turning out to be," I thought to myself.

Eventually we arrived back at the car and unloaded the gear. We loaded the canoe and we were off on our way home. A couple of hours later we arrived at my sister's house. Boy, did we have a story to tell the family.

We walked in the door, Mason with his gear on his back. My sister came and greeted us with her usual warm smile.

"Hi! Hi!" she said. "How was the trip?"

"You won't believe what happened to us." I said. She looked with an expression of apprehension and fear.

"No! Nothing bad," I said.

Her face softened.

"We heard voices at the campsite. It took us a while to figure out we were hearing the same voices at the same time. At first we thought the sound of the rapids was playing tricks on our ears but we checked things out. We definitely were hearing voices," I rambled. My sister looked intensely curious now.

"Yeah, and we saw an alien!" interjected Mason.

I looked down at the ground. "Mason said he saw an alien. I didn't see one, but Mason said he saw one," I said. I was embarrassed. I looked over at my sister. She was looking down at the floor the way I was. She paused for a moment. She didn't know quite what to do, then she turned around and walked away. I looked up at Mason. What I saw caught me off guard. Here before me, stood a strapping young nineteen year old man, his whole body shaking, tears streamed down his face.

"Nobody believes me!" he said. He looked devastated and so very, very hurt.

I didn't know what to do. I realized something had happened. I walked over to him and grabbed his left elbow with my right hand. "I'm not being a very good uncle here. Am I?" I said in a concerned yet disoriented tone. I desperately searched for the right thing to say. What would be an honest response to all of this? Finally I said, "I believe that you believe you saw something. I'm sorry. You know, I didn't see it. I mean an alien. I would have needed to see it."

I paused for a moment and looked at him blubbering and shaking. "Jesus. What did you see?" I continued in a tone of shock and disbelief, seeing my normally tough nephew's tearful reaction. He was not so tough now. Clearly he believed he had seen something very, very unusual. I felt bad. Frustrated, he walked upstairs. I went into the living room and continued telling my sister about the trip.

Mason and I spoke only one more time about the alien. It was about a month or so later. He challenged me about not believing him. I told him it was just too difficult, and perhaps he should just forget about it. He responded by saying that he was going to. He explained that he went to the police to report it and they just treated him like he was crazy.

<u>MICHELLE</u>
Dreams and Green Lightning

My dream of the Indian man giving me my name slowly edged its way into the back of my mind. My work continued and everything seemed to settle back down, or at least as settled as my life could be. My visits with the Rye-hun continued on a regular basis. Most of my visits were not your standard "abduction" type of experiences like you see on TV. My visits centered around the Gemini community (those humans who interact with the ETs on a less medical basis) and the work I was doing for the non Rye-hun ETs.

Between August of 1996 and December of that year I spent many a night in the company of these non Rye-hun ETs teaching lessons to human children who were "abducted" by the Rye-hun.

One series of lessons I worked on and took great pride in was the teaching of telepathy to a group of children about six years old. It is taught in an fascinating way. Simple in design but complex to teach and learn, it took quite a bit of my time to brush up on my technique enough to teach these children.

As you probably know, both the gray ETs and the human looking beings often talk with a form of telepathy. Even though, as you probably also know, people who have contact with ETs are generally very psychic in nature and have very good "seeing" abilities, often telepathy between humans is lacking. The ETs point out that we all have the ability to be telepathic, but for many reasons, here on Earth, humans seem to loose this ability when they are about five or six years old.

If you are a contactee, you probably remember a time when you just "knew" what people around you were thinking without much effort. But most of us start to loose the ability as we develop language skills and start school where we have more verbal stimulation.

In the ET world, to counteract this, children at "re-taught" to use their telepathic skills. This is done over a long period of time through a method taught to me by a human looking ET named Alex. Alex coordinates many of the classes taught to the children in the ET world.

The method is simple. The children are brought into a classroom. They are seated and the class begins. No words are ever spoken to the children. Not a single sound is uttered by the teacher at all. Rather the children are given a series of "hand signs" that replace words. These signs are similar to the sign language used by the deaf, in that hand actions are used to represent words and ideas, but as far as I'm aware, none of the signs were copied from one to the next.

As the teacher signs to the children the "concept" of the word being presented is relayed telepathically to the child. The words are not relayed, for there is no guarantee that the child can speak the same language as the teacher and for true telepathy one has to know what the other is thinking beyond language. Language and words are applied to the concept presented by the receiver not projected by the sender. The language one hears when receiving telepathy is applied by the mind of the receiver, not sent by the transmitter, if it is done correctly.

As the children become more and more familiar with the signs and the "thoughts" they hear as the signs are presented, the children are encouraged to communicate with each other, and as time passes the teacher slowly starts to omit signs and present more complex concepts until the children learn to rely on the the concept in their head. By then, telepathy is mastered.

Just about every member of the ET community has gone through this telepathy training and many of us have retained some of the basic sign language we learned at that time. Even into adulthood, the ETs will communicate with us or reinforce telepathic ideas with the use of signs. Many experiencers have reported to me that they recall being "signed" to by the Ets. Some knew what was being said, others did not. Other experiencers have even reported that they will sometimes break out into sign language when they are frustrated or excited and have no idea why or what they are saying with their hands.

The process of teaching telepathy took a lot of concentration on my part during that fall and into the winter of 1997. I used the sign language every chance I had. I even "sign sang" in the house and car when no one was around.

Still, it wasn't a quiet time. The Native American theme dreams kept returning through this time though none were as vivid as the one with the large man who turned into the white eagle.

In one dream I found myself standing in a run-down old wooden shack. The roof was rusted tin. I was looking out of a window whose pane of glass had long since been broken. There was a large illuminated cloud in the sky. I watched with amazement as the cloud formed itself into the shape of a beautiful white horse. My whole spirit longed to fly into the sky and ride that cloud horse. Just as I thought it, I was flying in the sky towards the horse. Then a voice in my head said, "Death rides a pale horse"

A pale horse? Was this cloud beast a pale horse? I became terrified that if I did ride it I would die. I thought about my children finding me dead in my bed that next morning. The whole idea terrified me and I "snapped back" to my flesh. I was shaking and scared. I looked around the room, for what, I wasn't sure. After a while I went back to sleep.

The next day I told a friend who is also a member of the Gemini community and who has excellent intuition about dream experiences. She told me that indeed, there is a Native legend that Death rides a pale horse. She felt I would not have died if I dared to ride the cloud animal. I would have transformed into something else. It symbolized my old life dying as a new one took its place. I didn't know it at the time, but she was correct. It didn't take a ride on the pale horse to make it happen.

One night, not long after this dream, I believe it was just before Thanksgiving, the house was very quiet and dark. I awoke to a strange sound, but by the time I was awake enough to make out what it was it stopped. Just as I was about to doze off, it started again. It was a songbird I was minding for my parents while they were wintering in Florida. It was singing.

It was the dead of night, completely dark, yet the canary was singing like it was a bright summer morning. The bird kept happily singing to the point where I wondered how I could quiet it down before it woke up the children.

The customary way to quiet a canary is to cover the cage or close the room lights because normally a bird will not sing in the dark. But it was pitch black in the living room and the bird was singing like a feathered Pavarotti. The bird stopped suddenly. Within a seconds time there was a huge crash of thunder.

Thunder and lightning storms are not very common in New England in the late fall and winter months, so I was taken by surprise by the crash of nearby thunder. I got up and pulled up the blinds of the bedroom window to see what was going on. The bird started to sing again.

As the bird sang, we experienced a storm like I had never seen before. The lightning was striking so steadily that the sky was almost constantly lit, and it was a very unusual color green. It was not a yellow green or even a grass green, but rather a deep pine green that shone bright with the intensity of each strike.

Then, in the distance I saw three large bolts of bright purple lightning followed by several bolts of cobalt blue lightning. The storm seemed to be over but the canary kept singing. Moments later as I was just getting up to close the shade, a large bolt of deep green lightning struck an area not far from the window where I stood. The whole house shook and the windows rattled. I was overcome with a feeling that the lightning wasn't just odd in color, but that it was trying to tell me something. I shook off the feeling and went to bed. The haunting feeling that it wasn't a normal storm stayed with me for a long time. It was some time before I fell asleep. Before morning came, I had two dreams.

I dreamed that I was standing in the green lightning storm. In a flash, I found myself sitting crossed legged in a field of tall tan grass. It looked like wheat or some other grain. There was green lightning branching out over my head in the sky above but it didn't come down to the Earth.

A group of people surrounded me. They were chanting something I didn't seem to understand. I dreamed that I fell into a meditative state and a swirl of wind whipped around me. There was also a swirl of bright light. For a moment I wondered if the lightning had struck me. Then there was only calm. I stood up and floated into the sky. Below me where I had been sitting was a fresh crop circle in the pattern of a heart with kind of lumpy sides. It wasn't the full "chaos" symbol; far from it. It was just a rough heart shape with rounded edges that were caused by the circles in the grain. The center had a perfect spiral, which I had been sitting in just moments before.

In the second dream, I was looking at a very ancient oak tree. The tree seemed so wise, so strong. I wanted to be "one" with the tree. I felt myself drift out of my body and soon I visualized myself turning into water. I became rain. I poured into the ground around the base of the old tree. It soaked me into its roots and I was drawn up into its leaves. From its leaves I burst forth into the sky like sunshine. When this happened I was overcome with a feeling of peace and happiness. Then I saw the face of the same Indian man who gave me the name. He looked at me with his strange green eyes. I looked back, transfixed on his eyes. His face changed. His eyes got dark brown, almost black. His face became old and wrinkled, and in a moments time his face changed to that of a totally different aboriginal man. An old man who said, "Come to me".

His words startled me. I found myself back in bed with a harsh snap. I didn't know who the old man was and I didn't have any idea I would be seeing him again really soon.

<u>*PAUL*</u>
November 1996
A Strange Dream

In mid November I had an unusual and strange ET dream that made no sense at the time. I was standing in a circular, darkly lit room speaking with a number of gray ETs. We were discussing some type of plan and my mind felt sharp. Everything seemed to make sense. Talk was soon finished and we walked down a hall into another room. In this room the round walls were a dark blue and purple in color and had a metallic feel to them.

As we entered the room, my perception began to cloud and my vision became distorted. I found myself standing with a group of ETs in front of a small woman. They exchanged some words. I was confused.

I heard one of the ETs say the to the woman, "Either take him or he's out."

"What?" I thought to myself with surprise. "What are they talking about? 'Either she takes me or I'm out!' This is not good."

The woman seemed to be arguing with the gray in front of her. I remember leaving the room afterwards feeling awkward. Something was amiss. It all made sense before I walked into the blue walled room, but the second I walked into that room my mind turned into mush.

The next day I awoke with a memory of this hazy, cloudy dream. I was tired, like I had been out all night. I felt emotionally distraught all day, as though something important had happened that I did not understand. It would not be until some months later that I would verify that this was in fact an ET contact experience. I found out because Michelle told me of the same experience. Only her view was from the perspective of the small woman in the room with me. She told me about this experience before I told her.

<u>*MICHELLE*</u>
December 1996
A Time of Strange Emotions

With all the things happening in my life, between my family here on Earth, my ET family and the holidays coming, you would think strange emotions would be the norm. But the month of December, particularly the end of December in 1997 saw me totally up in arms with emotions. I had no way of knowing that my link with a man almost a thousand miles away, and the tragedy in his life was affecting me.

Earlier, in November, I had an experience with a man on shipboard that had been haunting my thoughts. I was brought into a room and introduced to a man whom I knew during the experience, but back at home, I couldn't put my finger on who he was. All I could remember was thinking that he came back from the dead. I remembered being shocked to see him.

It was a strange event. I wanted to hold him and hug him and welcome him because I was so happy to see him, at the same time I felt strong hurt surrounding him. He seemed to have hurt feelings as well. We tried to talk.

Our attempt at discussion was getting us nowhere. Finally, Hetar said to me, "Either take him or he's out." The man looked at Hetar with panic and desperation on his face. It was obvious that he didn't feel it was fair that his fate was in my hands. I didn't feel it was fair either. I did not want the responsibility for his future. Hetar signaled and two little grays led the man away so I would have time to think before I decided.

I looked at Hetar and said, "What do you mean by 'he's out'?"

Hetar said, "He's yours. Either you take him and get to work, or we move him out of the way."

I remember looking deep into Hetar's eyes and thinking he was serious. I was angry with the man who I saw in that room and I felt very hurt. I wanted to tell Hetar "No. I never want to see him again. I don't care what you do with him." But just the thought of not seeing that man again made me shudder with deep and intense pain. I remember saying to Hetar, "How can I say no. He's my soul."

Over the next few weeks, the haunting feeling of this strange event faded and was replaced with a feeling that I had to get ready for Christmas. As the middle of December came and Christmas was drawing near, I totally lost my holiday feel. I barely wanted to finish my shopping, and if it were not for the fact that I had small children, I would have suggested giving the holiday a miss all together that year. My emotions were a wreck. I felt like I was slipping into a deep depression. I blamed most of it on my work as editor of the magazine and other writing projects which took a great deal of time when compared to the money they brought in.

It didn't help that I was still unable to rectify the Native American theme dreams I kept having. I wondered if they were somehow responsible for the deep, dark feeling I was experiencing before Christmas that year.

To make matters worse, it seemed all my friends needed more emotional support than I did. I worked feverishly to help them, but couldn't see I was on the verge of crashing myself.

Christmas came, and went. The holiday was very typical for my family. I was glad it wasn't anything special. The kids enjoyed what Santa brought them. The holiday meal at mom's house went off without a hitch and it was over.

The morning after Christmas I was taking the bulbs off the tree. By lunch time the tree was bare and in the bin for the neighborhood recycling program. I was glad to see it go.

I was edgy and nervous. It was hard not to cry. I had no idea why I was feeling like I was. The three days after Christmas were the worst of all. As I tore down the tree, I felt overcome with an uneasiness that is hard to describe. It was like my skin was moving on its own, aggravating my body's nerves. I tried to ignore it, but by the 28th I was so on edge, I was on the verge of a panic.

That night the kids were in bed sound asleep by 8:30 which was unusual. But I didn't care. I was glad. I needed to relax. I needed some time to myself. Maybe I could even get out of the edgy mood if I could have some peace and quiet. I thought about a relaxing bath, or maybe just going to bed early myself, but I was so restless and edgy that I couldn't imagine lying down and trying to sleep. I felt more like I was ready to run a marathon!

I decided that the best way to relax was to listen to some music. So I pulled out my rocking chair, collected up the CD's I wanted to listen to, shut the lights around the house, put the first CD on, grabbed my headphones and endeavored to try and relax.

Some time later, I thought for sure that I heard two voices talking to each other in the room. I couldn't make out what they were saying, but they were definitely voices. I took off my headphones to find out what it was, but there was no one there. I thought that maybe there was someone talking very loud in the hallway or outside. But by the time I had the headphones off the room was silent.

I put my headphones back on and within a minute's time I heard the voices again. I reasoned that I must be more tired than I thought and I must have been dozing off. So I decided I better go to bed whether I wanted to or not. I shut off the stereo, hung up my headphones and got up to walk to bed.

I was walking through my living room when, without warning, I felt like I turned into fluid flowing through a funnel. I truly felt like a liquid mass spinning and flowing through the hole of a funnel. This feeling, so strange then, has become very familiar to me in recent months. But then it was new and very disturbing.

Just as suddenly as it started, I found myself standing outside in the darkness. It was chilly but not cold. There was no snow on the ground. In front of me was a bright fire, making it hard for me to see anything else. I was really dizzy, like I had been on a spinning carnival ride.

My eyes slowly adjusted. As they did, I saw a Native American man draped in red shawls, crouched by the fire. He wasn't looking at me at all, but must have known I was there because he said, "Starwalker. Will you join a Landwalker at the fire?"

I didn't move. I was really confused, and more than a bit shook up. I was very disoriented. He asked me again to join him at the fire. He said, "It is a holy fire."

I still couldn't bring myself to move because I was too confused and too nervous. Finally I calmed down enough to ask him how I got there.

He said, "I summoned you."

He explained that for three nights he sat by the fire and sang a song of summoning and shook his rattle. When his song reached me, it drew me to him.

He turned and got up. When he faced me, he looked like a man about 50 years old. As he walked towards me his face seemed to change with each flicker of the firelight. I know this is hard to imagine, but I swear one second he looked like he was old, then young, then a man, then a woman and even a girl and a boy. It was as if the dancing of the fire light on his face caused it to change. Oddly enough, because of this, I didn't feel afraid anymore. But I was still confused and a bit dizzy.

He held up the big, terra-cotta colored rattle he had been playing. It had feathers tied to the handle. The top of it had some kind of design either etched or painted in it with a lighter color, probably white. It was hard to tell in the firelight. It had a design on it that I don't recall in detail.

He asked me if I knew what it was. I think I shook my head indicating "no." I'm not really sure if I moved at all. I'm not sure I could. Then he told me that it was a tool that the Indians use to help them bring their messages to the Grandfather Spirit. It could also be used to bring the "Starwalkers".

He explained that Grandfather Spirit had directed him to build it and use it to summon me.

I know I asked, "Why me?"

He said, "That's because it is you who came to its song. Grandfather Spirit didn't tell me that YOU would come. The one who came would be the one who the song sang to." Then he went on to tell me that when the Spirit told him to build the thing (he called it a name I can't remember now) he talked to the bugs in the ground and told them what the Spirit had said. He said that the bugs then went deep into the Earth and came back with small, rounded pebbles of different elements that make up man and the things of the Earth and gave them to him. He put them in the 'rattle' and after that he put the feathers on it. He explained that the feathers were the colors of the sky and the ground and the stars.

Then he walked close to me and asked, "Do you understand why the song called to you?"

I replied, "No, I don't understand, but I want to." I really did want to know more about this. I just couldn't understand why this was happening to me. I said something else to the effect of, "I cannot seem to become part of this world in my heart. I understand and I respect it, but I can't find it in me to feel this world as home."

He said in reply, "Starwalking sister, I am aware of the sins of the past. Forgive the children of the ground and soil for what we did so long ago in the stars. It's again time for oneness. Tell your sisters we offer this to you." He handed me the rattle, round end first.

I put out my hands to take it. As he put it in my hands, it dissolved into a bird. I was totally amazed. I slowly lifted the bird to my face to see it better. It was obviously alive, yet it didn't fly away.

I didn't say anything. I couldn't. I was so overwhelmed with feelings that I was numb. It was like I felt everything and nothing all at the same time.

Then he said, "Forever is a long time to walk in the stars without a mother's firm ground to hold you. The Indians know the ground and the sky. The Starwalkers know the stars and the many suns."

I understood what he meant in my heart. I held the bird to my chest, looked at the man and said, "I am you. You are we. We are one. One is all."

He nodded. Then suddenly, I was once again standing in my living room. My eyes were crying freely, but I couldn't isolate any emotions at all. I was still very numb. After a short while, I was overwhelmed with exhaustion. My body shaking, I went to bed.

While this was happening, I had no conscious idea of what was happening to the man who literally was the completer of my soul. I had no way of knowing that on the very same day, so many miles away he too was feeling extremes of emotion, and he made a Native connection that changed his life.

<u>PAUL</u>
December 1996
Death, Fire and Light

After the trip with Mason on the Moon river, I became more and more interested in the possibility that there was more to the alien thing than I was admitting. I started to wonder about the sightings I had as a child and thought I may want to explore more into what they were. So I decided to get an Internet connection and began to look into the alien abduction/contact phenomenon with more vigor.

I was amazed at the number of websites devoted to the subject. Quite by accident I came across the website of a group calling itself *UFOBC*. They were located in the Vancouver area. I thought it appropriate to contact them since my early childhood experiences occurred in that province. I also hoped that if anybody else had filed a report with them that corroborated what I had to tell them, it might be more readily accepted as scientific evidence and therefore be more useful.

I soon found myself talking over the Internet with a man called David and his partner Graham. Graham had over fifty years experience in researching the UFO phenomenon and I felt a little more at ease in speaking with him. Though hesitant at first, by early December of 1996 I felt comfortable enough that I decided to write down my experiences and mail a copy to David and Graham.

Within thirty-six hours of filing my report with *UFOBC* I arrived home from work exhausted and worn. I had been dealing with the stress of both work and the stress of spending the previous week typing up my experiences. The anxiety of wondering what the consequences of signing my name to such a bizarre document would be had taken its toll on me as well.

I walked into my house and noticed there was a message on my answering machine. I pressed the play button. It was my mother. Mason was in the hospital. Not only had he had a severe asthma attack, but he had to be revived because his heart had stopped beating. He was in Sunnybrook Hospital's Intensive Care Unit in a coma. I stood and listened in a state of shock.

It didn't make any sense! The shock began to build. I picked up the phone and called my sister's house. My brother-in-law answered. Speaking through tears, he told me my sister was spending the night at the hospital. Mason had been there since noon.

He said that around lunch time Mason came out of his bedroom to ask his brother Warwick to call a cab for him to go to the hospital. His brother called a cab and helped him to the door. When the cab finally arrived, Mason was worse. The attack was more severe than he anticipated and he began to pass out along the way. Mason managed to maintain some level of consciousness and staggered inside the hospital. He made it through the doors and collapsed. Emergency staff got him inside quickly and

45

somewhere through all the commotion his heart stopped beating. It took them thirty minutes to revive him. But he was in a coma. They feared he suffered extensive brain damage.

I told my brother-in-law that I would head straight down to the hospital in the morning. I hung up the phone and went to bed where I cried myself to sleep.

The next day I got up and headed south to Toronto. I arrived to find my sister sitting by Mason's bedside talking to him over and over about anything she could think of.

The next two days were a nightmare. We all took turns sitting with Mason talking to him and watching helplessly as his body endured almost continuous seizures. Nevertheless, I was convinced he would wake up. I told the family that if I could see three people descend on a cloud out of the sky above me when I was a child, then miracles were possible. Mason could wake up. I was hell bent on prayer and faith that we could somehow get him to revive.

Saturday morning came and I called down to my sister's place. My brother-in-law answered the phone. He told me he spoke to the doctor that morning. The doctor asked that we all come in for a family meeting. My brother-in-law warned me that a family meeting was usually not a good thing.

As I drove down, my mind was in a tailspin. I did not want to let them take Mason off life support. We could not give up that easily.

When I arrived at the hospital we all met and were filed into a separate room. The doctors explained that they had verified Mason was completely brain dead. There was no hope of recovery and that it was time to consider taking him off life support and letting him pass away naturally. I experienced rage and helplessness. I told my sister and brother-in-law they did not have to make a quick decision, then I left the room. Yet in my heart I realized he was their son and it was their decision. Maybe I was wrong. Maybe he wouldn't make it now.

I waited in the general waiting room for a few minutes with my mother. She spoke but my mind was elsewhere. This wasn't fair. He had his whole life ahead of him. My brother-in-law walked in a few minutes later and told us he hoped we wouldn't hate them too much, but they had decided to let Mason die in peace.

I now found myself having to not just put the emotional and mental brakes on, but I had to start charging in the other direction to support my sister and her husband's decision. The pain was unbearable, but in my heart I knew they were right.

None of the family wanted to stay. I insisted on being with Mason when he died. At the time, I could not understand why the family would leave, nevertheless a part of me was glad. I decided I would do everything I could internally to help his spirit pass through this final stage of life. Besides, there was a part of me that did not wish to fall apart in front of all of them as he passed away.

The nurse called me as soon as they disconnected life support. I rushed in and stood by his side. The nurse explained which instruments to watch and explained that he may well have passed already. I could see movement in the readings still. I had also seen a dead body before and I knew some part of Mason was still there. I could see it and feel it.

"He was my bowsman," I said to the nurse.

"Sorry?" she said quietly.

"He was my bowsman in my canoe," I said again while I held his arm.

"Oh dear," she said, not knowing what else to say.

I watched one of two young men who were the closest I had ever had to a son of my own die in front of me. The nurse closed the curtain around the bed and left us alone.

I spoke to Mason and apologized for everything I ever did to let him down. I told him how much I loved him and found emotions in my heart that I never knew existed. I began to sob and the nurse looked in to ask if I was okay.

"I'm okay," I sobbed. Again, she left us alone. At one particular point I looked down at his body and realized he was not there anymore. I looked at the monitoring instruments. They were all flat lines. I stood in shock for a minute.

After a long moment I came out and looked at the nurse and said, "He's gone." I walked away and froze in my tracks then slowly turned around. Something was watching me.

I looked at the foot of Mason's bed. To this day, as God as my witness, I felt his presence standing there watching me. I looked for a good thirty seconds in a state of shock as nurses walked in front of me. I stared straight through them.

I went to a phone. It was now 12:10 PM, Saturday, December 14, 1996. I called my sister's house where they all were waiting. I told them, "It's over. He's gone." A part of me was gone too.

Later my mother told me how at a few minutes after 12:00 noon that day, she felt someone running their hand through her hair the way Mason always did when he saw her. She knew it was him.

As I left the hospital, I stopped on the main floor again and turned around. Once again, standing in the hall I could feel a powerful presence watching me. It was Mason. I just knew it.

I stopped by my sister's house. I didn't stay long. I couldn't. Something was happening inside. I was decompressing from the last seventy-two hours. I drove home and collapsed. For the next three days it would take every ounce of energy I had to get out of bed in the morning and walk to my living room and sit on the couch. I put on the television but I could not hear it. My mind was in some other place. Anything that was of any psychological value to me was stripped away. Nothing meant anything anymore.

By the fourth day after Mason's death, I returned to work. Shaky and heart broken, I faked my way through the day. I didn't make it through the next day and had to leave. I had lost grandparents before, but this was so different. There is nothing, absolutely nothing, to compare to loosing a family member who is younger, and worse, still a young child in your eyes. I felt it should have been me who died. Though I was afraid, I told the powers that be that if I could trade my life for his, I would.

Over the next few days, the family talked about gathering the photographs together that we had of Mason for a scrapbook. We all thought that was a good idea. So I started to go through the hundreds of pictures of canoe trips I had until I found the set from the only trip I ever took him on.

I came across the pictures from the Moon River trip the previous summer. I remembered the voices and how we had been so freaked out. It was truly an adventure. If ever there was a trip to take someone on, that was the one. I was glad we had that trip together.

I looked through the photos and came across two where Mason was standing by the smoke of the fire during the daytime. One looked completely normal, but the other one contained much thicker smoke. I remembered standing in the smoke on that trip and looking down the river. The river looked different and I had thought at the time, "There's something in the smoke."

I looked at the smoke in the picture. Something didn't seem right. There were some odd things in it that looked like little balls. Since smoke does not normally travel in balls like these it struck my attention. I looked and looked. There was some type of feature I couldn't make out. I looked at the photograph, then put it down and walked away. A few minutes later I was drawn to it again.

"Is that an image of a deer's eye?" I asked myself. Then it all came together. There was a face in the smoke! It was only a trick of smoke and light, but it produced a three dimensional image. On the right side was a human face. On the left was something else. "It wasn't a deer. It was an alien!" My mind raced with excitement and amazement. "We heard voices! Mason said he saw something! Oh my God!"

I picked up the phone and made an hysterical call to David in British Columbia. As I recall, it was a Sunday afternoon. David did his best to calm me down. I told him I would send out a couple of copies of the picture for analysis. I told him I always thought we just camped on an old Native spirit place, but now, seeing the face in this picture, it may well have more to do with other things!

Over the next few days I got the photos scanned and enlargements done. I showed my family and friends the photograph. It became clear that some people would see the face, perhaps not right away, but after some guidance could clearly make it out, while others never would.

David at *UFOBC* was the first to coin the term "Rorschach Test" to me. I realized there was an element of truth to it. I began to realize over time, it was not enough proof for the scientists, but it was definitely enough for me.

During all of this, I began to recall not only what Mason said about seeing an alien, but also the incredibly clear dream I had that night of waking up in my tent and conversing with three large eyed, non-human beings at the tent door flap.

Once I realized the nature and quality of that dream, so many other dreams that were of the same quality and nature over the last three decades now made sense to me. This broke some kind of inner barrier. Clear memories began to emerge of experiences in another reality that had been buried in me for most of my life. I surmised that the shock of Mason's death, coupled with the finding of the photo, propelled sweeping recovery of huge sections of my memory regarding my alien contact experiences.

What I had once thought to be childhood memories now became an absolute physical reality in a way that they never had before. I was now on "a mission from God" so to speak, to find out the truth behind these memories.

As the memories flooded in, I wrote everything down. I did not understand what was happening to me, but everything seemed to be forming some type of pattern. I cannot adequately describe in words how the feeling of being compelled interlaced itself with my being and grew inside of me. I was driven like I had never been before.

I knew I had to go up to the Mohawk reserve with my picture and try and find somebody that could help me to understand what had happened to Mason and me when we were on their land.

I thought of knocking on doors, but then I thought that if I was not welcome I would soon find myself the guest of the Tribal Police. So it was my plan to go up right after Christmas and seek out the Tribal Police office. I was hopeful that I could convince a Police Constable to direct me to some Medicine People on the reserve. I was nervous about violating the privacy of a people who had been not only oppressed by European settlers, but discriminated against for decades. I had no idea how I might be received. I hoped they would not be too angry with me for intruding on them, and some of them might even help me.

Somehow, the family made it through Christmas. We made a place at the table for Mason. We all tried to make the best of it.

I tried to rest, but every time a sat still I found myself thinking of Mason, thinking of the photograph, thinking of the reserve and thinking about my report to *UFOBC*. On December 28th, I screwed up my courage and headed north. We had just had a snowstorm and the roads were not good, but I was determined not to let that stop me.

I got in my little car and fired along the roadway northward to the reserve. I knew of a place called *Mohawk Archery* along the highway beside the reserve. I thought that would be a good place to get directions to the Tribal Police office. As I drove I shivered with both nervousness and anticipation. I felt a deep-seated determination. I knew that no matter how weird my story was, it was the truth. I planned to make no mention of aliens, only the voices we heard, and that Mason saw what was in the left side of the face in the smoke in the picture I had. They could make up their own minds from there.

After a couple of hours driving, I came up to the archery place and pulled in. I knocked on the door and entered. I apologized for bothering the storekeeper and explained that I was looking for directions to the Tribal Police station.

He was friendly and open. He explained to me there were no Tribal Police on this reserve. My heart sank. I had to be more direct now. I began to explain, then quickly excused myself to get my picture. I brought it back in and told him how we had heard voices on the Moon River the previous summer and had just recently found this photograph contained a picture of a face. His wife came in at that point and I explained again to her as well. Neither could see the face in the smoke, but they could tell from my tone and my manner that I was sincere and really wanted to leave a copy of the photograph with someone on the reserve.

The man thought for a moment then suggested I go see a man on the reserve who had an interest in the history of the land and might also be able to help in relating some of the spiritual aspects of my experience. He referred me to the local Medicine Man, Tom.

"Great!" I thought. That's where I wanted to go anyway; to see a Medicine Man. Within five minutes he gave me a phone number and I was on my way.

I called the Medicine Man from my cell phone and explained to him what I wanted to do. I told him I didn't want to take up too much of his time and that I wanted to leave a rather unusual photograph with him.

I guess he was intrigued, because he gave me directions to his house and I was off. I got to Tom's in less than ten minutes. I pulled up and got out of my car. Eight rambunctious little puppies swarmed me. A larger dog, that was obviously the mother, came over with a curious look on her face.

I walked up the stairs and knocked on the door. I clearly heard a yell, "Come on in!"

I opened the door and stepped inside. The entrance was full of shoes and young children's boots and coats. Stairs led up. I looked up to find a very large man who appeared about forty looking down at me.

"Hello," he said with a friendly grin.

"Hi Tom. Thank you so much for seeing me during the holidays. I'm really sorry to intrude like this."

I walked in, put my briefcase down, pulled out my photo and gave it to him. It was an eight by ten enlargement. No sooner had I begun to talk, when a young lady came over to me and stuck out her hand. "Hi, I'm Lily," she announced. It was Tom's daughter.

"And this is Joe," Tom said pointing to his ten year old son. Then a woman, about Tom's age, came walking through the kitchen to the dining room. She had a friendly smile and penetrating eyes.

"Hi, I'm Lucy," she said. I shook hands with her and felt her eyes stare right through me. She exuded warmth and friendliness. I was nervous but felt a bit more relaxed now.

I began to explain again what happened. "Last summer my nephew and I went on a trip on the Moon River across the reserve..." It took a few minutes to give them the short version of the story of how we heard voices, my nephew's recent death and how I found the picture.

Before I finished, Tom interjected, "I'm having trouble seeing the face you're talking about but I can see two others here. Lucy, can you see anything?"

I was surprised he saw other faces. I wondered what was going on.

Lucy walked over and without any prompting of where to look, she pointed to the exact spot in the smoke on the photo and said, "Oh yeah. Look there's a face right there!" She circled it with her index finger.

"You see it?" I asked.

"Oh yeah. Look at that, eh? Wow!" Lucy said.

I sat back and took a deep breath. "Oh, thank God. Then you don't think I'm crazy."

"No! Look at that, eh, Lily," continued Lucy.

"I'm having trouble seeing it," said Lily.

Lucy went on to describe it and I felt confident that if Lucy could see it then eventually they all would see it.

"I was so worried I'd get here and you'd tell me I was nuts and to get the heck out," I said. We all chuckled. I was relieved. I realized that if at least one of them saw the face, I could now take a daring step.

"The night we were on that trip," I began to explain, "my nephew said he saw something outside of the tent. I didn't believe him, but what he said he saw is in the left side of the face in that picture. I feel very badly about not believing him now."

Lucy crossed her eyebrows for a second, looked at the picture and said, "Oh, you mean the alien half? You met the aliens when you were out there?"

My eyes opened up, my jaw dropped and I nodded in the affirmative.

She looked straight at me and said, "I'm an abductee! Many of my people here are abductee's. We've seen these things here for years. We kid that this is a UFO landin' pad or somethin'!"

What she said shocked me to the very core.

"One crashed here in 1947. Some people found a piece of it and sent it into the army and never heard from them again," she continued. She was obviously excited.

I just about fainted flat out on the floor.

"This has been happening to me all my life," I explained. "You are the first person I've ever met who has had the same experience!" I looked around in shock. We all were a bit surprised. I looked at Tom. His face was very serious now. His arms were folded and he was staring bullets into me.

He explained that he had seen several disk shaped craft and other highly strange phenomenon around the reserve. We talked for a good two hours then exchanged addresses and phone numbers. They described many unusual things to me and tried to help me make sense of my experience the previous summer.

I left with a feeling of tremendous gratitude. I thanked them for letting me into their home and apologized for bringing such a crazy story with me into their holiday afternoon. They were understanding and compassionate. I felt we would all become friends.

Driving home I was ecstatic. I could not believe what had happened. I was so exhilarated. It helped to deal with the shock and pain of losing Mason. It was one of the most incredible days of my life. Not only had I found a picture that twigged me off to what really happened on the Moon River the previous summer, not only did a flood of memories rush into my consciousness, but I also had met people who confirmed for me that it was real. It was something they knew was happening on their land and had been happening there for decades.

It was odd, I had sensed for so many years that my path would somehow cross paths with aboriginal people, and this day that had happened. I began to start to believe there was a real purpose in all of this.

<u>MICHELLE</u>
White Wolf Dreams part 1

For sometime after the event with the man in the desert who gave me the rattle, I struggled to make sense of what was happening to me. I tried talking to my grandfather about it. I hoped that he would give me some insight into the whole thing. But as I feared, my grandfather was not interested. Before I said more than a half dozen words I was stopped by his firmly stating, "I don't want to hear any nonsense." He tuned me out and turned away. Later when I brought it up again he said, "What do you want to go and tell people you're an Indian for? They are only going to treat you like dirt. Even the Indians will treat you like dirt because you ain't really an Indian anymore cause we became Catholic."

Daunted but not destroyed, I shared my experience with a few close friends and some of the people in the support group I was working with on the Internet at the time. No one I knew was involved enough with Native culture and lore to lend more than a few glimpses of insight. I needed to know more, but I was too nervous because of my grandfather's warnings of rejection to go into the Native community directly with my concerns.

I looked for traces of my grandfather's tribe and heritage and found very little. Though, I have to admit, I really didn't try all that hard. There was something inside of me that was truly afraid of all this. It seemed to baffle my friends that I ran gung-ho into discovering the ET experience, but I was very hesitant and even afraid of going forward with this more human based experience.

Despite my reluctance, the events continued. Many of the more amazing events that happened that winter involved a special animal. It was a large, rather impressive looking white wolf. Most of these events appeared to foreshadow a happening of great importance, yet I had no awareness of exactly what it was or when it would happen.

In the first event I was talking on-line via my computer with my friend, Diane. I was telling her about how edgy I was feeling. I was very concerned because it was the same kind of edgy feeling I had right after Christmas, only it was not quiet as intense. As I typed to her, I got very dizzy, then I was suddenly aware I was standing in a glade of some kind. It was sunny and warm even though it was cold and snow covered in New Hampshire at that time of year. I did not really feel like myself, meaning that my body felt different, but my mind was very clear and my awareness of things around me and my memory was very sharp.

There was a large, very old oak tree in the glade. An Indian man I saw in my first vision stood leaning against the tree. He was the same man who told me my name. Around me were all sorts of white animals. They were amazing to behold. Oddly enough, what got my attention was a group of white dog like animals. I remember thinking they looked like wolves but I wanted to believe they were dogs. Two of them were sitting watching me. Two of them were rolling in play together. One of them was standing at my side. He was a beautiful animal with ice blue eyes. I bent down and wrapped my arms around him. He pushed me over and started licking my neck. We wrestled in play like you would with a big friendly family dog for a short while.

Then the man near the tree called me. He asked, "Who are you?"

I said, "I am the Kristance." At the time I recalled this I was baffled that I used the word "the" in front of my "special ET name".

"Are you prepared?" he asked in short, firm words.

I said, "Yes, I am." But I was not entirely sure I was. Then, oddly enough, I turned to the wolf and asked it if it were ready. It seemed to reply in a way I understood. I turned back to the man. "Yes. Ready," I said with more confidence.

"Take this." He handed me a small box about one inch wide by one and a half inches long. It was about an inch deep. It was wrapped in a brown paper with what looked like twine tied around it to keep it closed. "Deliver it to them and come right back," the man said.

I nodded my understanding, and took the small box. I swallowed hard with nervousness, then I whispered to the white wolf at my side, "Okay, lets go." We walked through the glade and into some brush that was at the edge of the clearing. As we walked we entered a misty area, then back into a clear area. Soon after entering the clear area, the path we were on broke out of the brush and into another glade. This one was only about 12 feet round. A path across the way from us led back into the heavy brush again.

There was movement in the forest in front of us. I reached down and patted the animal's head nervously. I was a bit concerned about what was about to happen. The wolf at my side silently grew until its back was well past my waist. The hair on its back stood up and its lips rolled back baring its shimmering white teeth. It stood in a fierce position, ready to pounce.

In a few seconds, two human looking people came out of the brush and stopped at the opposite edge of the clearing. Both of them stared wide-eyed at my canine companion. I looked at them uneasily. They were quite the unusual people. There was a man and a woman. Both were at least 6 feet tall. Both were dressed in heavy black clothing. The woman looked about forty-five and had hair that was dyed bright red. She wore at least two rings of silver on each finger. Her eyes were heavy with black make-up. Several silver pendants hung around her neck. The man looked much the same. He was about the same age and was dressed the same in jet black with many silver rings. He wore a black cape and a hood over his balding head. They seemed like they were dressed to intimidate, but it was my wolf companion who was obviously intimidating them.

I said nothing to them. I simply walked forward and held out the box. As I approached them I could feel the tension in the wolf heighten. The woman reached forward and I gave her the box. No words were exchanged. If the man had walked forward, rather than the woman, I would have just as easily given him the box.

Immediately upon her taking the box into her hand, the wolf stepped forward and started to snarl and growl at them. His long white teeth shined with saliva. The guttural sounds from his chest were terrifying. They both quickly walked backwards into the woods from where they came, all the while their eyes were transfixed on the wolf's snarling face. After they were a few more feet away, the man and then the woman turned and walked quite a bit faster into the woods and were gone.

After they were out of sight I started to laugh. It just seemed like so much poetic justice for some reason I couldn't pinpoint that those people were intimidated by my wolf companion. Even the wolf seemed to laugh. I felt his amusement in his ice blue eyes.

After a few seconds, he silently shrank back to a normal size and I got down on my knees and hugged him around his neck and said, "I love you." I really felt it.

The wolf said nothing in words to reply. Rather, he rubbed his face over my face and licked my neck. I started to giggle, because it tickled. Then I pulled away.

"Come on we have to go back," I said. We walked back the way we came into the mist. Soon we were back in the glade by the oak tree.

"Did you deliver the package?" the man asked.

"Yes. They have it," I replied.

"Was there any trouble?" he asked, though I had a feeling he already knew the answer.

"None at all," I said.

The man nodded and I felt like a great task had been accomplished. I was overcome with a feeling of excitement. I ran to my wolf friend and started to play with him. The other animals joined in and we were rolling in play. It was party time for a job well done. We played until I was all out of breath and then some.

How I got back from the glade I have no memory. But the next thing I was aware of, it was morning and I was sleeping on the sofa. My computer was still powered up in the dining room.

Another time I found myself in the same glade with the same man and wolf. This time started with the same uneasy feeling. I felt like I knew something was going to happen, but I didn't know what it was. Sure enough, about 11:00 PM that night I couldn't sleep and decided to get up and watch TV. I was sitting on the sofa when I felt this sudden 'whoosh' like feeling. In a moment's time I was standing in the glade again by the oak tree. This time there were at least a dozen, maybe more, different kinds of animals around me. They were both weird and amazing. All of them were pure white. I recall there were all types of creatures, including at least two pure white deer, a pure white bear, three white wolves and even a pure white tiger whose stripes were almost sliver. All the animals seemed to be very calm and at peace with each other. I greeted the wolf with the ice blue eyes as if he were a human. I talked to him like he understood English. I felt like he was "my wolf" some how.

The same man was there. He told me I had to follow the wolf and he would take me where I needed to go to do what I came there for that night. I was not thrilled about the idea. It was like I knew at the time what I was going to do, but I did not really know. Nevertheless, I felt resigned to doing it and followed the wolf into the woods. Again we walked into a thick mist.

I only took about ten steps to get through the mist. When I came out of the mist I realized I was standing in the dark of night, in the shadow of a large pick-up truck that was parked in a driveway to my right. It was a dark colored truck, either blue or black. There was a small wooden fence between me and the truck. In front of me was a one story tan house with a darker red-brown trim. It had a flat roof and looked rather run down. Broken, white, plastic lawn furniture lay near a door. There was a porch light on to one side. It was casting the shadow I was standing in. The ground below me was dirt. It was rather muddy in some spots but seemed to be frozen or close to it in others. It appeared to be cold, but I felt no sensation of temperature.

Not more than ten yards from the house, four men sat near a fire in a semi-circle, side by side to each other. They were facing out, away from the house and in my general direction. It was clear that they were human men. The four were wearing jackets and jeans. Two of them had all kinds of logo patches on their jackets. One of the men was wearing a hat made of leather with side flaps that were folded up, like a hunting cap. They were talking, but I could not hear more than an occasional mumble because they were too far away and talking quietly.

I thought about things and realized I wasn't totally sure what I was supposed to do or say. I was more than a bit nervous. Still, something inside of me told me it was okay. So I figured I would know what to say and do when the time came.   I took a deep breath and I walked closer to the men.

When I walked into the light, I became aware of myself. Now, I know this sounds a bit strange, but I am sure I didn't look like me. I was smaller and thinner; maybe more like an ET halfling (hybrid) than human. I felt very petite. I know I had straight long hair and I was wearing a straight white dress that had no details, no buttons, nothing. It was just plain white cloth. It seemed to shine on its own, it was so white. The really odd thing is that this didn't seem unusual to me at all at the time.

I looked for the wolf, but it was gone. It was too late to turn back, so I continued to walk out of the shadow of the truck towards the men. I must have been something to see. The second man to the right jumped to his feet, shouted out a startled profanity and ran into the house. The other three stayed where they were. They starred at me with shock.

The man on the right from my view seemed to be in his late twenties or early thirties. The one next to him looked about forty. The last one was older, maybe sixty-five or more.

Before I could say a word, the older man spoke to me. His voice echoed with anger and he seemed more than a little hurt. He said, "For many generations my people called on you for help. We suffered and died without you. We never spoke badly of you. We gave you our gifts and we believed in you. Yet you did nothing. Where were you then?"

I didn't know what to reply. I stood there speechless.

Then he said in a very sarcastic tone, "So now you dare to put your silver feet on this filthy Earth. How thankful we should be to you?" Then he spit on the ground.

How could I reply to that?   I could understand. I could feel his pain and I knew exactly how he was feeling.   I've felt the same way at times with different but similar issues.

I decided I had to say something. So I told him I understood how he felt and that I didn't blame him for his anger. I also said, "I don't have any excuses for the things you accused me of. No explanations as to why. I am only here because I have a message I am suppose to give you."

"I do not recognize you as a holy messenger. You will have to prove that to me," he said with a firm but shaky voice. "How do I know you are a holy messenger and not a bringer of lies?"

His words gave me reason to pause and think. How did I myself know I was not a bringer of lies? I mean, I wasn't even sure why I was there. I didn't even know that I was supposed to be some holy messenger. For all I knew, I could have been a bringer of lies. I just didn't know what to say, so I shrugged my shoulders, with my hands out, like I was saying, "I don't know".

When I did that, all the white animals that had been standing around in the clearing appeared around me. I knew the men saw them because they startled and became even more visibly shaken. The animals remained for just for a moment, then they faded away slowly. All except for the wolf with the ice blue eyes. It stayed there at my side.

The old man started to apologize. He was shaking and his cracking voice lacked the firmness it had before. I told him it was okay, not to worry. I didn't know what else to say. After a few seconds of re-organizing my thoughts I said, "There is no need to be sorry." I understood how he was feeling. "It is good that you want to know if what you are hearing is the truth. And if what I tell you does not ring right in your heart, do not listen to it."

He bowed his head and rocked slowly, "I will gladly take your message," he said. "Thank you for coming to me."

I told him, "Go tell them that the pieces are in place. Tell the Landwalkers that all the pieces are there, in place, waiting to be found; waiting to be called. Tell them the time of unity is at hand."

As I finished speaking, all three men's eyes turned to the sky above my head. I looked up too. Above me was a very large space craft. It was totally smooth and silver-white with no markings. It glided over my head silently and slowly.

Despite his cracking, shaking voice, the old man managed to ask me, "Are you a sky sister?"

I replied, "I am a Starwalker."

I know at that point I was picked up by the ship. The next thing I recalled was looking out a window at some tiny lights far below. The being, Alex, put his hand on my shoulder and thought to me, "You did good."

I thought back, "Thank you." I felt I did do a good job.

The next thing I recall was waking up in bed, even though the last place I was before all this started was on the sofa.

The same blue eyed wolf would show up in many of my experiences. Sometimes he would be accompanied by another wolf, just as white but slightly larger with bright green eyes. I would often see the green eyed wolf in my home when I was drifting off to sleep. It became very common and very comforting for me when it happened. I would be drifting off to sleep and I would become aware that one of the wolves was in my bedroom. It was usually the green eyed wolf at the beginning. Later the blue eyed wolf would be more and more common until he would be in my room each night.

The green eyed wolf would come into my room, climb up on my bed and cover me like a blanket. Sometimes he would remain a very physical feeling wolf presence. Other times he would seem to dissolve into a warm, safe, not totally physical feeling over my body. Still at other less frequent times he would turn into a man and hold me in my bed.   The visits happened night after night.

Several times I found long strains of coarse white hair in the bed. This always amazed me. I collected them for a while with the idea of having them analyzed, but over the next few months it didn't seem as important and I stopped.

Sometimes only the blue eyed wolf would come by at night. He seemed so much shyer than the green eyed wolf when he was in my home. He would quietly walk to the side of the bed, gently lick my face and neck then lay down on the floor by the side of the bed.

Several times I woke in the middle of the night to see the tall green eyed Native man standing by the foot of my bed, the blue eyed wolf at his side.

I didn't know what to make of these experiences. I was overwhelmed by them most of the time. Yet, I found such comfort in these nighttime visits that I wished they would never end.

MICHELLE
THE TIME of UNITY is at HAND

The months of February and March are always times of increased ET activity in my life. I don't know exactly why that is, but it seems to be consistent. So I wasn't very surprised in the beginning of 1997 when my ET activity became extra busy. It was a very busy time for me all around. The Hale Bopp comet was coming and everyone was excited about it. Speculations seemed endless and I was working hard to keep up on the latest details for the magazine.

In late February, I started to feel very concerned. I was not sure what I felt was going to happen, but whatever it was, it was going to be a big thing. I started to wonder if I got caught up in "comet mania", but what I was feeling didn't seem to be directly connected to the comet. I didn't seem to feel that the comet was at the center of my concerns.

By the second week of March, my anxiety had grown to such an extent that I was spending hours on the phone talking to friends about things, all the while hoping that someone could help me sort it all out. Finally, on March 19th, I had an experience that helped me understand a bit better.

I remember the date well because it was the night after my birthday. I was lying in bed when it felt as if I was being watched. I opened my eyes to find two smaller grays standing by my bedside. I asked them what was going on and what were we going to do. They told me that I had to come with them, and that Hetar wanted to talk to me about something that was very important.

I got up to go with them and was transported to the ship where I found myself sitting on the edge of a table like object, feet dangling down. Hetar was standing in front of me. He was holding what looked like a digital thermometer attached to a clip board of some kind. He kept touching my leg joints with the device. There was no feeling at all. Maybe it was recording something.

After a few silent moments watching him touch me with the device, I cleared my throat and he looked up to meet my gaze. "One moment, please," he thought to me. "Be a good girl and sit still," he added.

I waited the moment longer. Then he asked, "Are you feeling well?"

"More or less," I replied. I had been suffering with one of my many winter colds. It was beginning to clear up.

"Good. You need to be well for the meeting." He continued his work then put the thermometer-like thing into a holder on the clip board and walked away.

"A meeting," I pondered. There was some kind of meeting coming. It had to be the reason why I was so restless and uneasy. "What kind of meeting?" I wondered.

I knew without a doubt that it would have to do with the Native experiences I was having. I had no idea how important it would be or how it was a milestone in the changing of my life.

The next few days, the tension inside me grew with each passing moment until I found myself on the phone with my friend, Dee, telling her all my suspicions. Dee and I would talk for hours on-line each week chatting about our experiences and the days events. Since she lived in Wisconsin at the time, and we talked out just about everything on line, it was rare that we would call each other on the phone. Still, I was to the point where I had to hear a voice tell me it was okay. It was the day of the 22nd of March. Several friends insisted that what I was feeling was anxiousness because it was the closest approach of Hale Bopp. Even though it seemed to make sense, since so many other contactees were feeling anxious about the approaching comet, I just couldn't accept that this was what was bothering me. I knew something else was going to happen that night. I didn't know what it was, but I was sure it had to do with the events that I had seen. It was going to tie together everything, the men in the field by the little tan house, the darkly dressed people I gave the box too, the tall Native with the green eyes and the old man with the rattle. Everything.

The night of March 22nd I planned to stay up late and wait for whatever it was. I assumed I would get at least a visit from the Rye-hun. It was no use. By 12:30 AM I was in bed trying to find sleep. I have no idea how long I lie there with my eyes pasted open and my body too tired to move. Since I had a feeling that something important was going to happen that night, I started reasoning to myself that what I was feeling was just nerves. It was just my imagination because I was expecting something to happen.

I don't know how long I had been lying there, when without warning, I saw a flash of blue light coming towards me. It was round and in a burst like you would see a phaser blast coming at the old Enterprise viewing screen in Star Trek. It startled me and my whole body jerked. After it passed, I took a deep breath and tried to relax. Relaxation wouldn't come.

In a few seconds I had the very strong impression that someone was talking to me with their thoughts. I felt like they asked, "Are you ready?"

I thought back, "Okay. Let's get this done." I felt resigned to whatever it was I had to do.

I took a deep breath and became aware that I was standing very still in some place. There were people standing by my side, but I couldn't see anything but heavy fog. I heard chanting that sounded like it was coming from in front of me.

It felt like I was totally out of body. It was like I had total awareness, but not really physical awareness. It was like I could sense everything around me, but I didn't really physically feel anything. The chanting seemed to be getting more clear. I could hear it, but couldn't understand it. It was in a language I did not know. It went on for several lines, then repeated itself. The parts that I remember sounded kind of like this: (phonetically) ...ba..baa ta hee. (Short pause) Nima nana hi (pause) Ba baa baa ta ma heeaaa. Then it started again. There were other sounds being chanted in time with those sounds that I could hear but not make out as clearly.

Then I became aware that the person, who was without a doubt a female, on my right side started to move forward. I started to move with her. After a few steps, the woman on my left started moving. I got the sense that there were more. We drifted, rather than walked, forward in the fog in the direction of the chanting. We emerged out of the fog into a huge high walled canyon. The walls and ground of this canyon were rusty red in color.

I'm not totally convinced it was an actual physical place you could find on a map, though it really looked like Earth. It almost looked like "*Red Rocks Venue*" I saw the Moody Blues play at on TV. Still, there were several things that led me to believe it wasn't a physical place in the strictest sense. The first was that it was very dark in the sky, yet the whole canyon was warmly lit with an orange, fire like glow, even though there was no fire or other source of light I could see anywhere. The second was that the stars overhead where streaking across the sky like shooting stars. So rather than having twinkling dots in the sky, it was filled with gently arcing streaks of white, yellow and pail blue.

The walls of the canyon where very steep and perpendicular in front of me. They were far from smooth. Behind me the walls were the same. These two walls of rock curved in on both sides creating a canyon with an entrance to my right and to my left that seemed to lead into the night's darkness.

When we moved out of the fog, I realized to my amazement that we had just passed through the rock wall itself. It felt really warm but otherwise gave no resistance.

In front of me, on the far side of the canyon, were hundreds of people. All human and all from different indigenous peoples of the Earth, not just Native Americans. There were all kinds of people. Each in groups of two or three. They were all in different outfits. Some were even without clothes. Some had their bodies painted or tattooed. There were so many of them. They were the ones who were chanting.

In front of them, in the center of the canyon, were two people. The first was an older woman with several layers of clothes and rough cut fur on. She had her hair tied back and had feathers braided in her hair. She wore several pendent like things as well as a small pouch that seemed to be made of leather around her neck. At her waist she carried a large leather bag that hung from a strap that was slung across her chest and over her opposite shoulder.

The second was a man. He appeared to be in his late forties. Had some kind of bells on the top of his boots. I don't know why this fact caught my attention so strongly, but it did. He, too, had many things hanging from his neck and had a bag slung over his shoulder. Both the man and the woman were scooping white sand from the bags at their hips and letting it run through their fingers, creating a picturegram on the ground. The white sand showed up so beautifully on the red ground.

It looked from where I was standing, that they were drawing a large circle, I would guess to be about 12 feet or more. It was inscribed inside of a bigger square. The woman "drew" lines cutting the circle like a pie, then the man drew more lines. Before they were done the whole circle was filled with small triangles, almost like a geodesic dome. The outline of the bordering square was probably about one and a half feet wide of sand. At each point there were long lines that went off towards the canyon walls.

At the end of each line stood a young man with no clothing on except feathers around his groin like a loin cloth. Each one had his chest and face painted with red paint that was the same color as the ground. They each held a long stick in their right hand. The sticks were smooth like spears. Each stick had three white feathers hanging from its end.

As the circle was being formed, the four men walked closer to it until the feathers at the ends of the sticks where hanging over the points of the square on the ground. All the while, the chanting continued.

Then when the circle was done, the woman turned to face the people with her back to me, and said something in a language I didn't understand with my ears. Nevertheless, I knew she was saying a prayer to the Mother Spirit. She prayed the bringing together of this day would never be forgotten in the souls of those who attended it and that the twelve tribes will make a lasting peace.

She turned back towards the circle. I just stood there in total awe as she reached into the same pouch she got the sand from and called to the sky for the power of the Grandmother Spirit to come forth to join the peoples. Then she tossed a handful of sand into the center of the picturegram. The circle in the center burst into a huge orange flame. In seconds it turned bright green, then rose into the air and was gone. When the flames cleared, I saw that the sand picture wasn't damaged, but there was now a hole about a foot across in the ground at the center of the circle. I was speechless with wonder.

The man who had helped draw the picture of sand then came forward with a tree branch. It looked a bit crooked. At the top, it flanged out into three smaller branches similar to a ring setting. I noticed that he was careful not to walk on the lines of sand as he approached the center of the circle. He placed the branch into the hole in the center of the circle. When he did, the chanting stopped. The canyon became strangely quiet.

There were seven of us who came out of the rock wall. We all looked very much the same. Our faces were different, but everything else was exactly the same; same long straight hair, same fair skin, same plain white dress. We were even all about the same height. The woman in the center was a bit taller. She was on my right. There were two more woman on my left, and the three others were on her other side.

The Native woman who drew the circle said, "Welcome the Seven Sisters of the Stars. We who walk the land honor you."

The tall woman from the center of our line stepped forward and bowed a bit. She said, "We are honored to share this most holy of grounds with you. Thank you."

The other woman said, "The time of oneness has come. As with all children, there comes a time when they leave their arrogance behind and seek the wisdom of their parents once again. The time of the new energy is now. This is an energy that can only come from the womb of the Mother. The energy that brings together, not sets apart.

"Before you stand the children of the many tribes of man. Standing beside them are the souls of the ones who have passed into time and darkness." She spoke a few more sentences, but I can't recall what they were. Then she went up to the stick in the ground and put her hand on top of it and announced in a very loud voice, "This is the beginning of the time of unity! Let all understand that!"

The taller woman in the center of the seven of us walked forward to the edge of the picture of sand and began to talk. She talked about how proud she was that the children of the Earth have kept the sacred words. How they have protected and healed the pain of the soil and how they have kept the seed alive despite the incredible forces against them. She talked about how the Starwalkers acknowledge the great strife the Landwalkers have endured in order to bring about the time of oneness, and how strong they are to have come to this point. She spoke about the twelve tribes, and how they were called to this place this night, some not even knowing the reason why. How we each are bound to each other and how we are stronger as a whole than we are as the sum of our parts.

She said, "You have honored the stars with your love. They shine down on you with their love."

Then she said, "The time of bonding has come. All tribes are one tribe this day."

She said, "From the stars and the mother tribe." She produced a large shining, faceted crystal orb seemingly from nowhere and she placed it in the tree branch. It fit perfectly. It actually appeared to become oblong to fit firmly into the branch. It was glowing a warm white color. She backed away.

The woman with the sand said, "I bring to this unity the Landwalkers of this Earth! Many in name, yet one in origin! I bring forth the seed!" The people behind her all lifted their arms up and she shouted, "Na Da Ma Day!"

Then the center woman from my group said, "I bring to this unity the Starwalking Sisters, and the tribes from the skies who planted the seed." Then we six stepped forward one step and said something. I believe it was "Na Da Ma Day" also.

Then the center woman turned to me. I walked forward to the edge of the sand circle and announced, "I bring to this unity the four winds of chaos, and all that remains of them. Those who have blown the seed to the reaches of the land and beyond, challenging it to grow."   And from the shadows of the canyon entrance to my right came in a large group of Rye-hun ETs. They said nothing. They just walked into the light of the canyon and stood there. One of them came forward and stood on the line behind the young man who was holding the feathered stick to my right.

Then, the woman who was standing on the other side of the center sister came forward. She announced, "I bring to this unity the life giving water of the rain that washes over the seed and brings forth growth."

Then from the shadow of the canyon on the other side, came forward a group of angelic, human like ETs. One of them -who I called Paul- came forward and stood on the line to my left.

The woman who was on my left side came forward and said, " I bring to this unity the tribe of the triangle. Those who have tended the seed so that no weeds could destroy it."

Then several very tall gray looking beings came forward but they were a lot taller than normal Rye-hun. As they walked forward, they shrunk into these shriveled old man type beings. One came forward and took a place across the circle from me on a corner line.

The woman on the other side came forward and said, "I bring to this unity those who tend the soil. Those who dig so the seed can have freedom to spread its roots, that it might grow strong."

From the shadow walked out several extremely tall beings in robes. As they came forward they dropped their robes and they were just blobs of light. The light kept changing form and shape. As I looked at them, I thought I saw a figure or shape in the light, and it seemed to turn into whatever I thought, though it's appearance never really changed.

One of these beings came forward and took its place. I was just in awe of it. The light was so bright, but it didn't hurt to look at.

The next woman came forward. She said, "I bring to the unity the predator of the vermin. Those who protect the seed from those who would consume it."

When she said that, a group of beings that looked a lot like preying mantis came forward. I had spoken to people who had seen beings like this before, but never saw one myself. They were very large and for some reason, were wearing large hats that looked like the kind Catholic bishops wear. One took a place on the line by the circle.

The woman on the end of my side came forward. She said, "I bring to this unity all those who aid in the growth by virtue of their patience or nature, though they may not know their deeds."

A mixed group of beings came forward.

Then the last woman from the opposite end stepped forward, She said, "I bring to the unity those who are the lost tribes. Those who have damaged the seed from spite or ignorance. Those who have come to learn, and are ready to do so now."

Another mixed group of beings came forward. The being that caught my eye in this group was a rather large very muscular looking tall being that looked kind of like a mix between a man and an iguana. It even had a tail.

Even though my mind was spinning with awe, a part of me was thinking, "You're nuts, this looks like something out of the bar-room scene of Star Wars or from an episode of Buck Rogers." Still I couldn't deny my own experience.

When everyone was in place. The taller of the seven of us said "Let us be joined in unity. Oneness in the Mother and God has become reality once again."

She walked to face the Indian man with the sand. The rest of us Starwalkers stepped back. Then I walked forward onto the line of sand that made the thick square. The Indian woman walked forward across from me onto the opposite end of the square. She winked at me and said, "It's not polite to stare, dear." That broke the tension I was feeling and I actually laughed a bit. Then I realized, I must have been staring, and apologized to her.

She said, "It's quite alright," and winked at me again. I felt a bit embarrassed. But, frankly, there was a lot going on to be staring at. It wasn't every day I saw an eight foot human iguana and a twelve foot tall praying mantis with a bishop's hat on.

At this point the beings that were standing on the lines behind the square's corners walked onto the broad lines of the square, too.

Including the Indian woman and myself, there were twelve of us there. Three standing on each length of the square. I was in the center of the line where I stood. The gray stood to my right. The being I called Paul to my left. To Paul's left, on the next line, was a tall almost human looking being, who was extremely thin with a blue robe on. He must have been ten feet tall. Next to him was the praying mantis being. Next to that being was what looked like an octopus type of being. It didn't stand on the ground, rather, it was hovering. I know this sounds strange, but it was orange with red spots and had many more than eight legs. I had never seen anything like it before.

On the next row was what I guess could be called a bigfoot. It was a large being with a hairy body and a clean smooth face. He had heavy features and very kind eyes. Next to that being stood the Indian woman. The old shriveled being that started out looking like a gray stood next to her.

On the next row was the lizard type being. In the middle was the incredible light being who had been robed before. Then another being who looked rather human but had strangely colored hair and eyes.

In one stroke at the same time, the young men who held the sticks at the corners drove them - feathered end down - into the corners of the squares. I got the impression that the symbology was that they "closed" the square. At that point we all stepped forward into the circle. Even though it was obvious that we were not moving, I had a strong sensation that the circle was turning.

The taller woman from the Starwalkers started saying a long prayer. She asked each of us in turn if our people would agree to join in oneness for the benefit of the seed of life. Each of us agreed. The Native woman put her hand on the ball that sat in the center branch, then me, then the other beings from the middle of each line, and so on with those on the sides, until all were touching the ball and each other in some way.

When everyone had an appendage on this ball the center woman said, "Unity has come. The twelve tribes once again are one." With her words, the ball lit up with an incredible blue light. It was so awesome. My mind was spinning. It developed into the most wonderful feeling. It was the total of what pleasure is.

For a short while I understood exactly what it was like to be part of the whole consciousness of the universe. I understood without boundaries. It was incredible. Everything made perfect sense. Everything! I realized I wasn't a single person. We, all of us in creation, were one person.

I don't know how long this state lasted. If it was minutes or seconds, I have no idea. Eventually it stopped and I opened my eyes. The ball in the center of the branch still glowed blue, but the intensity was gone. We all put our hands down. There was a brief moment of silence that was broken by a booming voice. It was as if the voice of the canyon spoke. It said, "One is ALL!" and then the walls of the canyon started to move.

I was amazed, terrified, enraptured and totally confused all at one time. The Landwalkers started to chant again and the rocks of the walls came alive and formed into beings as tall as the canyon itself. These rock beings walked out of the walls of the canyon and stood there. They gave off the most intense loving feeling. It was like the Mother Earth herself was in them. Maybe she was.

They started to sing. Their voices sounded like strange harmonic tones, like a finger on the rim of a wine glass. It was spooky but very beautiful.

I heard a voice in my head say, "You truly are welcome Starwalkers". With that, white flashes of light started shooting through the canyon. I stood in total amazement and totally enraptured as I watched the lights fly by. Where ever the streaks hit a wall, beautiful white animals came running out the rock face and into the middle area. There were all kinds of animals. Everything you could think of, even giraffes. All were pure white.

The people began singing with the canyon beings. "Baaa ta ma da Kaaaaaa.... Oooo mai lai a."

I just stood there, still in the center of the picturegram feeling all of the energy and excitement. I was trying to absorb it all and remember it all. Then a white streak flew close by my head. I followed it until it hit the wall. An animal appeared. It was the white wolf with the green eyes. He ran towards me and I heard him think to me, "I'm proud of you!"

I thought back, "We did it again! We did it again!" I was overcome with bubbly excitement.

The wolf turned into a man and he hugged me. I just stood there feeling complete in the universe around me.

I began to feel like I was melting into this man. I found myself getting dizzy. I closed my eyes. When I opened them I was home sitting up awake in bed. It was 4:47 AM.

After this event, the world seemed very different to me. I realized that something important to all of mankind had happened and very few people knew about it. That next morning I wondered if I were the only one in the world who remembered. Later I found out I wasn't. There were others who remembered. At least they remembered parts of it.

It seemed that each turn brought more questions than answers. Now not only was I totally confused about my Native American theme events, I was now completely baffled as to why it seemed I held such an important roll in whatever it was that was unfolding.

PAUL
March 1997
NA DA MA DAY

One of the people who was a great help to me was a man named John. John worked with a support group over the Internet and had been doing research for years. John lived on the west coast of the United Sates and was himself an 'experiencer.'

John and I communicated for some time back and forth. The data he collected about what an 'experiencer' would go through adjusting and dealing with the experience of being an abductee was invaluable in helping me make it through the winter. He shared some of his theories and interests and communicated in a consistently thoughtful and polite manner. It was nice to know there were some level headed people out there.

One day John forwarded me a message that was sent to him by a woman he knew. He told me very little about her except that she had been having some unusual experiences that involved aboriginal type images. He explained that she was experiencing anxiety and fear over trying to understand what was going on.

The message John forwarded me described a very long and detailed experience. It was clear the teller was uncertain as to the nature and substance of the experience. She described both non-humans and humans alike. She described, in detail, various Native ceremonies involving drawing mandelas with sand as well as a single phrase that would make all the difference, "NA DA MA DAY."

I printed off the message and took it up to see Lucy and Tom. Tom was working out in the sugar bush making maple syrup when I arrived, but Lucy and her sister Lisa was there. I showed them both the printout of this woman's experience and they read through it. Lily, Lucy's daughter, read it all first then began to tell me how many parts of the experience reflected with accuracy many parts of Native ceremonies from different tribes. As Lily was speaking there was some commotion on the other side of the table. Lucy and her sister Lisa were talking back and forth in Innuit, their native tongue. Lisa looked up and said, "Our mother used to say this to us."

"What?" I said with surprise.

"This here, 'NA DA MA DAY'."

"Yes," said Lucy, " this is an Innuit expression for which there's no English translation."

We all looked at each other surprised and somewhat stunned. It took us about five minutes, but I eventually was able to get them to loosely translate it. It meant, "You young people come here and look at that way over there."

Looking at the letter I noticed that 'NA DA MA DAY' was said by an older woman in charge of the ceremony to a number of younger people as the ceremony began to change and was said in context so that the phrase was accurately used. I was shocked. How could a woman who lived in the United States, send a message to a man who lived in California, who would then send it to me asking me to 'run it by' my aboriginal friends, have known how to use or say such an Innuit phrase. The Innuit generally live in eastern and northern Canada. Where did this woman learn Innuit?

I rushed home and fired off the news to John in California.

A few day's later I got a message forwarded to me from him that had been sent by the woman. She asked him to thank us for our efforts and said that she wasn't afraid anymore. She now knew there must be some actual substance to these intense recurring experiences. She told me that her grandfather was a Native from Canada. He had gone back to visit last summer. Interestingly, that was about the same time her Native theme experiences started. She went on to say that she he was from a town called 'Penetancushin.' When I read the name 'Penetancushin' I just about dropped on the floor. She had incorrectly spelled the name of a town called Penetanguashene on Georgian Bay. It was just down the road from where Tom and Lucy lived on the Wahta Mohawk Reserve.

I fired off another message to John and felt good that I had helped someone. I knew something unusual was going on. This was too coincidental. I waited on the edge of my seat a week and half for a response from either John or the woman I only knew as Michelle. I tried not to think about it and turned my attention to a Mohawk social coming up that weekend. I would get to meet more people on the reserve. Including one of the few living relatives a man who supposedly witnessed a UFO hit the ground of the reserve in 1947.

<u>*Michelle*</u>
Enter the Twigman

For some time after the meeting that heralded the time of unity I found myself struggling as to how much I wanted to say and to whom I wanted to say it. I published an abridged account of the event in the next issue of the magazine, hoping that someone who was there would see it and contact me, but there were no helpful replies. Several people wished me well, called me blessed and said they were honored to know me. Some even told me they envied me. I found that hard to understand. I didn't talk about it in hopes of being honored or envied. I was hoping to find some answers. So far all my reaching out lead to no solid leads. Despite the beauty and awe of what was happening to me, I was still experiencing the fear of the unknown and unfamiliar. In fear, it was hard for me to conceive of how meaningful the experiences truly were.

In April, a friend of mine on the Internet named John, told me he knew someone who was involved with some medicine men. He had taken the liberty of forwarding my letter of the experience of March 22nd-23rd to him to see if he could make heads or tails of it. I agreed but was cautious with my hope. It seemed that no one so far, no matter how much they claimed to know, was able to answer the questions I needed answered. Still, I waited anxiously for a reply from John's contact. I had no idea who this contact was or what part of the world they were in.

Finally, in early April, 1997 I received a letter from John in which he forwarded me the reply I had been waiting for. The person, who identified himself as "Twigman" brought up many points of interest between my experience and actual Native American ceremonies and languages.

I had such deep mixed emotions. Of course I was excited that some of what I said seemed to make sense to the people this fellow spoke to, but I was also afraid. This message confirmed to me that it could not have just been imagination. If it were just a vivid dream, then why would I have remembered it so clearly? Why would I have known about ceremonies from people I had no knowledge of? Why would I have quoted words in their language?

I must have read the reply he sent six or seven times before I wrote up my own reply in return.

What could I say? The dreams and events I now had with a Native American theme numbered well past twenty, maybe past thirty. A stranger from who knows where was writing me, telling me that there is likely more to these events. My friends were telling me I was blessed and special for what was happening to me. Yet through this all, my grandfather's words kept coming back to me. After all, his words were things I heard far too many times growing up - things that hurt to think about like,"Never tell anyone you have any Indian blood in you. People think Indians are lower than dogs. It's a shame to be Indian."

To make matters worse, when I started to tell friends about what was happening, and about what this mystery "Twigman" person said about my event, one of my close friends didn't believe a word of it. She told me that she was convinced that the person John sent the letter to was making it all up. She would say time and time again that there were no Natives of any kind, never mind medicine men and this guy was just another "Internet looney".

With all this in mind, I wrote up a reply to this "Twigman". I had serious questions and wanted serious answers. My friend's scoffing put just enough suspicion in me, and my heart was burning for answers with such a fever that it was impossible to be subtle. I sent back a letter full of questions. I wanted to know everything. I wanted to know exactly what everything that was happening to me meant in clear detail. I wanted to believe that this person could help me, still all the while I was suspicious that this was just one of a hundred dead ends I had run up against in my quest for answers.

Twigman didn't know my background with the ETs and his reply was, in a nut shell, to suggest to me in a very delicate way that he and his contacts believed maybe I would be contacted by ETs, and that I should keep an open mind about the existence of aliens. He also suggested that maybe I should take a walk in the woods.

It was not a bad letter by any means if it were being written to someone who had no idea about the reality of ET contact, but I had been having ET contact all my life.

I read the letter with a heavy heart. To say the reply was less than I had hoped for would have been a big understatement.

I read it several times trying to find meaning in it. Still, no matter how many times I went over it, all I could get out of it was that this person was telling me that everything that was happening to me meant that someday I might actually see aliens. "Wow, you really mean it?" I was tempted to write back. "Someday, possibly, maybe, actually SEE aliens!" I laughed bitterly. After all, I had seen them on a regular basis since I was a baby.

It was difficult, but I tried to face the idea that what seemed to be promising was just another dead end after all. In frustration, I wrote back for what I thought was going to be the final time.

In my letter I mentioned to Twigman that I knew about ETs and had actually written a book on how to cope with ET experiences. My letter reflected the emotional disappointment I was feeling.

A few days went by when I got a reply from John's friend. I sensed that my frustration with the situation had come through loud and clear. It was obvious that he was feeling like he couldn't help me after all.   I believed he was probably right. He asked me several questions about ET contacts he was experiencing and asked me if there were any ideas or tips I could give him. He explained to me some of the things he learned about levels of consciousness and asked if any of the ET memory of lessons and teachings I had could help him to learn to master the higher of these states.

Several days went by and I couldn't find the energy to reply. I wasn't sure if I even wanted to. There was so much going on in my personal life. My home life was miserable. I was working very heavily with several very distressed abductees one-on-one. To my horror, a man who I had been helping through some tough contact related issues in his life had taken an unwelcomed shine to me in a bad way that was verging on obsession. I was starting to feel afraid he could quickly become a threat. The only comfort I had was that he lived over 1500 miles away. And of course, the Indian visions and events kept coming fast and furious. I just did not feel I had the time to deal with this new person; with this Twigman.

I tried to forget about this "empty lead" and get on with things. I began to look for new avenues. Try as I might, they all seemed to be dead ends and once again I was left with the scant chance that I missed something along the way. Every time I examined my trail, it came back to the Twigman lead.

The main thing that kept drawing me back was that I'm not one to believe in coincidence. I believe that things happen for a reason. Was it just pure chance that a friend over three thousand miles away from me who I know from chat rooms on line just happened to send a telling of my event to some guy he knew who lived in Canada, who just happened to find and become friends with some medicine people who just by chance lived on a reservation outside of where my grandfather was born?

Was it just pure, dumb luck that I remembered and wrote down real Innuit words and the woman who he asked to read the event was fluent in Innuit, a very difficult and not widely spoken language for that area.

It seemed the more I looked into things, the more and more coincidences I found. In a short time I had counted up ten seeming coincidences. This could not be just acts of random chance.

The next time I was with the ETs I asked a human looking ET named Alex what he thought about it all. Alex smiled at me with his typical warm, compassionate eyes and said, "This is your journey, child."

His words didn't say much. He didn't tell me if it were right or wrong. He told me to make my own choice. Later that night I asked Hetar the same question. Hetar said, "What do you lose writing E-mail? A few moments time. And at the very least you may be able to help him with his experiences."

I knew Hetar was right, but I have to say it did bother me. I know it was terribly selfish, but I felt like I was the one who needed help, not Twigman. I went to this man for answers not the other way around. Yet, Hetar was right. If a fellow experiencer needed help and I could give it, there was no reason why I shouldn't.

The next morning I sat down and re-read the E-mails that had passed between us. Then I wrote once again. This time I decided to put it all on the line and tell him about everything I knew. I wrote to him directly, without going through John. I outlined some of the coincidences and told him I did not believe that they were random chance. I decided to tell him everything I knew about things, but first I had to find out how much I could trust him. I told him I had to tell him things that would probably make him believe I was crazy. I needed to know that my E-mail would never go past his eyes.

His reply came quickly. I was really surprised. There was a part of me that wasn't expecting a reply at all. In his letter he admitted he felt my frustration and also felt that there were too many coincidences, but didn't know how he could help me. He also gave me several phone numbers I could reach him at.

I copied the phone numbers onto a cardboard box I had on my computer table. I wondered if I would ever get the nerve up to call. That day we exchanged several pieces of E-mail about the things I felt I needed to tell him, about my grandfather, my feelings about my Native theme experiences and my connection with the ETs.

He told me about his trip on the Wahta reservation with this nephew and tried to offer some insight into what was happening to me. In that one day we must have exchanged five rounds of E-mail before lunch time. Yet with all those typed words, I couldn't say what I felt I needed to.

Finally, about 3:00 PM that afternoon, and after picking up the phone and putting it back down several times because I just couldn't formulate anything to say that made sense, I called him. I knew everything I had to say would sound crazy, I was sure. Should I tell him about the other dreams? Would he be able to help me if he knew about all the times I saw the white wolves? Would he think I was crazy if I told him about the man with the rattle and about how the rattle changed into a bird? And what about what Hetar showed me just two nights before when I asked Hetar who this man was. Hetar touched my forehead and made me dream about a big hotel full of birds. Each room had hundreds of tropical and non-tropical birds in it. I was running through this hotel looking for "Twigman" who I now knew as Paul. What did that mean? Should I tell him about the dream Hetar provided? Should I tell him about the being named Rovere and how Rovere asked me to say hello to him?

Of course I asked Rove why he would want to send his greetings to this man. Did he know him? I even half expected a helpful answer, but Rovere just smiled and said, "Rove knows everyone."

I felt for sure I was either going to say too much and sound like a lunatic, or say too little and learn nothing from him. For that matter, I wasn't sure what it was I was hoping to learn at all. I really didn't believe there was anything he could do to help me at this point and there was little if anything I felt like I had the energy to help him with. Nevertheless, something inside of me was driving me like wild horses. I needed to hear his voice.

Our first call started rather strained, but within a matter of minutes we were chatting like we were old friends. His energy seemed very familiar and comfortable to me. Even his voice, and the particular way he said the word "process" seemed very familiar to me. I concluded that we must have met in the ET environment at one time.

Over the next few weeks our phone calls became more and more frequent. We talked about our experiences and I shared with him as much of what I knew about methods for regaining memory and coping skills. He wasn't afraid of his experiences, even when he didn't understand them and I found that refreshing. He was anxious to learn and that sometimes put me in a teaching position. This often made our early phone conversations feel more like lectures on my part.

He taught me quite a bit about the belief of the people in the Gurdjieff school, which he had attended in his twenties. After a while, our conversations became less a formal transfer of information and more a friendly interaction of energy and information. We started to relate to each other's experience and condition better. I found that I really enjoyed my new friend, Paul. There was something so strangely familiar about him, the way he talked, the expressions he used. I knew that somehow I knew this man a long time.

One day while talking on the phone, we got on the topic of how some abductees are very psychic, and how many of us even communicate long distance without the use of phones. We seem to "know" and "feel" the others we call friends. I told him how I was able to do this with several of my contactee friends. Since his motto was - and still is- "verify everything" he approached this with skepticism. He asked me if I were willing to try and contact him in this way. I told him I would think about it. A few weeks later, we connected by accident while I was shopping and he was meditating. We started trying for real after that. We called the sessions "powwows". We both knew it was not the correct usage of the word, but it felt strangely appropriate.

Our first powwow session was interesting. We both felt we connected to each other in some way, but nothing seriously tangible happened. By the third night we tried, we were making real progress. We were seeing similar things and picking up on the same feelings. I had a strong sense of his presence and he knew that I had started about ten minutes late that night. I was seeing things, and he was hearing and sensing things. The amazing part was that they were the same things.

With each powwow session our connection grew to the point where we were so aware of each other that I knew the moment he awoke and "came on line" in the morning, and he could tell when I was upset or excited almost a thousand miles away.

For example, It was often our habit to follow sessions with either long detailed E-mail or long phone calls (for which our bills were phenomenal, seeing they were at international rates!). One evening I was talking to him on the phone in the bedroom when I heard something bang in the other room. The children were yelling incoherently and I said to Paul, "I have to go. I'll call you later." I didn't even wait for a reply. I just hung up the phone.

The bang was my son falling down and hitting his face on the kitchen floor. My son, was crying. Blood was everywhere. I didn't know it at that moment, but he had only split his upper lip and given himself a bloody nose. There was a lot of blood but no serious damage.

I rushed my son into the bathroom and started to wash the area with a cold, wet towel in hopes of being able to clear some of the blood and assess if he had knocked out any of his teeth or worse. I was sure I would have to rush him to urgent care at the hospital. There was so much blood. My son was in hysterics. My daughter was crying too from all the panic going on around her. I was on the verge of losing it to panic myself.

I couldn't stop the blood from flowing and was getting ready to rush him to the hospital when I heard the very loud, very directed and very unmistakable voice of Paul in my head say, "Mick, Calm down! Focus! Calm down! Focus!" The voice repeated for several minutes. It was so clear it was almost physically audible.

I thought for a moment that I must be crazy or imagining it, but it didn't matter. Hearing his voice in my head, breaking through all the confusion and yelling around me that was driving me to panic did help me focus and calm. I focused my energy on the voice and my calm on my son and what I had to do. I was able to regain my total composure and clean him up. I discovered he had just split his lip and had a bloody nose. It seemed a lot worse than what it really was because of the blood. I managed to get the child calmed and the bleeding stopped. Soon the whole house was quiet again.

After the house settled down, I was sitting at the dining room table sipping my tea and trying to relax, when I realized that I had so rudely hung up on Paul. I put my tea down and called him back. The phone barely rang one full time when he picked it up. I didn't have time to even say hello when he, in a very urgent, very concerned voice, blurted out, "How's your son? How's his face? There was so much blood!"

"How did you know?" I asked. I was floored with amazement. Then I thought, could it really have been his voice I heard in the bathroom?

Before I had a chance to say more than, 'How did you know?' Paul replied, "I saw that there was a lot of blood. I could feel you panicking as you were cleaning him up. Did you hear me trying to calm you. I kept telling you to calm down and stay focused."

He knew about the voice. There was no longer any doubt in my mind, for I didn't say a word to him about any of it and he was telling me exactly what had happened. He had no way of knowing that my son was hurt when I hung up the phone, because at that time I didn't even know. He had no way of knowing about my hearing his voice tell me to be calm and focus unless it really was his voice.

We both knew that we were connected and that the connection was growing through our powwow work and this confirmed it for both of us. It was only a matter of days after we started to powwow that we realized that we had a connection that was different from what either of us had ever had with anyone else in this Earth-life. We became, in a very short period of time, each other's best friend. We realized in a very short period that no matter what happened in the future we would have to keep in touch. We even started making plans for keeping in touch through any series of *earth changes* we contactees are told about. We knew that we had to stay connected no matter what. We knew that the connection we were discovering between us was strong. What we didn't know at that time was that this connection had always existed and we were not forming it, we were simply re-discovering it.

<u>PAUL</u>
April 1997
Indians and Aliens?

Some days after the Mohawk social I received a long message from Michelle. She was extremely nervous about writing me and felt bad about what she had to communicate. She had not been able to write for several days and had been struggling with her Native ancestry and with other Native influences that were not particularly wholesome or trustworthy in the manner in which they were marketed by certain quasi-evangelical Native individuals in the United States.

She realized that there was something amazing going on after reading my last message to her, interpreting the words "NA DA MA DAY" from Innuit into English.

I had thankfully not encountered any uncomfortable Native influences and had only nice things to say about the aboriginal people I met. I wrote her back and told her not to worry, that I would not abandon her for her honesty in expressing her rather humiliating feelings of being ostracized by certain Native people in the United States.

We took several days passing large messages to each other and catching up on our backgrounds. I soon discovered that Michelle was a published author and had an extensive background in the extraterrestrial field.

I, for one, found it extremely helpful to speak to her about certain things that happened to me as she had quite an understanding of what people go through who had been in contact with these beings. Her recall of her experiences was phenomenal in its detail. I started to believe that it was more for my benefit than for hers that the connection was made between the two of us.

One thing we both shared in common was the connection between aboriginals and aliens. Somehow, our paths had crossed these two elements. Trying to ascertain the relevance of this connection stymied us both.

Just about this time, I had to go to the hospital for some overdue hernia surgery. When I went, they found a second hernia was developing. They were not able to operate on the second hernia for various reasons. I would have to come back later to have that one repaired.

After surgery, I tried to go back to work as soon as possible, but found that my body wasn't ready. I collapsed on the floor at work and was unable to get up. I ended up staying home for the remainder of the week. In the middle of that week something strange occurred.

Late one evening while I was sitting in my living room pondering the recent events over an espresso, I heard fast footsteps on my roof that sounded just like the ones my nephew and I had heard outside of the tent on the Wahta reserve. They were quite loud, very fast and distinct, like a biped, not a quadruped.

I launched myself off my couch. I tried to ignore the sensation that my stomach was going to split open from the recent surgery, whipped on my running shoes and ran out on my front lawn only to see a cat looking down at me from the roof. I was a bit surprised to see anything at first and a bit frightened. I did not understand how a small cat could make such loud footsteps on my roof. What I heard were steps that sounded like a sizeable person, not a small cat.

I moved back on the lawn to see if I could see anything else further back on my low laying roof. Above the trees behind my house, I saw three lights in a triangle formation travelling from east to west at a high rate of speed. The triangle formation looked to be quite large. The lights faded out as they passed over my house.

I tried to find reasons for the lights I saw. My first idea was it could have been birds, but they were moving much too fast to be birds. Then I thought about the fair that was in town. Could it have been a spotlight? Spotlights travel in an arc not a straight line. Besides, the fair's lights appeared as one round sizeable light, not three small lights that could disappear in flight.

I realized that I might have been encountering some type of screening illusion so I followed the cat. I walked along the front yard to my neighbor's side and watched the cat jump down. I called the cat with a friendly 'kitty, kitty, kitty'. It blinked affectionately at me and stopped, but would not come over to me. I started to question my sanity as I stood there wondering for the first time in my life if I was seeing a cat or something else. The cat sat there starring intensely at me as I walked back to my house, clinching my stomach in distress.

As the next few weeks passed, my body continued to heal. My energy level increased slowly. Some days were good, some not so good.

On one front, and what would prove to be the most important and enduring part of both Michelle's and my work, she and I began to meditate simultaneously each night. We spoke about trying simultaneous meditation and decided to work seriously with it after an usual occurrence.

I was sitting in my living room, quietly meditating, when suddenly a great peace came over me. My energy level increased dramatically. My state of awareness altered. I could feel Michelle. It was an incredible feeling. The experience lasted about five minutes and I thought it was something exclusive to myself until Michelle called a while later to explain to me she had the most incredible state come over her while she was out shopping.

I explained to her I had been meditating and had the same experience. It was as if a huge light bulb went on over our heads. We were forming a psychic connection different from any that we had experienced with anyone else in this life before.

So every night that we could, we meditated. We labeled our meditations "powwows." Though an improper use of the term "powwow," it served its purpose as a useful and playful code word.

One of us would telephone the other and we would arrange for a suitable time to meditate. What we began to find was that we would experience the same or similar sensations or images at the same points of our meditation. We were able to verify this with each other because we would sit down at the end of our meditations and send an E-mail message to each other, outlining the events of our meditation that night. More often than not, we would find strikingly similar experiences occurred during our meditations. We began to understand we had a unique ability with each other that neither of us had experienced with another human being before.

I spent my days scanning the Internet and continuing my research. Early in the month of May, I came across a message on a newsgroup from a person who was doing research on the west end of Lake Ontario. This person claimed to be sighting and videotaping UFO activity out over the lake. I had read about stories and reports of a supposed "extraterrestrial base" in Lake Ontario in an old Canadian UFO Research Network interview some years earlier, but had never taken it seriously.

I became intrigued to say the least. So that night I drove down to Oakville, Ontario and sat on the lakeshore. I faced out towards the opposite shore which was approximately thirty miles away. There was a mist on the water when I arrived.

As I looked across the lake I saw an orange light sitting on the water. "How odd," I thought to myself.

I got out a set of high powered binoculars so I could take a closer look. I couldn't believe what I saw. There, out on the lake, was a round and brilliant orange orb. It simply sat motionless on the water. There was no boat around it. It was simply a brilliant, shining light that sat on the water. I observed how people walked along looking in the direction of the light, but not really noticing it. Without binoculars it merely looked like a light from a boat.

Over the coming months, I noted how people looked at lights like this and said, "Oh, that's just a boat light," not realizing what it actually was, or allowing any challenge to their paradigm that would disturb their evening walk.

I sat that first evening watching the lake as the sun went down behind me. While I sat, I began to meditate. During my meditation, I heard a voice in my head that sounded exactly like the voice I heard from the being that sat in the door flap of my tent on the Wahta reserve. The voice said, "Keep watching, and tonight you will see something you have never seen before." I took the words with a grain of salt.

As the sun went down, I began to notice lights from the horizon coming on. It was odd though. I could see lights from the far shore that were from buildings, then I could see other lights mixed in with those lights that were much brighter and appeared to be closer than the far shore lights.

Indeed, if my vision was accurate, what I was seeing was a grid of red lights that formed about six to eight miles out on the open water. Still, I kept my skeptical hat on. I was looking for something that was unmistakable and clear.

Between 9:00 and 10:00 that evening I got what I wanted. I saw a light I had been observing for about ninety minutes suddenly split into two. One part hovered over the top of the other. Even without binoculars I could clearly see that it was now two lights. With binoculars it was more astounding. The two lights pulsated wildly. The brightness increased tremendously.

Then I noticed something larger flying low over the water to the right of the two pulsating lights.

I watched with total amazement as a triangle shaped craft with five lights along the front of its hull, flew up to the two pulsating lights, hovered, then flipped completely upside down so I could see three lights at each point of the triangle on one side of its hull. It looked very much like what flew over my house some weeks earlier.

The object sat there and appeared to emit a dull, strange glow. Gradually, over the space of the next few minutes the object faded then disappeared into thin air. Soon after, the two lights on the water to its left rejoined and their brightness faded back down to match those around them.

I looked at all the other lights on the lake with a new perspective. Some, like the one I saw divide into two, were clearly not normal lights. I was hooked.

After that first night, I spent almost every weekend for the next four and a half months down at the lake, observing, watching and listening with my head and my heart.

One night, after a trip to the lake, I had a vivid dream. Later, I verified it was not just a dream.

I found myself standing in a crowd of people in a room that was all white. The walls were modern looking and there seemed to be some type of instrumentation on the walls. The people were all busily talking to one of the taller gray type aliens, who was standing in front of them. I raised my hand and said to the being, "Excuse me, would it be possible for me to see Michelle LaVigne if she's on board?"

"Her name is Kris," he responded.

"No, I want to speak to Michelle LaVigne," I reiterated.

"Her name is Kris," he replied once again.

"Could I speak to Kris please?" I asked.

"Yes," was his response finally. Then he turned and began to communicate with the busy crowd of people standing in front of him.

The next thing I remembered, I was sitting in a white room by myself. The chair I was in was comfortable and I was relaxed. A woman with long, dark brown hair entered the room. We began to speak. The nature of the conversation was about our friendship and honesty.

The next day when I woke up, I was groggy. I knew something had happened, but I wasn't totally clear on what. Many times after a night's experience, it would take up to an hour for my memory to come back. Sometimes the memory would be right there as soon as I woke up. This morning I was groggy. I remembered speaking in the crowd. I remembered sitting in a room with a woman, talking. It was hazy. I struggled to remember what we spoke about, but for some reason could not quite get it clear. Yet other parts of the experience were very clear.

Several days later I was E-mailing Michelle about the basic ideas that I had spoken to the woman on shipboard about, though I didn't mention to Michelle about the woman or about being on shipboard. In her return E-mail she asked, "Do you remember sitting in a chair telling someone this a few nights ago?"

I wrote back right away.

Her response was, "Hey there Paul, we have to talk. Call me." That was all.

I called Michelle on the telephone. She began to tell me of an experience she had several nights before. She had not told me about it before this in the hope that I would remember on my own. She began to describe the conversation we had. As she did, I began to remember in even more detail and more clearly. I started to finish off her sentences as she recounted our conversation.

Then I jumped and yelled, "I remember this! How did I forget this? I remember our conversation. It was real! It wasn't a dream!"

"That's right," she responded.

"Send me a picture of yourself," I pleaded. "I've got to see if your face was the face of the woman I remember sitting with." Michelle and I had only ever communicated via E-mail and telephone. Neither of us had any idea what the other looked like.

Michelle was hesitant in sending a picture. Even with all my prodding and pleading, she did not send a photo for some time to come.

Michelle
Summer of 97:
A Time of Discovery

During the Summer of 1997, Paul heard about a person who had been viewing some amazing lights that may have been genuine UFO phenomena at Lake Ontario. Paul and I were still working with our powwows on just about a nightly basis and were such good friends there was nothing we couldn't talk about in great detail with each other. He would tell me every single thing about his trips to the lake. We would talk for hours about what he saw. It all seemed so very amazing that I wanted to jump in the car and drive the eight hundred or so miles out there to join him at the lake to see for myself. I knew there had been reports of strange phenomena and UFO like orbs on the Great Lakes for decades, but until this time, I never knew anyone who had seen anything there personally.

We talked about everything and anything. We were so comfortable with each other, as if we had been best friends together forever. Our friendship seemed to have no boundaries or limits. Our phone conversations lasted for hours and both our phone bills were in the hundreds of dollars a month just in calls to each other alone.

Sometimes the energy generated by our powwows became very sensual in nature. We would experience what could be called creative energy. Some of the feelings that came up during these sessions were very strong, maybe too strong for people who were "just friends" to experience. Even so, we were able to talk about these times with each other openly. We had a more open and honest relationship, even at that distance, than I think I ever had with anyone.

The strangest thing also started happening in my night-time encounters with the ETs. The ETs kept bringing me to spend time with a person who I was not allowed to touch, but I could talk to. I knew this person really well. For some reason though, it was like my memory of this person was scrambled when I awoke in the mornings, and I kept thinking I was seeing the musician, Phil Collins, in these events.

I knew it wasn't really Phil Collins because he didn't really look like Phil Collins except in a vague sort of way. Despite how strong my memories were that it was Phil Collins, I was rather sure it was not really him. But who it was, I had no idea. All I knew was that he looked vaguely like Phil Collins and like the performer, he played the drums.

I saw "Phil" night after night. Sometimes I had strange dreams that I was running through big buildings looking for Paul only to find Phil Collins at the end of my search. Other times I believed I was talking to Paul, but he didn't look like what I pictured Paul would look like or what I saw in my mind when I thought of him. For that matter, he didn't look like Phil Collins. He looked like Andrew, my life long friend from the ET world; Andrew, my friend from my childhood who was now a man. None of these dreams or events made much sense to me, so for the most part, I documented them and then tried to forget about them. Sometimes I would tell my friends about them, but by and large, I put them on the back burner of my mind.

When I asked Hetar about them, he would just smile and say things like, "You ask me questions you know the answers to."

In the meantime, Paul and I kept talking and powwowing. After about a month or so of hearing him talk about all the great things he was seeing at the lake, he finally got his act together and sent me a video tape copy of some of the stuff he saw at the lake. He prefaced the tape with a bit of video of himself and his home which I had seen in several powwows and was able to personally confirm by seeing it on the film. When I got the tape, I eagerly popped it into my VCR and turned it on.

As soon as I saw his face I knew who he was. All the dreams made sense to me. All the strange visions of the guy who kind of looked like Phil Collins made sense. I sat there, watching the TV screen, transfixed on his face. I knew this man. I had known him for a long, long time. Something inside of me tightened up with a deep pain and my stomach turned. Could he really be who I thought he was? Could he really be Andrew?

On the tape, he took me on a walking tour of his home. The tour finished with his music room where he sat down at his drum set and played a short lick for me. He was a drummer. He was the mysterious "sorta Phil Collins".

I ran the tape over several times. I barely even cared about the lake footage, which was intriguing in itself. There was something more about him that I couldn't let myself believe. I found that as I watched the tape and I looked into his eyes I was mumbling things to myself like, "this can't be," "you're going crazy," and "don't even go there." Believe it or not, even though I made the connection and knew who he was, I still could not put all the pieces together; or more accurately, I could, but refused to. I knew who he was without a doubt, yet at the same time I did not really know anything for sure except that I knew him from the ET world and I had several clear memories of talking to him there.

I knew there were many more memories. If I thought about his face, memories would quickly come to mind and I would be overcome with frustration and sadness. I would become very upset and stop my thinking on the spot. As soon as the memories would start to come, they would be shut off. It was as if the ETs were working on me to make sure I did not think about any memories involving him. Or, I ponder now as I look back, maybe I was blocking memories of him myself, because once I stopped denying it all with phrases like, "don't even go there" and "you're going crazy", the memories filled in fast and furious.

As I watched the tape over and over I sat there knowing all but not truly allowing myself to know anything.

The next day I called Paul and told him that I received the tape and did indeed know him for a long time from my ET experiences. For some reason I was terrified to tell him. I didn't know what his reaction would be. I recalled to him an event that came to mind in which I was talking to him in the ET environment. I hoped it was unique enough that he may have remembered it.

I told him about this memory I had of a long debate I was having with him on shipboard several years back about Star Trek. I recalled to him about how I was in a rather playful mood and kept taking contrary points to him no matter what he said. Before I finished telling him, he told me of a vivid dream he had of the same exact thing. He never forgot it but he thought it was just a dream. He stopped me and finished the telling of the event based on his dream. His dream and my memory of the event were identical even to the smallest details. It was confirmation that we both needed. We did in fact know each other in the ET world.

This confirmation put me in a strange position. If he was the person I was having the Star Trek debate with- which it was now apparent he was- then there were other things about him that I recalled that were going to be difficult to deal with. The hardest probably being that he was more than my best friend, Paul or my long lost friend, "Andrew", he was also the first and probably only person I had ever truly loved. The ETs told me he had died when I was a young teen, only to bring him back into my life years later just to take him away again. In all that time, I never stopped loving him and in the depths of my heart I believed, somehow, I would find him once again, and now I had.

I remember the last few days Andrew and I had together before the time he was taken away from me. The last night we spent together in the ET world was one of wonder and amazement.

That last night, we met on shipboard. I was all excited and wordy about something that happened that day in school. My energy was off the wall, and my tongue was going a mile a minute with endless words. Andrew was not his usual self. He seemed rather serious and blank of expression. His mood seemed to change quickly and he - as he usually did when I was talking so much - kissed me in the middle of my sentence. Then he said, "Come on. I want to show you something."

I followed him to an observation type of room. It was a small room with a domed ceiling that was made of a clear glass like window. There were two formed chairs in it that could be tilted back so you could see the whole view from the window. There were also several control panels there but they were dark and inactivated. We sat down and looked out the window at the bright blue and white Earth below us. It was an amazing view. The white clouds were so bright that at times it almost hurt my eyes to look at them. It truly looked like a bubble of water floating in the blackness of space.

As we sat there, touching, loving and playing with each other, Andrew's mood changed. Again he seemed solemn and quiet. He almost seemed to be sad. He looked at me with far away but very intense blue eyes and said, "Never change. Promise me you will never change."

"Change? What are you talking about?" I replied.

"Just say it. No matter what happens, you will never change. You will always be like you are today." His eyes were afire with an intensity I had not seen before. His words reflected the intensity and I was verging on fear.

I believe I said something like, "What's the matter?" or "What are you talking about?"

He insisted, "Promise me."

I promised him. It was then I knew that something was very wrong, but I had no idea what it was.

I asked if everything was alright.

His mood changed again and he became light and playful once more. He promised he would love me forever and that we would be together, "Batman and Robin" until the end of time. He reminded me of our shared fantasy to live on an island and raise puppies, and vowed that someday we would do just that. We talked about how we planned to have five children, a big house, a bunch of dogs and a few horses and live happily ever after. He held me and said that he wanted to always remember me exactly as I was that night. He also said, in a rather strange and melancholy tone, "Even the darkside of the moon faces the sun sometimes."

The next time I saw him was far less pleasant. I remember being in a room. I was confused as to why I was there. I did not know what was going on, but I suspected it was something big because Alex, Molanie and Hetar were all in attendance, as were several grays. All of them seemed focused on something serious. Not one of them smiled or greeted me.

Alex and the others went into another room. After a few moments Molanie took me into that room too. Andrew was there. He seemed different. He was cold and angry looking. I could not understand why I didn't feel his presence the way I always did before. They told me he was leaving. With their words I was overcome with a strong sense that it would be forever. I questioned why. I wanted to know how long he would be gone.

They explained that he was being sent away to do something special. That it was something he had been getting ready to do for a long time. I asked him if it were true. He nodded silently. I started to cry. I could feel something was seriously wrong. I stood there looking at the person I was closest to in the universe; the person I loved; the person who was the other half of my being, and I felt nothing from him. It was as if he were dead already.

I sensed that he was not just going away for a while, he was going to be gone forever. I was verging on hysterical panic. I said through my tears, "But what about our dreams, our island? What about our future?"

I don't recall exactly if it were said to me in words or thought to me in telepathic concepts, or even who said it, but I heard someone reply, "You have no future."

I didn't take it very well. Frankly, I threw a fit and begged him not to go, because I knew he wouldn't be coming back if he did. Rather than feeling love and compassion from him, as I literally cried at his feet, I felt like he barely knew me. He said nothing and walked away from me.

Not long after, the ETs told me that he had died. Later I learned that they knew I was trying to search for him and decided for my own protection I should be told he was dead so I would stop searching before I found him. Nevertheless, I could not bring myself to believe he was dead; not in my heart. I always sensed he was alive and near, just past my point of memory. Maybe because of this or maybe because love is eternal, I never stopped loving him. No one in my life ever came close to the emotions I felt for Andrew.

My thoughts returned to the present. So there I was, sitting in front of the TV, looking at a video tape of my long lost Andrew, who I found through a series of strange events and coincidences. He was alive and well and on video tape. There I sat, almost a thousand miles away, feeling helplessly trapped in my situation, with only the shreds of my self esteem left after so many years of abuse. I couldn't help but remember all the times I lay awake at night, wondering if Andrew was still alive, where he was and if I would ever see him again. But my sense of self worth at the time I watched that tape was such that I couldn't help but feel like the universe was playing a horrid trick on me to bring him back into my life. At that moment, I did not know if I should rejoice at finding him, or cry my eyes out. I opted for the latter.

I know it sounds strange, but if only for copings sake, I found that by the next morning I had convinced myself I was wrong. Paul was not and could not be Andrew.

I knew for sure that I knew him in the ET world, but told myself he was not, could not be MY Andrew. I do not know quite how, but I managed to push the whole idea out of my head.

The Star Trek discussion caused us to start questioning other "dreams" and "events" we recalled with people in the ET world. Then one Saturday night I had another event where I was brought into a small room to talk to "Phil Collins" again.

The next time I talked to Paul he recalled being in a room and having a woman come talk to him. He was pretty sure it was me. He said he told her three very personal things about himself.

In my event, Phil told me three very personal things about himself. I told Paul of the event with "Phil" and told him the two things I remembered out of the three things Phil told me in the room. They were very specific, personal things he did during his younger years. They were things Paul did. They were too specific to be coincidence. It was clear we had been talking that Saturday night.

Paul said he had a really good visual memory of the woman in the room, and he needed to see what I looked like. So after getting up the nerve, which took some time, I sent Paul a computer scan of a photo of me via E-mail. He recognized me as the person he was having a discussion with. He also recognized me as the "Star Trek" person. He indicated that he felt there was something else, but didn't seem to have a clue. My knowledge was so buried deep inside and it caused such pain when I tried to look at it, I couldn't say a word to him about it.

In the meantime, we kept talking and working with each other through the summer. As we did the wall of denial came down, and more and more memories of our relationship came forward in me. As the days went on and the memories came back, it became clear to me that Paul was remembering our connection too. We would have powerful powwows in which he would experience visions of our connection but the total nature of that connection still seemed to allude him. At least it appeared that way to me.

In one very vivid image, Paul recalled the following to me in E-mail. *"I saw images of wolves faces. Next, you, me, and the wolf were standing in an opening. Then Hetar showed up, almost out of the air. I was looking at you. The wolf was between us. Hetar said the wolf and you are tied together, the wolf and I are one, we all need the other, and without the stars the wind would stop, the sky would no longer be and the water disappear. As the wolf moved into the sky, I saw a beam of sparkly, blue white light. It was almost like ethereal water going up to the sky and spreading out like a mushroom the way you'd expect ozone atoms to spread out when they reached the atmospheric edge. It was beautiful.*

There was a lot of wild imagery. At times the energy was extremely erotic and enjoyable. I saw the Indian. There was singing and drumming. A small boy squatting beside him with his head between his knees. Then the Indian hit me in the side of the head with the rattle he was shaking to the beat of the drums and told me to wake up.

Finally the wolf appeared again, rolled over in the sand and left an imprint that it motioned with its nose for me to look at. It looked like a circle with two upturned wings swooping outward. I looked closer and closer in the circle. I saw it was my face. In front of me was the wolf face at about my chest level. It became an emblem that emerged out of sand and turned into gold. As I moved back I could see the whole thing was a medallion and the swooping wings were connected to a chain. I saw that it was around your neck."

When I read this telling of the vision he experienced, I knew that he was making the connection on a deep inner level that he was not aware of yet in a more conscious state.

The Indian he referred to in the vision was a being that we sometimes saw when we powwowed. He was much like the Native man who gave me the name. When he did appear in either Paul or my visions, his presence was so overpowering that we would feel him around us for hours after a session.

The more we powwowed the more we became tuned to each other. We were so in tune to each other's feelings and consciousness that we use to joke that if he stubbed his toe, I would feel the pain and if I sneezed he would catch a cold. The most amazing part of all was that it wasn't really a joke. It was the truth. Over the summer and fall of 1997 there where countless times I would call him and say something like, "What did you just do to your hand?" after he just whacked his hand by accident; or he would call and ask, "Can you do something about your headache? It's giving me one too."

Still, I could sense an intense fear in him whenever he tried to explore the depths of our connection and it drew up more intimate feelings in him. It was as if he was convinced that if he acknowledged those feelings, or even attempted to try, he would lose his best friend. I knew he was feeling that our unique and very intense friendship was far too precious a thing to risk. He didn't have to tell me this, I knew it. The feeling from him was so intense at times it would have been hard not to know.

One morning, we were talking on the phone about the ET related events of the night before when we got onto the topic of "having one's lights on." Having one's lights on was an expression we used to indicate that the person was awake and aware during a contact event. We remarked about how at times people who seemed to have all their lights on sometimes lost control suddenly, like someone or something turned off the lights. I told him it can happen and I had seen it happen to several people before. He started to recall to me an event he had many years before where he started to experience something and his lights went out. Without going into detail, for the details are of a rather personal nature, the event involved him, a woman with long hair and the concept that he was actually dreaming.

He had barely started to describe the event when I knew exactly what and when he was talking about, because I was the woman. Before he finished, I stopped him and told him what happened and what was said. He seemed a bit confused and maybe even shocked that I was the woman in the event.

This got us talking about things. He knew that the woman in this event was someone special to him, and he had many memories of her as a teenager. Now he knew that woman was me.

We talked a lot through the next few months about memories from our childhood, memories we have of each other as teens. We shared memories of being kids holding hands, running through the hallways of Rye-hun ships playing Batman and Robin; memories of sitting in the observation room looking at the Earth, shinning blue and white in the dark night sky; memories of sharing and loving as we grew. It was hard to realize those memories and still keep perspective on who we were and what lives we had. I was quickly remembering and developing for Paul here on Earth, the deep feelings I always had for Andrew in the ET world.

<u>PAUL</u>
Lights on the Water

During the August long weekend, a civil holiday in Canada, a group of my canoeing buddies and I paddled to a place called Rosebary Lake. We found a beautiful campsite next to a long sandy beach where we saw several moose come to drink over the next three days.

On one of the nights, during the height of the new moon, one of the women in our party got up in the middle of the night to tend to something. When she stuck her head out of the tent she looked up and saw a large full moon in the sky.

The next morning she asked all of us if we had seen it. She said she didn't have her glasses on so she could not make out any of the moon's features. She only saw its large, white presence in the sky. We told her it was a new moon and it was physically impossible for her to see a full moon that night. I knew what it was and jokingly said to her, "Gee Diane, maybe it was a UFO or something?"

No one in the party knew that I was an "experiencer." My paddle partner, Peter, knew of my interest in the subject as a result of what happened on the Wahta reserve, but that was the limit of his knowledge. I had a hearty chuckle to myself. Unfortunately, I remembered nothing but sleeping through that night. I had no dreams, no experiences, just sleep.

On my return home, I spoke with Michelle. She told me that she had another Native theme experience the very night the woman in my canoeing party saw the full moon. She said she talked to a Native looking being about some kind of event that was about to take place. She told him that she was worried about me. She said the being in her experience responded to the effect of, "Do not worry. Grandmother Moon watches over him."

When I heard this I laughed and said, "I think it was Grandmother Moon hovering over the lake."

A few weeks later I made a small film of myself to send to her.

Despite the earlier experience we shared in the room with the chair, I did not expect something about my face would seem familiar to Michelle. It just seemed unbelievable that she would know me from an alien encounter. The next time we spoke, she told me that my face, seen in this reality on videotape, appeared to be very familiar to her.

A couple of days later she told me of an experience she had with me years before when we were in our twenties. She said that we spoke about the old Star Trek series one night while we were on shipboard.

I jumped back. An old dream, or what I thought was a dream, triggered in my head. Some dreams are just dreams, and some dreams you remember forever. I remembered a very long and annoying dream of speaking to a woman about the old Star Trek television show one night years ago. I was able to remember the face of the person in the dream. I needed to see her face. Once again I started bugging her for a photo. After some prodding, she agreed and sent me an electronically scanned photo attached to an E-mail.

When I opened up her picture and viewed it on my computer screen I could not believe it. It was the same woman I had seen in the Star Trek dream and the same face from the experience in the room with the chair several weeks before. I called her up immediately. This was incredible to me. I had found someone who not only was an experiencer, but someone who I now could establish had experiences the same time I did even though she lived over eight hundred miles away. I was ecstatic. This was yet one more verification for me. It was my own personal proof. I knew I was not crazy because now there was somebody else who was able to tell me about a conversation that took place during a strange dream-like experience that I had shared with no one.

When I called her up, I was in an excited state. We spoke for a good hour on the telephone about more and more things. It now became apparent that we had known each other for some time. Our memories of each other were beginning to click.

Over the next few weeks I noticed Michelle's attitude toward me changing, as though she knew something I did not. Michelle began to tell me how she was remembering more and more about me, but she would not tell me what. She said it was important that I remember on my own. She told me that we used to call each other by different names and that she would not tell me what she used to call me. That it was important I remembered on my own. Michelle told me that the ET she commonly worked with, named Hetar, had told her not to say anything. She was to let me remember on my own. She promised him she would follow his instructions.

I found this period of time frustrating. I began to notice it was even more frustrating for Michelle for reasons that I did not fully understand.

Then one day she told me something that Hetar had told her. It was something personal about me. There was no way she could have known what she told me, or the ramifications of his statement. She relayed it to me and unwittingly cut me to the very core.

We had both agreed some time before the only way we were going to figure all of this out was to put "all the cards on the table." I knew what I had to do.

On my drive home from work something cracked inside me. In an instant a flood of memories forced there way to the surface. My name was Andrew! There was a young girl I used to spend so much time with. The long dreams! They were not dreams! They were real!

It was hard to concentrate with the flood of memories that were pouring back to me. Somehow, I managed to drive home. I was excited.

"My God, can this really be happening? I'm getting my memory back like I wanted and asked for. I didn't expect this. How could I have forgotten? It was so long ago. Oh my God," I pondered in shock.

I sat down and wrote a long message to Michelle entitled, *"The Story of Andrew"*. I remembered when she and I were seperated as teenagers. I had never really healed from it. Recovering the memory exposed the pain. I sent the E-mail.

A few hours later the telephone rang. It was Michelle. She spoke to me in an understanding tone. She reassured me it would be alright. The event was something that happened over eighteen years ago. We talked for a long time about it and other things that I remembered that day.

The next day I felt a bit better, but something was different. I kept remembering things from the past. I kept experiencing memories of being in a place where there were trees and gardens, of playing with a young girl, of being in love. I had memories of being in a place where the walls were white and everything was rounded. I had clear recall of times when I lie in a room embracing a lovely young lady as we watched the Earth from orbit through a large clear dome ceiling. I recovered many more disjointed memories of a life somewhere else. I did not know what was happening to me, but these were clear memories, not dreams. I remembered these as real, physical events.

Over time, I was able to verify these memories as I recounted the beginning of these events to Michelle, and she would finish the recounting of the memories from the perspective of the young lady I called Kris. It became an incredible journey of discovery for both of us.

As I was dealing with the recall of these memories, my Earth-life went on. At the end of August, I went on a three day canoe trip to Franklin Island on Georgian Bay. At the start of the trip, as I was putting my canoe in the water, I bent over and heard a tearing sound in my left hip.

"Aaah, shit!" I yelled. "That would be the second hernia," I thought to myself. I reached down and felt a lump that had descended several inches down the outside of my hip.

"Damned ET's! Why didn't they just fix the damned things?" I muttered to myself. I was beginning to dislike some of the verifications I was getting.

When I returned from my trip, I went down to Lake Ontario. As I stared into the mist with a high powered view scope, I saw a cigar shaped craft which appeared to be metallic. It had lights on it and it was hovering just above the water. I watched as the cigar shaped craft moved in a downward motion from approximately ten meters over the water and into the humid mist over the lake.

After that, I sat and waited for some time. Then, just after 9:00 PM, I spotted a light approximately five degrees above the horizon coming up the Niagara River. I watched the object fly out over the lake. I followed it with my view scope as it approached the surface of the water in slow descent. Then a beam of light appear and reflected on the water. The object paused for a moment, then in an instant, it descended into the water without causing any waves. I laughed with excitement. I was so elated. It was magnificent to see such technology so close.

That night I watched four different objects fly up low over the lake. Three of them flew into the water. The fourth one turned so I could make out what looked to be a long row of windows or portals along its length. It was massive and very low over the water.

One object was brilliant, blue-white light that seemed so incredibly bright, yet it did not hurt the eyes to look at. I felt so peaceful as I watched it. After a while nothing more happened and I decided to pack up.

Over the next few days I took a copy of a film made at the lake to show to Tom and Lucy on the reserve. I wanted to see if any of the craft on the film compared with what they had seen hovering over the Wahta reserve.

After viewing the film, Tom sat down and appeared very introspective. His body started to shake, his eyes bulged and he closed them then dropped his head to the table. A moment later he looked up and said, "It is an ancient life form. They've been here for thousands of years."

I was disappointed with his analysis. It wasn't until some time later that I understood how accurate Tom was with respect to some of the lights I was seeing over the lake. At that time I was thinking they were all mechanical devices. I soon learned that some of them were not.

I returned from the reserve somewhat disappointed. But I knew, regardless, I was dealing with a series of connections that was leading me somewhere important. First there was the unusual way in which I met Tom and Lucy. Then there was the phenomenon at the lake. Plus there was Michelle and our shared memories. Somewhere in this there lay a pattern. I felt like I was getting closer.

Michelle and I continued to remember things. On recovering my memories of being with her as a child and in our teenage years I remembered, in much more detail, the time we were split apart. Michelle had always remembered, she had never forgotten. As I remembered more and more I started to understand what an incredible shock it must have been for her to realize who I was. Not only that, it must have killed her to sit back and say nothing waiting for me to remember by myself. Most certainly, when I connected the memory in my own mind, it broke my heart into little pieces.

<u>PAUL</u>
Memories of Home

As details started to fill in my memory, I remembered that long ago in my childhood and teenage years, an extraordinary series of alien contact events occurred. I remembered going to sleep and having long dreams that seemed to go on for several days at a time. I dreamed of living in a beautiful place with a young girl who was my best friend. It was a place with green grass, gardens and trees. There were people and animals, places of work with modern instrumentation and classrooms with simple chairs. Even though these dreams seemed to last for days, I would wake up and it would be the next morning. The beautiful feelings would quickly pass, along with my memory of where I had been.

Some of the memories to come back were painful. I remember being called into an area where there was a group of beings that were familiar to me. One was a small gray being, another was a tall blond man, there were several others. I was told there was a considerable job that had to be done. It was very important to a lot of people. It would affect the world. They asked me if I was willing to do it. They told me it would be very difficult, more difficult than I could imagine. They said they would have to train me for it and they would have to lie to me to protect Kristance and me. They also said I would be angry about it afterwards, but in the end it would all work out.

I told them I would need time to think about it. It was a big decision. I remember I put it out of my mind and joined my friends again to enjoy the days of play and fun.

Kristance, I called her Kris, and I would spend days painting the surroundings with creative energy. We were in love in the most beautiful way possible between a young teenage boy and girl.

A period of time passed and I remember being called to the group again. They asked me if I had made a decision yet. I thought for a minute. I didn't like thinking about it, but I could emotionally feel from everyone how incredibly important it was. I asked them once again about its importance. I asked them if it would help Kris and me in the future and allow for more possibilities in our growth. They responded in the affirmative to both. I finally told them I would do it.

They all seemed pleased. There was further discussion later where it was decided that Kris would not be told about my leaving for the mission until the day I left. I felt bad, but I was also afraid that she would hate me for choosing to leave.

I remember the day before we were separated. We were lying in a room in each others embrace, looking through a transparent, domed shaped ceiling. It was beautiful and peaceful. Through the dome was a vast sea of darkness out of which emerged a beautiful blue ball that filled the sky. It was the Earth.

I exchanged some words with Kris. I remember thinking how I would be leaving soon. It was our last night together for a while. Though I didn't know how long, I had the sense it would be a long time. I made some comment that alluded to my leaving. She asked me if I was going somewhere. I thought for a moment, then I decided to lie and tell her no. I didn't wish to destroy our last night together.

At one point, I was thinking about where I was going and I looked into the sky and said with melancholy and sadness, "Even the dark side of the Moon faces the Sun sometimes."

"Don't ever change," I said to her. Some part of me knew I was about to change and I wanted to believe that she would never change. As we lie there I felt love and joy in my heart at being in the arms of my love. Little did I know how my love would be wrenched from me the next day.

In the next conscious memory I have of being with the ETs, I was standing with Alex, Hetar and Rovere. There were also several small gray type ETs there.

Hetar said to me, "We're going to have to make you angry now." At the time, his words made sense to me.

I nodded and watched as Hetar held out his hand and a ball of light emerged from my solar plexus and flew horizontally across the ground over to his open hand. As this happened, I felt like I became half of what I was; half the person. Hetar held the missing pieces all in the palm of his four fingered hand. I looked at the ball of light and felt so incredibly vulnerable.

They instructed me to follow them. I was brought to a place that was all white. Someone was walking with Kris as she approached. We told her I had to leave to perform a mission. She started to yell and scream. I couldn't understand what was going on. What did she know about my leaving that I didn't?

She was crying. She was in deep emotional pain. She waived her arms around wildly. The person with her restrained her. She was a wreck. I felt a great desire to say something. I felt like I was going to cry inside. I wanted to say something, anything, and was about to when I heard a strong voice order me to say nothing.

It was heart wrenching to remain silent as I watched Kris scream in pain and shock in front of me. I could not understand why she reacted so strongly. Did she know something about my leaving that I did not? How long was I going for?

A few minutes later they took her away and I found myself standing with the group of beings again. They explained how they would have to lie to me to protect me, and that I would go through periods of hating them. I stood in horror and shock. It did not make any sense. I felt so empty. Why did Kris yell at me so much?

"How long will it be before Kris and I are together again?" I asked.

"Twenty years," came the response.

I was horrified. "She won't last that long," I said.

"We will take her memory away," one of them said.

"No!" I replied, "She has to remember me."

The next thing I said was, "Then I will feel things and she will see things."

I looked at Hetar and said, "I'm going to kill you when I come back."

Hetar looked back and nodded at me in acknowledgment. It was a horrible experience; a dark day in my memory and my life in both the ET world and here on Earth. I felt rage and hatred at my ET family that I had never known before.

In my earthly life I fell into a deep depression. For reasons I could not understand, I suffered a tremendous feeling of loss. I experienced long periods of knowing there was a place better than Earth, a place where there was a young woman I loved, but my memory was shaky at best. The heart knowledge was strong, but the mind knowledge was weak.

Next I began the side mission that I had been split from Kris to do. It was something no one should ever have to experience, but looking back now with the understanding I have gained, I realize how important and how necessary for the future it was. It seemed like forever until it was over.

All of this tied in with an early morning sighting that I had in Toronto.

One morning at 6:00 AM, I awoke from a dead sleep and literally leaped out of my bed for no apparent reason. I ran to the window and looked up at the sky. I saw a small black dot underneath some very high clouds.

The clouds were moving from northwest to southeast. The small, round, black dot I observed was moving very slowly from north-northeast to south-southwest. It moved in that direction for about twenty seconds, then turned suddenly and continued in a straight line in a west-southwest direction, almost at right angles to the wind.

I experienced a feeling of elation. All through that day I was filled with energy. It was extremely unlike me to rise before seven-thirty in the morning at that point in my life. All morning long the words went through my head, "It's over. The darkness is over. It's time to heal. Thank God, it's over!" Chunks of my memory regarding my ET experiences began to return after this point in my life. Understanding their nature took some time though. This is only a sample of the difficult memories both Michelle and I were trying to deal with through the fall of 1998.

By October, Michelle and I were working closer together as friends and exploring the memory of our past love as we continued to meditate simultaneously. From a distance of eight-hundred miles away, her in New Hampshire and me in Ontario, we discovered our connection was strengthening and growing. We saw similar images in our head and felt the same sensations and feelings.

Looking back I can see how hard this time was for Michelle, because she remembered me as Andrew and remembered her love for me. I did not want to let myself feel what I was really feeling inside. I kept telling myself our love was a thing of the past that had changed and grown into something else. Most of all, I did not want to risk loosing my best friend if our attempt at a relationship did not work out.

Besides, my life was my spiritual work and I concentrated on that. Meanwhile, Michelle kept her feelings to herself and suffered silently. Little did I know how inevitable the heart-swell of truth inside me would be as this part of our friendship and work continued to grow.

October afforded me a bit of rest from my day job and I was able to spend some more time watching the phenomena at Lake Ontario, comparing notes with Michelle, and meditating in the evenings. I also went up to the Wahta reserve once or twice to visit with Tom and Lucy.

Something incredible happened that month. On the evening of October 22, 1997 I went down to the shore of Lake Ontario just west of where I would normally go. I was fiddling with something and when I looked up there were fifteen lights spread across the harbor that I had never seen before.

"Where did those come from?" I wondered.

For the next two hours I sat and stared in awe. These lights were different from any I had ever seen before. They completely blocked the view of the opposing shoreline lights. They must have spread across an area of three to five miles. Moreover, I could 'feel' these lights.

Through high powered binoculars, I saw the fifteen lights reflecting off of the water. As darkness set in, something remarkable began to appear between and behind the fifteen lights. I saw what looked like rows and rows of beings. They had on robes and appeared to have faces that were similar to, but not the same as a gray type alien face. There was something familiar about their faces I could not quite put my finger on.

What was remarkable was that the rows of beings seemed to recede back into eternity. The rows of beings went on forever. Tears ran down my face. I was awe struck to the core of my heart with wonder.

Taking a very rough guess, it seemed to me the beings must have been visually between thirty and fifty feet in height. The only words I can find to describe what I saw is that it was as though I were looking into another dimension. I wondered if the fifteen lights spread across the lake created a type of viewing portal through which the beings could be seen.

Eventually it grew late and very cold. Reluctantly I decided to leave.

"What are they doing out there?" I thought. Though I was not aware, in a few months I would have an answer.

MICHELLE
Fall of 1997
White Wolf Dreams part 2

By the early fall, the memories were so strong and the powwow energy and visions so intense that we knew we had to meet. Paul started talking about flying down from Toronto to visit me.

The complexity and detail of our memories together were beyond the point of denial. It also seemed that we were still in contact with each other in the ET world. We would see each other at night on ET ships or bases and the next morning quickly grab the phone and call the other up to talk about what happened. Sometimes my recall was better than his and this seemed to frustrate him. Other times he would recall things I only had a sense off. Still, more often than not, we recalled the same things.

Again I saw the white wolf in my dreams, meditations and events. Sometimes the wolf had green eyes, but more and more often the wolf had ice blue eyes. One night I was on shipboard with Hetar. The blue eyed wolf was also there. He came walking into the room I was in and put his head on my lap. I looked over to Hetar with surprise and said, "How come I can touch him when he's in this form but not when he is in his body?"

Another time, after being a bit miffed with Paul over some little thing, I dreamed that I was walking on a hard surfaced, red sand desert that had a few shrubs and some tall cliff like rock hills. There was a building, almost like a cabin or a shack at the end of a dirt road. I walked to the cabin and went in. It was empty. So I walked back out into the middle of the road about twenty feet or so from the building and then laid down on the ground.

The blue eyed, white wolf was there. He came over to lie down next to me. I pushed him away. I snapped at him that I was mad at him and didn't want him to be close to me. He paced around me whining with his tail low, but still wagging.

Despite his pleads, I refused to let him come close. He persisted in his whining. After a few unsuccessful tries at getting close, he started to yap playfully at me. I looked at him with his beautiful blue eyes. Despite the fact that he was an animal, it seemed clear that he was smiling at me. I could not resist his charm and said, "Well, okay. Come on." He ran over and licked my face and neck feverishly, then he cuddled up with me. I felt completely safe and secure. Together, we fell asleep right there in the middle of the dirt road in the desert.

Then next morning, even before I told Paul about this "dream", he told me about an experience he had the night before where he saw me. He was sure it was a real experience and not a dream. He said that he was in a desert and there was a building in front of him. He knew I was in the building. I came out of the building and he knew I was upset with him. He said he spoke to me, then went up to me and kissed me and hugged me and everything was better. He did not recall being a wolf in the event. Still his event and my dream were very close. They were too close to be coincidence.

Another time I dreamed I was a bird. I was flying very fast over the two white wolves as they ran across an open plain. Rainbows of colors like condensation trails from a jet formed behind us as we went.

I told Paul about my dream of flying, not mentioning the wolves right away. But I didn't have to. He told me he had a dream he was running. Then, with some nervousness, he confided that it was one of his wolf dreams.

"Wolf dreams?" I asked.

It seemed he had been having dreams of being a wolf for some time. As we talked more and more about the wolf dreams he had, it became clear that many of them could be and likely were connected to the events I was having with the white wolf with the blue eyes in particular.

I asked Hetar about it. He was rather helpful. He explained that there were several layers of things going on and went into a little detail about those layers. He said that the "wolf manifestation" was one of the layers. Then he directed me to Rovere for the answers to my wolf related questions.

Rovere explained with an analogy that was less clear than I hoped for. He told me about the wind and the water and the sky. He said that Paul was the water, I was the sky and together we join with the wind. He also reminded me what Hetar had told me some time back when I asked him about Paul. He said Paul was spiritually a fish and I was a bird. But now I was starting to believe that Paul was actually a wolf. Before long, I knew it was true without a doubt.

MICHELLE
Meetings

One night, as Hetar was sending me home, I asked him about my connection to Paul. He told me to remember what happened the night of the total lunar eclipse back in 1989. I had no idea why he would want me to remember this, but it got me thinking anyway. I didn't tell Hetar anything that I remembered from that night, nor did he ask for details. He just told me to recall it.

It wasn't very hard to remember that night. Because of the eclipse, it stood out in my mind. It was the summer of 1989. August I believe. Still, I had not thought about that night in years. It was a night that I had a very unusual encounter.

I recalled I was sitting up that night. The room was, for the most part, dark. The only light in the room was coming from the lights on the stereo's control panel and the lights from the 12th scale doll house that was sitting on a table behind the couch. I had wired it with tiny electric lights and it gave off the most prominent lighting in the room.

I remembered a man coming down the stairs of the house. I remembered thinking he was then husband, George, but also thinking he wasn't. It was strangely confusing, but then I decided, it had to be George. Who else could it be? The man walked over to where I was sitting and brought me to the sofa. There we made love. It was probably the most intense sexual experience I had known to that date.

I kept thinking, "This has to be George". But he didn't make love like George. His body didn't feel like George's. He was much more animated and vocal than George had ever been. The energy that was pouring from his body to mine was beyond physical, it was so incredible and intense. It was something I never recalled experiencing before. It was not at all like any time I was with George.

After the encounter, the man looked me in the eyes and said, "My God, I've missed you." I thought those were odd words coming from George who had seen me just a few hours before. Even odder was that as I looked at the man I thought was George, I knew in my heart he was not George and this did not disturb me.

It was not just that the man I was looking at was the wrong height and his eyes were not the same, it was that I felt such a strong love and passion for this man. I was experiencing feelings for him of such a depth, I am sad to admit, I did not feel for the man who was married to at that time.

Why Hetar asked me to recall all this was not a mystery for long. A few days later I was on the phone talking to Paul. Our conversation took its usual unpredictable course and somehow we ended up talking about our most unusual and hard to talk about memories.

After some dancing around the subject, Paul asked me if I ever had an event where I was in someone else's house, because he had been thinking about something he always thought was an intensely vivid dream, but now realized was probably not. He started talking about how he found himself in a house at the top of a staircase. He walked down the stairs to find a woman sitting in a chair in a living room. He said he knew that he was somehow very close to this woman, but in his memory of the event he didn't know why or who she was. He started to tell me how he brought her to the sofa and began to make love to her.

My heart skipped a beat. Could he be recalling to me the night that Hetar asked me to remember? Could Hetar have known that Paul had such a vivid memory of that night that it was only a matter of time before he brought it up in conversation?

I nervously asked him if he recalled anything particular about the room. Was there anything unusual about it? I made very sure that I did not give him any hints or clues. He had no way of knowing that at that time I had a doll house in the living room. As a matter of fact, at the time we were recalling this event the doll house had been in storage for several years.

He said, "I know this might sound strange. But the couch was pulled away from the wall and behind it was some kind of table with a lit up object on it. As I recall, I believe it was a big doll house."

Before I could bring myself to even speak any words, he went on to describe how the stairs turned at the bottom and what the rest of the room and the sofa looked like.

I was amazed. How could he have guessed about any of that, especially the doll house? I told him about what I recalled from my event. I told him about my house at that time. I told him the way the man made love and what the man said. This time it was his turn to be left without words.

He did not tell me, but rather I told him what he already knew about kissing the woman and saying "My God, I've missed you." I told him how he lead me back to the chair I was sitting on when he first arrived and how he quietly walked back up the stairs. I also told him how George had no recall of the whole thing the next day.

We both continued to recall these types of unmistakable memories. We were also experiencing very deep, strong memories of some kind of "job" or "mission" we had to perform together. The need to find, develop and fulfill that mission was so strong that it became the driving force in both our lives. It was clear we were connected in a big way, and we knew that our mission, whatever it turned out to be, had to be accomplished as a team.

By November, Paul said he couldn't wait any longer. He had to see me face to face. He had to know if it were all true. He had to look in my eyes and know it was all real, and maybe find out exactly what the mission was.

I felt the same way, but I knew that once he came I would know without a doubt if he was truly Andrew, then I could never be the same. If he was Andrew, then I had literally found my soul. If he wasn't, then we must both be having some crazy delusions to have so many memories in common.

I didn't have any kind of relationship with Paul that could have been considered remotely romantic at the time. Moreover, I didn't believe anything would ever come of him and me. I believed that he would never remember the total of our connection and things would never be like they were when we were teens again. Yet, my emotional bond to Paul was so strong I couldn't imagine life without him. He felt the same, even though in this physical life we had never even spoken face to face.

One morning I was on the phone with Paul talking to him about my overwhelming feeling of being trapped like a bird in a cage by the problems I was dealing with. Paul was my best friend and it was not uncommon for me to cry on his shoulder. He kept telling me that I was strong enough to deal with anything. He reminded me that I had the strength to do what I knew was best for me and my children. He challenged me to stay strong in times when I felt like I had the fortitude of a worm. He never tried to convince me to run to him, nor did I have any intention of doing so. He and I both wanted to see me and my children independent, strong and safe.

Still, this particular morning had been very bad, and it had been a very hard week, and I was really feeling down. I kept repeating to him, "You don't understand. I'm a bird in a cage. It's impossible to get out of it."

After I said it for maybe the tenth time, Paul said, "Mick, no cage is escape proof. You can do this." Just as he spoke those words I heard a thump.

I looked over to where the thump had come from and one of my society finches was sitting on the window sill where it landed after running into the glass. I was astounded. The finch had been in a cage that not only was secured by regular means, but had locks on all the doors to keep my four year old son from opening them up. I knew it was in its cage just moments before, because I was looking straight at it.

I picked up the bird and checked it for damage. It was no worse for its little jaunt. Then I looked at the cage very carefully before I removed the locking device from the cage door and replaced the bird safely inside. The cage was totally and perfectly closed. I checked all the locks and doors to make sure they were firmly in place. They were.

There was no way that bird could have gotten out of that cage. Yet it did, and so would I.

Each day that passed, the psychic and emotional bond between Paul and me grew stronger. Both of us found we were dealing with emotions that were hard to come to terms with.

These emotions confused us both because this was happening well before we established any physical relationship or even admitted to each other we had any emotional one aside from intensely devoted best friends. This happened even before we met face to face in our earth lives. It became clear to us that we both felt that we were inseparably bonded for the rest of existance.

The situation was so obtuse that both of us preferred to talk on the phone to each other about practically nothing than to be with anyone else in any way, including romantically. The intense sensation that we needed to be with each other and not with anyone else was overwhelming and baffling.

Through the fall of 1997 I was not working aside from my writing, which did not make enough money to pay the rent and feed three kids. So my main focus was to get a job so I could survive with my children on my own without public assistance. To make matters worse, I did not have my own car so I had to depend on public transportation and friends for rides.

The powwow events between Paul and I kept getting more and more intense. The energy seemed to be developing into a frenzed state. We were connecting each morning and staying connected all through the day. When we meditated together we could feel a huge, very aware, consciousness around us. It was like our energy was spinning off and attracting these presences or maybe even creating them. We would talk for hours. Sometimes we would just sit on the phone and meditate together in verbal silence.

I say verbal silence, because even though our mouths said nothing, our minds were ablaze with shared thoughts and ideas.

Our connection was so intense, I could not put off meeting him face to face any longer. So, I invited Paul down to spend time with me so we could explore the energy between us as friends.

Back in Canada, Paul arranged to get some time out of work and made his plans to come visit with me from Dec 28th until Jan 2nd. He was going to stay at my house and sleep on the couch. As the time approached, we both became more and more nervous. Our connection was becoming more and more intense. Our energy more and more melded together. We were getting together not just to find out what our "mission" was, but also to test if any of these intense energies we were feeling were truly because of our unique connection, and not just some reaction of being both abductees personified by imagination. Neither one of us had any romantic ideas or plans. We joked with half seriousness that there was nothing a man and woman could do together that could possibly match the energy we were likely to generate when we touched palm to palm.

For weeks before his visit, the ET's kept telling us that we had to "put all the cards on the table" with each other and talk about everything regarding ourselves and our relationship. For days we talked about things. Not just good things. We forced ourselves to examine the deepest reaches of our fears and our expectations of mission, self and one another. We both had very difficult things to work through, but we somehow managed to keep working at it until we had just about every conceivable issue out in the open and hashed out. Later we found out how incredibly valuable this time was. It saved us from having to face all the issues that usually come up in the beginning of a relationship later on when we had more pressing, larger issues to deal with. I am convinced that if we had to face all the "cards on the table" issues and the later ones at the same time it would have been disastrous.

The few days before he arrived were difficult. We were both feeling terribly nervous and sometimes our nerves caused us to get a bit on edge with each other. Our phone conversations were just as long and as involved, but the energy was skittish. To make matters even more strained, by this time I had complete and full memory of exactly who he was and what relationship we had since childhood.

I was doing my best not to expect anything from him, but it wasn't easy. As I said to my friend Dee, "I know exactly who he is. If he does not remember me then I will feel empty and incomplete for the rest of eternity." She assured me that if it were meant to be, he would remember. I tried to be hopeful.

Sunday the 28th came. I picked up Paul at Logan Airport. When I got to the terminal, I found the door to the customs area where I was told he was coming out. I stood there watching the door. My heart was pounding in my chest. There was an energy to the air around me. It was very familiar.

I stood there alone and waited for Paul to come out of the door. The energy grew more and more intense. I was well aware that my life was about to change, one way or another. As far as I could see, either way I was about to be hurt. If he didn't remember the emotions I did, I would be devastated. If he did, I would be even more devastated because I promised Andrew I would never change, and I had changed. It was not a little change either. I grew twenty years older and quite a bit heavier. I was convinced he would hate me for changing.

"Shé-ko," a voice behind me greeted me in Mohawk. I turned and hugged the body that belonged to the voice. I didn't have to check. I knew it was Paul. Our first hug in this existence was a confirmation for me. The feeling, the energy, was exactly the way I remembered it. I knew at that exact moment that he was who I knew he was. He was Andrew.

<u>PAUL</u>
The Visit

Through the month of December we all prepared for Christmas. Michelle and I both wanted to meet each other quite badly. We decided that I would fly down to visit her between Christmas and New Years. It was the first reasonable chance for me to take some holiday time and we were both eager.

Most of the month, Michelle and I spent on the phone each evening talking to each other. We spent a certain amount of time meditating together, then one of us would call the other and we would debrief each other on our experiences during the meditation.

Sometimes the meditations would be full of imagery, other times they would be more emotional. Often the imagery became quite detailed. For instance, in one meditation I began to concentrate. Soon I fell into a deep, restful state. I began to make out an image in my head of a being that Michelle and I have our own name for. He was standing in front of me. Next, I sensed, then could see Michelle standing to my left.

The being in front of us then took both our hands and carried us at an incredible rate of speed through what seemed like space. I could see sparks and flashes go by as we travelled. After approximately thirty seconds of travelling like this, we stopped in an area that was filled with brilliant white light.

When Michelle telephoned me that night, she began to describe exactly what I had experienced during the meditation; the same thoughts, feelings and sensations. Clearly, something was going on. Again, we had tapped into something important.

We hoped that with the energy we were experiencing and generating from over eight-hundred miles away, we would be able to experience something incredible when we were physically together.

One ET contact event that proved to be most interesting caught both Michelle and I off guard. Early one morning I experienced an event where I was standing talking into some type of control panel. I was listening to someone speak who had an unnatural and high pitched, nasal sounding voice. They were telling me something important. I was straining to listen and having even a harder time understanding and remembering what they said.

Later that day Michelle telephoned me at work to tell me that Hetar had just picked her up and asked her to relay some information to me. On a hunch, I asked Michelle what Hetar's voice sounds like.

She responded, "He has a kind of high pitched, nasal sounding voice."

"Dear God that was him this morning," I shot back.

"Oh!" She gasped.

We both just listened on the phone in silence for a moment. We both wondered more than ever how involved the ET's were and how much they were watching as Michelle and I pursued our spiritual connection and history.

On December 14th I went to Mason's gravesite, it was the anniversary of his death. I burned some tobacco and performed a *Mohawk Thank You Ceremony* the way Tom had taught me. I had not been able to return to Mason's gravesite without breaking into tears all year.

After I finished the ceremony, I looked up at an area where I thought I could sense Mason's presence and said, "Come on. Let's get out of here."

I got up and we left.

Christmas passed by with my family and it was peaceful and pleasant, but all the while I was anxious to meet Michelle. I could remember what the young girl from my memories as a teenager looked like. From what I had seen of the pictures Michelle had sent me, she looked like she could be the Kris I remembered.

In late December, I got on a jet and flew to Boston. I was very nervous. I hoped everything would go alright. When I arrived at the airport, I walked out from the jet and along the walkways into the passenger pickup area.

Michelle had told me she would be wearing a big yellow coat. I looked around and saw a woman with a yellow coat. I recognized her profile from the picture I had.

I sneaked up stealthily behind her and stood for a moment.

"Shé-ko Michelle," I said. It was Mohawk for hello.

She turned around and I immediately recognized her. It was Kris from the dreams of my youth. I was in shock. She was a bit older, but it was Kris.

Michelle threw herself around me. I grabbed her with both arms and we shared a long, long hug just like two people who had not seen each other in twenty years would.

On the way back from the airport, Michelle and I stopped off at a restaurant to eat and talk. We were both hungry and excited. As we sat there and talked, we both fell into spells where we just looked at each other in shock and disbelief.

"How could this be happening?" I thought over and over. It was like an unreal dream. But there I was, sitting in a restaurant, talking to a woman who had finished the stories of my dreams and ET experiences as I was telling them to her over the last ten months; a woman whose face I remembered; a woman who I loved so much a long time ago.

Then, as we spoke, something unusual happened. Michelle's face began to change in front of me. The energy around us had risen dramatically since we met at the airport. Now I found myself looking at the face of an old Native woman.

I shook my head. I had seen this type of phenomenon before, but not for many years. I used to look into the eyes of a friend back in my twenties and we would both experience seeing each other turn into Natives.

"What's wrong?" Michelle asked.

"I just saw you turn into a Native, I haven't experienced anything like that in years. It just caught me off guard."

"I just saw you turn into a Native as well," she shot back with surprise. "You mean you saw it too?"

"Yes! Let's try it again," I answered.

So we sat and concentrated. Sure enough, after a few seconds we both observed as each other's face appeared to turn into a North American aboriginal face.

We talked excitedly some more. We were anxious to get back to Michelle's place so we could begin working.

That evening we stayed up late. We found our energy level was many times what we experienced when we were so far apart. Michelle was anxious for me to experience some of the ET events that commonly occurred in her home.

That evening we drove out to the countryside to do some UFO watching. We found a large open field underneath a beautiful starlit sky. It was bitterly cold, about twenty below zero Fahrenheit. We stamped our feet and concentrated on calling the ET's in our head. We saw many planes come over the horizon but nothing out of the ordinary. After approximately thirty minutes a white light appeared above the horizon. It was a soft, white, diffused light, similar to what I had seen over the lake. Unlike the jets we had been watching, this one flew directly towards us. It had no blinking lights on the way jets do, but rather was one solid white light.

"Why don't we look at it through the binoculars just to make sure," suggested Michelle.

"Good idea," I replied.

We both turned to get the binoculars off of the hood of the car. When we turned back around we saw that the light had completely disappeared from the sky. A second before it had been right in front of our field of vision.

"Oh, they're playing games with us!" Michelle snapped in a disappointed tone.

"They like to play silly buggers, don't they?" I remarked.

A couple of weeks later I read on a news group list that the very evening Michelle and I observed this object, a man from Newmarket, New Hampshire observed a UFO near Exeter, New Hampshire. I found this particularly amusing since I was from Newmarket, Ontario.

At the time I thought, "Hum, the ET's really do like to play silly buggers with us."

Michelle was disappointed that I slept through the first night without being awaken by the ET visitors that frequent her house. Actually, I was only half asleep when I heard the sound of one of the ET's voices. I was sure it was Hetar. His high pitched and very distinct voice was easy to discern. During the experience, I could hear the sound of many people moving around the living room. I heard Michelle and Hetar's voices. I struggled to wake up. Finally I jolted myself up and turned around, there was no one there. They had 'zapped' me. I thought I was waking up when they were there, but they had taken us, returned us, then let me wake up thinking only a few seconds had passed when in fact a couple of hours had.

The next day Michelle described for me, in detail, what had happened the night before. She told me how Hetar and a number of little grays ran around the house. Hetar used his physical voice rather than telepathy to speak that night in the apartment. She explained how we had left for several hours then returned.

Through the week we had many interesting meditations. I once again saw Alex, a being that always seemed like a father to me.

On the last night of my visit I took a hotel room. I wanted some space from the apartment so I could take the last night to get my head together. I also wanted some privacy from the children so that Michelle and I could work quietly.

That night we worked. Michelle directed the work, acting on instructions she had received the night before during an experience.

As I lay on the bed, Michelle sat beside me. Gradually, slowly she verbally walked me into a deep meditative, almost hypnotic state. I was aware of everything around me. I was sensitive to all sounds and completely coherent, but relaxed and open. Through this session something remarkable happened that was to shape our work throughout our lives.

Michelle first noticed Alex's presence in the room. "Do you feel Alex here?" she asked.

"Yes," I said. There was a massive and powerful presence at the foot of the bed. Michelle was asking me questions. Later I found out Alex was guiding her through the questions, suggesting as she went.

Suddenly, Michelle's whole personality seemed to disappear. Her voice changed and her whole persona was that of a man. Now, she seemed to have a subtle English accent. Her vocabulary was completely different. I realized it was Alex!

He put his hand on my chest and I felt bright, intense energy. I saw with closed eyes a spiral of energy circling above me.

"Dear one," were the words that came out of Michelle's body. Only now, her voice was not hers. It had a masculine quality. The tone was different, the inflection not hers.

"Yes," I replied.

"What is it that bothers you about all of this?" Alex asked.

"This is all so odd. My state of awareness feels very strange. All of what is happening is so fantastic. We both remember the same things and one part of me knows it's real but another part of me wonders if I'm going mad," I said from a strangely floating state of awareness

"This is real," Alex stated. He enunciated every word one at a time for emphasis. Then he took a deep breath.

"What is it about yourself that bothers you?" Alex asked.

A number of embarrassing images were flashing through my head. I kept my thoughts to myself as I struggled with the images.

"You worry too much," Alex said as though sensing what I was thinking, "There are no secrets. Now what is bothering you about this."

"I'm afraid I'm going mad."

"Noooo!" Alex said in a long drawn out tone. "Paul is angry with Andrew."

"Angry?" I asked. "But why?"

"Andrew made two of you."

I felt a rush of shock. Alex was right. I was angry with myself. When I was with the ET's I had everything I ever wanted. I was awake. I had my memories of my life with the ET's. I had kept the identity of Andrew from myself all through my life and did not piece together all the ET experiences where I had been called by the name of Andrew until my late thirties. There was a part me that was furious with myself for having denied a part of my life to myself, a very important part of my life.

Alex continued asking me questions. I answered. When my answers were not clear, he guided me. Soon I could see some of my major emotional and spiritual blocks sitting in front of me. They were out in the open and I could deal with them now.

Then one of the most incredible experiences of my life happened. I began to see the faces of grays, dozens and dozens of them. I saw them working and standing at control panels. Some were sitting in long horizontal chairs looking at some type of viewing screen above them.

I saw a huge golden dome or ball approximately ten stories in height with honeycombed black lines supporting its structure. The gold ball seemed to pulse. There were many Rye-hun around. Somehow I knew it was a kind of power source. I had been there before. I was recovering some more of my memory!

After Alex left, I was shaken. It was an incredible experience. Michelle asked what was going on. She said she blacked out and was clearly upset that someone had been in her body. My body was physically strained and in pain, though my mind felt free and incredible. It took some time for Michelle to get herself together. My body felt like it would the day after a ten mile run. I was physically exhausted. However, emotionally I was on top of the world.

Over the next while Michelle had great difficulty accepting that being whom she trusted had entered and taken over her body. It was a phenomenon that would prove very hard for her to accept as a part of herself and her being.

The next day Michelle came over in the morning. It was my last day there. When Michelle arrived she seemed anxious. She told me she had been picked up by the ETs. She said that Hetar had instructed her to do one more thing. He said that we were not finished and that it was important. She was reticent to do it, but Hetar had reassured her everything would be alright.

I wondered what it was she would not tell me. She only indicated she would show me. We sat and meditated. Michelle moved her arms in a particular fashion I had seen her use in the past to generate energy. Suddenly, she put one of her hands over my solar plexus and I felt a ball of tremendous energy enter into me. I knew what it was. It was something I remembered Hetar had taken away from me and given to Michelle for safe keeping almost 20 years ago. Once returned to me, I felt emotions that I had not felt in years. Over the next few days I felt energy so intense at times that my solar plexus would work itself into a knot as I acclimated to what was inside me.

We sat and looked at each other for a while. Neither of us wanted to part. Still, I was anxious to get home to Toronto to deal with some work issues and get some real sleep, but knew I would miss her terribly.

I began to realize, through the material which I sometimes refer to as "the dense male brain," that Michelle's heart was stirring from friendship to something much more than that. Michelle was my best friend and I loved her deeply. I remembered her from my past, and I would be there for her as a friend. Little did I realize how my heart was beginning to stir and how unsettling it was for me.

I packed up my things, checked out of the hotel and we drove back to Michelle's apartment to say good-bye to the children. As we walked up the hallway to her apartment Michelle ran her hand over her forehead and said, "You know last night really bothers me. I hate the idea of 'channeling' anything. I felt so out of control last night. It's really annoying."

I looked at her and laughed. Then she laughed seeing me laugh.

"I experienced one of the most incredible experiences of my life last night. There's no way you could have known some of the personal things that Alex talked to me about last night. You couldn't have because I never told you or anybody else on this planet. Alex answered questions and responded to statements before I vocalized them. You have no idea what a confirmation this has been for me!"

She looked at me and said, "I'm glad it helped, but I still don't like loosing control of my body like that."

We entered the apartment and gathered up the children. On the drive to the airport Michelle and I talked and talked. When there was nothing to talk about we would always find something to talk about regardless. Boredom never existed when we were together. When we got to the airport we all hugged each other and I departed. The week had been an incredible adventure; an adventure that was just beginning.

MICHELLE
The Fire Pit

The four days that Paul was here were incredible. Our connection was so strong there was no need to work up a rapport. We connected immediately. We spent all our time together playing with the energy between us, exploring our connection, and trying to awaken spiritual growth in each other.

The second day we were together we went to the ocean and played a bit on the beach. It was cold, but it was wonderful. I was still not sure how much he recalled emotionally about our relationship, but it stirred a lot of memories in me of our childhood when we use to play on the ET made beaches.

Our actual meditations were far too intense to capture in words. On the third night he was here, during a meditation together, he was compelled to put his forehead against mine. When he did, the energy I felt from him spiked, then spread through my whole being. It kept growing and spreading to the point where, despite myself, my body and being experienced a profound and extremely intense physical orgasm.

I cannot begin to explain the feelings this created in me. How could this man put his forehead to mine and create such an intense physical reaction? I didn't know if he knew what he had done to me. Could he tell by my physical reaction and verbalizations? Should I say something to him? If I did, would he think I was lying or crazy? I don't remember now if I said anything about the physical reaction - meaning the orgasm- at that time. I do not believe I did. Though I know we talked about the intensity of the meditation.

On New Years morning, Paul and I decided to find a spot in the wilderness that felt good and perform a *Mohawk Thank You Ceremony* that we were instructed to do by the medicine man in Canada.

The ceremony itself was a beautiful and wonderful thing. The memory of its beauty and power was one of the few things that helped me through the next two days, which were destined to be some of the most difficult of my life.

January first was a very cold day in New Hampshire. The weather was minus five degrees Fahrenheit. There was little wind, but when it blew it was bitterly cold. We got on our winter gear and drove out into the woods to find a place that felt right to build our ceremonial fire.

I joked with Paul that you know you really trust a man when you let him bring you into the wilderness in the middle of winter with only a shovel. That was pretty much all we took with us. A shovel, a lighter and some tobacco for offering.

We found a spot away from the road, but not too far off as the snow was three feet deep. We cleared out an area that ended up looking almost like a formed hot tub in the snow when we were done. Paul showed me how to build a fire in the winter from natural materials around us and we performed the ceremony.

During the ceremony, we offered a gift of tobacco and our thanks to many things. Starting with the smallest things, like the bugs, we worked our way all the way up to the Creator of life itself. At one point, we thanked *"The Wind Spirit"*. When we did, a very strong wind blew through the glade of trees where we were standing. But it was not just any wind. It didn't move the trees around us, and it was warm. It warmed my face as I looked directly into it. With the intense cold of the day, that wind should have been sub-zero, but rather it felt like a warm spring breeze.

It was then I saw them. In a moment's time, it seemed like every single tree around me was a conscious being. I don't mean in the way that some feel plants have feelings and can sense things. It was like they were all huge human type beings in tree form. It was like each tree had eyes, ears, a face, a name and a personality. I could feel them all around me. I could see them as clearly as I see the words on my computer screen as I type this now. I was in awe.

Then, I looked into the sky and saw three huge face masks in the clouds. They were not formed from the clouds but rather where detailed colorful face masks which seemed to be made of painted wood. They were just hovering in the sky. They were happy and inviting in appearance, despite the fact that one had a very fierce expression. The first was shaped like a rectangle, the second like a triangle and the last like a circle. I heard a voice say they were faces of the Grandfathers.

When the ceremony ended and the fire was burned away, I looked down at the beauty of the fire's remains. The snow around the fire pit was still pure white and unmelted. The center of the pit, where the fire once was, was filled with ash white sticks that darkened as they went outwards from the center to their chard black ends, forming a brilliant star that was surrounded by the deep rich green of the pine boughs we used to keep oxygen under the fire and stop the melting snow from putting it out. It looked like a gorgeous flower of some unknown species floating in a field of white snow. The vision of it burned into my mind.

The night of the first, Paul and I were both agreed that with the intensity of our work, it was getting difficult to work in my house with the kids. He had only one more night in New Hampshire, so he decided to listen to Alex's suggestion. While with the Rye-hun the night before, Alex told Paul that he knew what he had to do. Paul believed he was being told to find a quiet place where we could work undisturbed, so he got a hotel room not far from the house for the night. The next morning he was going to be leaving.

We worked on our meditation and connection that day in the privacy and quiet of the hotel room. Many times during the few days we spent together we felt a strong presence of beings around us. Several times in the hotel room, the presences returned. One time, it was very clearly Alex. He wanted to talk to Paul about something while Paul was in a deep relaxation state.

As Paul relaxed and I helped him put himself into a deep meditative state, I listened to Alex's voice. I could actually see Alex as a spectral blob of light and for the most part his words were clear to me. I repeated everything as best I could. Before long I found myself getting very dizzy. It was as if I were being drawn into something. The next thing I was aware of, I was no longer sitting on the end of the bed. I was sitting by Paul's side much closer to the head of the bed. My body was shaking and trembling and Paul was crying tears of joy.

He started to explain to me that Alex had been inside my body and had talked to him. He explained to me that Alex spoke to him about things I had no way of ever knowing about; things he never told me or anyone else about. He explained how clear Alex's energy was and how much my body changed when Alex was in it.

I did not know quite what to say to him. I did not know what to make of it all. I had never been a fan of *channeling* and felt that a great amount of it is purposely faked or at least questionable because of the host tainting the information. I was far from thrilled with the idea that I was subject to it. I think I even started to cry. Paul explained to me that it was okay. It was not a bad thing at all. He also told me that he believed I was not a sick person or lying. He knew it was not me. It was clearly Alex.

This helped me a great deal because I had no memory at all of what happened to me in that time, and it seemed like only a few seconds had passed. I wondered if I didn't black out and go into some kind of strange seizure that created a multiple personality manifestation.

Paul was sure it was not me he spoke to. He remembered Alex from previous contact events in his life, and he was sure this was him. Also, Alex spoke to him about things that there was no way I could have known. As Paul said, "Either you have an I.Q. of 2000 and are the best psychic on the planet, or it was really Alex." I would have to say it was more likely the latter.

After Alex was in me, I was charged up with energy and could barely sit still, but Paul was exhausted and needed to sleep. So I returned home. I had the hardest time sleeping that night. Not just because I was trying to digest all that just happened, but also because I felt something had to be done that wasn't being done. That night Hetar's people picked me up.

When I saw Hetar, he asked me if I had given "it" to Paul yet. I knew what "it" was. It was a small ball of light that was somehow a connection to my soul. It was a part of me that use to be inside Andrew before he was sent on the side mission when we were young. Now that he had returned, I was suppose to give it back to him, but I was reluctant to do so. Not because I didn't want to loose it, or give it away, rather because I was still not totally sure that Paul remembered who Kristance and Andrew truly were to each other, and I could not bare it if he rejected that part of me that was connected to this ball of energy and light.

Hetar explained to me that life was risk and that taking risks was sometimes the only way we can get difficult things done. I knew he was right. The next morning I called up Paul at the hotel very early and was over there before long.

He was in the shower when I arrived, so I sat down at the desk and waited for him to finish and get dressed. I was shaking so badly with nerves that I could hardly sit still. I was terrified about what I was going to do next and did not know how it would be received, if at all. I thought about what Hetar said about risk and knew that I had no doubt in my mind who and what Paul was. Of course this meant that I had no doubt in my mind that the energy ball I was holding belonged inside of Paul.

I told him I needed to speak to him about something important. I explained to him what Hetar had told me the night before. I told him there was something I had to do, but first I needed to know if there was any doubt, even the smallest bit, in his mind that I was the little girl he knew so long ago before he went on the side mission. I told him to think about it good and hard, not to answer quickly.

He stood in front of me, tilted my head up and looked me deep in the eyes. It was as if he were searching the depths of my soul with his gaze. I could feel his energy flowing through me. After a long moment of silence and contemplation, he said, "No doubt at all."

"Good," I replied. Then, as if by total instinct, I surrounded myself with energy, reached over my body, as if pulling something from my throat and chest, and produced a ball of bright white light in the palm of my hand. I could see it clearly. I knew Paul felt it without a doubt, maybe he saw it too. His eyes were wide with wonder. I reached forward and with one motion of thought and intent, pushed the ball of light into the solar plexis area of his body. He gasped when it went into him and I could feel it spreading out and fill him. His whole being seemed to change. The energy around us melded into something more intense than ever before. We hugged each other and spoke about it a bit, then I returned to my house to make the kids breakfast and get ready to drive him to the airport.

About an hour later, Paul was all packed up and ready to go back to Canada. I was trying to find a method of keeping myself from bursting into tears when I had to watch my newly re-discovered Andrew- my newly re-discovered soul - get on a plane and fly back to another country.

Just before his flight boarded, we said goodbye. He hugged me. It was all I could do to make myself let him go. As he walked away he motioned to me in the sign language the ETs use to teach telepathy, "You belong right here". He pointed to his solar plexis where I put the bright ball just that morning , then he walked away. I watched him for a few moments. He didn't look back.

By the time we got home, the pain of separation from Paul was so strong that I went into the bedroom and cried for a solid three hours. I ended up calling my friends Dee and Diane trying to find someone to talk to about it all. I couldn't believe what a mess I was in. I was living through one of the hardest parts of trying to rebuild my life and recover from a terrible marriage, with the well being of three young children to consider. I had no job or way of supporting them and myself as of yet. I was hopelessly in love with a man in another country. I felt like I had nothing left in my life that was stable. I had only my inner strength, and that was shaky on the night of the second of January 1998.

Over the next few weeks problems with George returned. After a terrible and dangerous psychotic outburst, he was hospitalized. It was clear then that my life was in danger. During this time, I barely slept and hardly ate anything. My ET contacts completely stopped and the intensity of the spiritual energy between Paul and I faded to just about nothing. I realized that the energy issues were, in part, due to my struggle and emotional condition, but also, it was explained after, that Paul and I were learning that our friendship was based on more than just the spiritual fireworks that we could so easily generate. We spent hours on the phone, talking about what happened when we were together, exploring our selves, our thoughts, and ideas with each other. He talked to me late into the night as I cried about what was going on and about my fears and uncertainties. More than ever, despite all the terrible things going on, Paul kept encouraging me to focus on the positive and keep my eyes and mind on the bigger picture. He kept me on spiritual track when I felt like all of creation had it in for me. He never offered me a hand out, rather he offered me a hand of strength. He said time and time again, "Mick, you're the strongest person I know. You can do this." He was right.

Still, through the beginning of 1998, I was constantly on the height of my nerves and many times I found that the vision of the fire pit from the Thank You Ceremony, and my memory of the energy connection Paul and I shared that day were the only things that I had left to hang on to. I came back to them again and again in my mind to give me strength and hope. Seeing the picture of the fire pit in my mind's eye and remembering and knowing the magic of that day, made me realize that there was something better out there just waiting to happen; not just for me, but also for my children.

<u>PAUL</u>
January 1998

After I returned to Toronto, Michelle and I went headlong at the telephones again We spent our evenings talking and processing the information from our meditations.

George had been the source of some terrible issues for Michelle, and I feared the situation was coming to a head soon. I tried to be supportive throughout it all. It was very difficult and painful to watch my best friend suffer while I sat in a different country, helpless do much more than listen and offer support.

For some time we had been experiencing strong psychic connections through the days, but now, it seemed as though we were decompressing from our experience of having been so close and feeling such intense energy together. It took a full two weeks until Michelle had a contact where Alex spoke to her and explained that they needed us to see and understand what it would be like to be together without the magic, or rather, feeling our spiritual perceptions so strongly.

We both realized, magic or none, we would still be best of friends and would continue working on ourselves until our deaths. Our work was too important. For the first time in both our lives we found another human being who understood the nature of the work we felt compelled to pursue, as well as someone we could explore our experiences with. We found someone who understood the nature of the ET phenomenon and how it was influencing our lives.

Alex explained to Michelle that it had been a test for us and that we would soon start to feel our energy again. He explained that being apart was a weaning process and we had to take the time to process what had occurred when we were together. He said that in order to learn to value what it was like to be together we were seeing what it was like when we were apart.

By the end of January, I felt it was time to get my second hernia fixed and went in to schedule surgery. While I was at the pre-examination, my doctor checked me out thoroughly then said, "Ah, here you see is another one."

"What?" I asked surprised and disappointed.

"Yah. Feel here, a small one," he replied.

"Damned aliens," I thought, "always right about everything. They said I would have three hernias in total and that I would get the third fixed when I got the second one done.

So I scheduled myself for a double hernia operation in February. I began to brag to family and friends that I liked to try something two or three times just to check it out to see if it was something I wanted to pursue full time or not, nevertheless, I was not looking forward to the operations.

It was during this period that the next major phase of Michelle's and my work became very clear to us. During a conversation on the telephone one evening Michelle was talking and suddenly told me she was feeling dizzy. A moment later I heard her speaking, but her voice was not quite right. She had a accent and was speaking out of character.

"What are you talking about?" I asked her.

She chuckled and said, "Always ignoring my voice." I felt a massive presence of energy that I knew was Alex, then the presence left.

Michelle regained herself and heard me on the other end of the phone.

"What is it?" she asked.

I knew she could sense the energy.

"What? Oh God, not again!" she began to cry.

I felt stupid for not picking up on who it was and Michelle felt used for having her body invaded and taken over without anyone asking for permission.

That night, Michelle and I were both picked up. My memory was cloudy the next day. I only sensed the generalities of the night before, however Michelle's recall was crystal clear. Michelle had walked by Alex and me as we were talking in a garden area. I was asking him why he said I always ignored his words when I try very hard to hear him. He responded that he knew I tried very hard to hear his words, but that he also spoke with sounds, patterns, events and colors. He was trying to emphasize the depth and methods of communication outside of typical vocal and telepathic converse. He was describing the use of imagery in life on the Earth by the higher elements to communicate with us.

Michelle said that at one point Alex stopped and said to me, "One moment. Your reflection wishes to say something."

Michelle burst in from where she was listening. She was bothered a great deal by being referred to as a "reflection". Neither of us understood the acronym at that point and the only place Michelle heard it used before was when somebody would activate communication with an implant.

"What am I, his implant?" she yelled at Alex.

I tried to calm her. She continued expressing her anger at Alex. Finally I called out, "Kristance!"

She stopped and looked at me. I grabbed her hand and placed it over my solar plexus where she had put her energy in me during my visit to New Hampshire. Michelle calmed right down. She said the next thing she remembered was waking up in her bed. I woke up with a hazy memory of having spoken with Alex.

The next day as we spoke, the both of us realized that we would likely be speaking to Alex in many different ways in the future.

Business at my day job began to slow substantially. The company's ability to meet payroll became intermittent. By the end of January I found myself laid off and out of work.

Michelle had several intense experiences through this period. Molanie spoke to her about allowing Alex to speak through her again. It took some time for Michelle to come to terms with the idea that she was channeling the ET's she spoke with during her experiences. She called channeling the "C word" and disliked the idea intensely.

We decided we would try and do it intentionally. So that night we called each other on the phone.

"Hi Paul," Michelle said.

"Hi Mick," I replied.

"How was your day?" she asked.

"Are you kidding? All I could think about all day was trying this. Are you ready?" I asked.

"Ya, okay. Let's try it," she said with trepidation.

There was a moment of silence. I concentrated on assisting her in her efforts in anyway I could, offering her my energy. A few moments later I felt something odd happening around me. The energy level in my body and around my living room changed dramatically. Suddenly, I heard Michelle take a deep breath.

"Hello, dear one," I heard the voice on the other end of the telephone say.

"Alex?" I asked. It was Michelle's voice, but it was different somehow. The tone and the inflection were completely different. There was a male quality to it.

"It feels like you. There's so much energy in the room here. This isn't normal. Your so far away."

"I'm right in the room with you. Don't you feel me?"

"Yes," I answered. "This is just so incredible."

"Indeed," Alex said with a sly and playful voice. "Some might say miraculous." He paused for a second then asked, "Questions?"

"Are you kidding? Yes, I have a million questions! Where do I start?" I blurted.

I heard Alex chuckle, pause for a moment, then say, "Perhaps we should start with the most burning questions first."

"Okay," I said. I took a deep breath. "How is this possible? How can you be here like this?"

"I have done this with her all her life. She does not even know it. It is by design. You both know it when you are home with us."

"We do?" I asked surprised.

"Yes," Alex responded.

"Why don't we remember?" I asked.

"You don't remember because you don't want to remember."

"What do you mean I don't want to remember? I want to remember everything!" I said with excitement.

"I know that you may not believe this, but before we bring you home you have never asked me not to remove your memory. In fact there have been several times when you have asked me to take your memory of an experience away."

"Really?" I asked somewhat befuddled. "Why would I do that?"

"Perhaps you realized that memory of the event would be too hard to assimilate in your daily life and you are protecting yourself so you can function when you return to your house," Alex explained.

"Michelle has told me that she was told we are the ones who determine whether or not we want to retain our memories of an experience. You're saying we are and that we do so to protect ourselves so that we can function when we get back home?"

"That is one of the reasons you and many others do not remember," Alex said. "In many cases we take people's memory away because they might not understand what has happened in the fullest context. Many people who claim to have bad experiences are remembering only part of their experience. For instance, a person might remember receiving an injection with a long needle. They might wake up thinking some type of test has been done on them when in fact it was an injection that would help their immune system deal with a particular virus or bacteria we knew they were exposed to."

"So you are helping us. But to do what? For what purpose?" I asked.

"You have work to do. All of you," Alex stated.

"Ah, yes," I said, "we have to wake up." I somehow could feel what Alex's intent was. It was as though a secondary layer of communication was going on.

"Yes. You have to wake up so you can do your work," Alex continued.

"But isn't our work to wake up?" I asked.

"Yes, that's part of it. You have to wake, which is no small task. Once you wake up then you can do your work for the Earth."

"Work for the Earth? You're talking about all the changes we're expecting and what's going to happen soon?" I asked.

"Yes. We can talk more about that later. I must go now, dear one. My presence places a certain amount of stress on her. It will get better the more we do this."

"Okay," I replied. As we spoke I noticed there was indeed a secondary layer of communication occurring. Alex would say something, and even though he would not explain everything in words, I emotionally and or spiritually understood what he was saying. It was a very odd experience. Had I not lived through it first hand, I do not think I would have believed it possible.

"Good night, dear one."

"Good night, Alex." I said, and then the phone was silent. After about 20 seconds of silence I became concerned as I could not even hear breathing.

"Michelle?" I blurted. Then I heard Michelle make a deep gasping sound as she started to breath again.

"What? What is it? What happened?" she managed to say from a disoriented and groggy state.

"You are not going to believe this," I said. I began to explain to her what Alex spoke to me about. It was an incredible evening, and one that I will never forget.

We continued to try every night we had the time. During one exercise, something new occurred. After Alex spoke through Michelle, she became aware again and was speaking to me. I told her I felt quite dizzy and was not myself. I felt the massive presence of Alex envelope me. Next I heard clear words in my head and I found that Alex and I were sharing the same body, and Alex was speaking through me!

This came as quite a shock and took me some time to become used to. I also found that depending on how clear I was, so too would be the connection between Alex and I as he spoke through me.

In the case of Michelle, she would loose all contact with her body. In my own case, I would remain conscious of still being in my body and feel another presence join me.

"Hello, dear one," I heard myself say. It was not my thought, but the thought of a consciousness that was inside of me. I felt both connected and distinct simultaneously.

"Hi, Alex," Michelle said.

"How are we doing this evening?"

"Well, thank you. Is it really you Alex?"

"What do you feel? What type of energy are you feeling?" Alex asked.

"I feel you, Alex. How can this be?" Michelle inquired.

"The same way I come through you, I come through him, your Completer. Only when I come through him he is still in his container." Alex always calls our bodies containers. "You had a dream last night?" Alex asked.

"Yes," Michelle responded, "I had several."

"You saw a dog last night," Alex stated. I felt disoriented hearing these words come out of my mouth.

"Yes," Michelle answered.

"It wagged its tail but you did not hear it bark," Alex said in a somewhat melancholic tone.

"Yes," Michelle said with slight surprise. "What does that mean?" she asked.

"What do you think?" Alex replied.

"I don't know," Michelle responded.

"I must go now, dear one. There will be some stress on his body the first time we do this. With practice we can do it longer. Goodnight, child."

"Good night, Alex." Michelle said.

I felt Alex's presence slowly leave the room. It took a minute or two, then my body began to feel achy and extremely tired. I felt physically stressed, as though I had just jogged five miles. It was a state similar to what had occurred in the hotel room when I visited Michelle at Christmas time.

I was exhausted so we called it a night soon after. My physical reaction was so strong it was impossible to deny that another presence had utilized my body. Besides the physical effects, the state of consciousness Alex's presence created in me was unmistakable.

Michelle now had confirmation of a process she would eventually find out had gone on throughout her life.

MICHELLE
Visitors

One night, late in January, Paul and I were talking on the phone. I had been having some really difficult times on the home front and was exhausted emotionally from all the strain it was was putting on me and my children.   Still, I tried to do my best to keep on top of my spiritual work. Often it was the only refuge I had.

This particular night I was very edgy. I didn't know what I was going to do about things and I knew Paul was getting a bit annoyed with my almost constant whining to him about how helpless I felt. His attitude, which I found out later was the right one for the situation, was "just do what you have to do." My attitude at that time was, "how can I do anything?"

Our conversation started to get a bit heated. I had just been at a meeting with the police domestic violence officer and was learning very quickly that the choices I had to make were very serious and very unpleasant ones. I was terrified that my children would hate me for the rest of my life if I did what I had to do. It was also difficult for me to understand why Paul didn't appear to comprehend how painful making those decisions was for me. I didn't realize that as I complained to him about the situation and the threats against my life, he was feeling more and more helpless being so far away. He was enraged about it all and was just about ready to jump in his car and drive down to put a stop to all the madness. But I was so lost in my own head, and without our typical strong connection working at its best, I failed to see this. Because of that fact, that night I felt his emotional distance was from disinterest in my well being rather than the true reason, which was exactly the opposite.

With this fundamental difference of opinion, and with both of us over tired and stressed, it was clear we were on the verge of a big argument. As things escalated, I became very dizzy. I was sure I was going to pass out. I said, "Paul, I'm really dizzy. I can't think straight. I need to stop for a moment and get my head together," or something to that effect. I took a deep breath and tried to relax in hope that the dizziness would pass.

The next thing I was aware of, I needed air. I instinctively gasped for a breath. I could hear through the phone that Paul was in tears.

"What happened?" I asked. I was totally disoriented.

Paul explained that Alex was just there. He told me that Alex said we were going to hurt each other if we continued. He stated that Paul never listened to his voice.

I started to cry too, but for a different reason. This was all I needed. Not only was my life falling apart and my world crumbling down around me, but I had ETs invading my most personal of space. Now, even my own body was no longer a refuge. I had no control over what happened that night. I realized as I lie in bed sometime in the middle of that night, I had just lost control over the very last thing I had that was really mine.

It's often said that you have to break down everything that is in your life in order to make a fresh start. It seems the ETs are firm believers in this. For in the year of 1998, absolutely EVERYTHING in my life changed in a matter of a few short months. Aside from my children, there is nothing that I had that identified me as an individual in my own mind -nothing that defined my sense of self and reality- that has remained the same. Not even my name. The same holds true for Paul. Though his name is the same, before the spring of 1998 he was in a different country, in a different life, in a different world.

The restructuring of our lives happened through the most incredibly stressful series of events we have ever endured. As the old structure was taken apart, it was replaced with a new and indescribably magical structure. As we both let go of who we thought we were, we discovered who we really are. It has become an immeasurable blessing in our lives. For me, it is a blessing I would not give up for a million dollars or a million stars to call my own. Yet, in January of 1998 I didn't see it like that at all. In January of 1998 I felt like I was the most despaired and wretched individual on the face of this planet.

I knew I had a mission. I knew I had some good friends. I knew Paul was Andrew and he knew it. I also knew I had been hopelessly in love with Andrew since I could remember. Moreover, I was hopelessly in love with Paul and I was convinced without a doubt that I would have to settle for being just his buddy for the rest of existence. George was threatening and a clear danger. It seemed like the only option I had to escape that danger, was a life of hiding in a woman's shelter with my children, and living on public assistance. I was afraid for my mortal life and my spiritual life as well, and now my own body was no longer a safe haven. When I thought of the future I saw only darkness. To quote Hetar, "How dark the problems are when we are standing in them."

Paul seemed excited about what was happening with Alex. He could see something I could not to it. It was clear that I was going to be a channel of some kind for these ETs whether I liked it or not. The idea of channeling still upset me. I couldn't even bring myself to say the word and would call it the "C word" when referring to it. What baffled me even more was that I was not being entered by some strange nameless force or some archangel as it seemed most people who claimed to do this were. I was being entered by ETs I had known all my life. I had known Alex since I was a child. He was a real person to me, not some spirit from the unknown.

It was very difficult to accept at first. I went through several phases. At one point I felt like I was destined to be a telephone of sorts. This made me angry. Often when Paul and I talked on the phone, it would end up becoming a conversation between him and Alex and I would black out.

Paul and I learned that we could start contact from our end. Sometimes Alex would come just long enough to tell us he was very busy and would be back later. Still, the fact that we could call when we wanted to gave us a sense of control that helped me, at the very least, deal with some of the feelings of violation the experience created in me.

One night, Paul started asking me questions about what I recall, if anything, when he talked to Alex. I told him I didn't really experience anything. On very seldom occasions I would have a short sense of time passing. "You must go somewhere. Don't you? Maybe you go to some dimension that can't normally be reached by the living. It's too bad you can't remember," he said.

His words intrigued me. After we spoke, I became determined to find out what happened to me when I was out of my body or "away from home" as I would call it. The more I worked at it, the more I could start to sense the passing of time. Also, I began to see things. Mostly I saw colors and vague shapes at first. Sometimes I would see visions of faces. There was no sound, at least not anything I could identify as sound. I say that because there were times when the colors I saw seemed to effect me as if I were not looking at them, but rather I was tasting them, smelling them or hearing them. This sensation, though unusual was not totally foreign to me because often during meditative states, I will actually see sounds.

I learned to relax when I was in this limbo like world. It was a very comfortable place. I felt a strong feeling of unconditional love while I was in this place. I felt like I belonged there. Still, I had an underlying fear that I would not be able to return to my body.

One evening when I was talking with Paul, Alex asked if he could speak with us. He said that he wanted to try something different that night. So Paul and I agreed. Alex talked in my body, then I became aware that I was in my body again.

I heard silence at the other end the phone, then some heavy breathing. Then I felt Alex say in my head that he was now in Paul's body.

I was amazed. I was sitting there talking to Alex while he was in Paul's body. I was totally stunned. I had many, many experiences over my lifetime with Alex. I knew Alex well. I had no doubt at all that the person I was talking to was Alex. That fact was very clear.

Talking to Alex in this way was reassuring to me because I knew that many of the things Alex talked to me about were things that Paul had no way of knowing. They were things that I had never told anyone but possibly Alex, Molanie and Hetar. It felt good to know that I wasn't crazy. If Alex could talk through Paul the way he was, then it must be true that Alex was actually talking through me when I was blacked out.

In February, Paul went into the hospital for a double hernia surgery. I wanted to go up to Canada to nurse him back on his feet, but couldn't afford to. During that time, by the most amazing luck, I managed to find access to an AutoCAD system and was able to brush up on my mechanical design. I worked up a good resume and portfolio, and against all odds, I managed to land a decent paying job. I was able to support my children and I would not need public assistance. I was starting to see light at the end of the tunnel.

By the end of February, Paul was healing from his surgery and I was healing from seventeen years of ill-treatment. Paul and I had managed to support each other through probably the most difficult times of our lives. All the while we both worked hard to keep our sights on our spiritual goals. It was starting to pay off.

I was feeling so much stronger. Amazingly, the children had not been as upset by the events of the month of January and February as they could have been. They did well dealing with issues that concerned what happened with George, which I will not go into here, but suffice to say that they were exceedingly difficult. Finally, there was peace and quiet in our family life for the first time that I could remember, and my ET contacts started again. More important than that, the work Paul and I were doing consistently through the hard times was paying off. Our connection was coming back stronger than before. Our vision of our selves and missions was becoming clearer and we were developing a new type of relationship. It was a relationship based on our deep and strong friendship that had been tested and proved to run to our very souls. It was quickly becoming more. Paul was realizing and sorting out his true feelings and I was learning a new love for my soul mate. It was a love that was aware of our past relationship, Andrew and Kristance, but built on our current emotions. I guess what I'm trying to say, corny as it sounds, is that we fell in love all over again.

By March, Paul and I knew that no matter what form our relationship would finally settle down into, we were partners in something very special and we both knew, even then, that we could never be apart.

We decided that it would be easier for him to move than for me to uproot three children, so Paul started making arrangements to find work in the United States. We knew we had to be physically close to one another to do our work. Besides, our phone bills alone could pay for really a nice apartment for him here in town. By a stroke of fortunate timing, Paul's employer in Canada had some problems and he was laid off, so he had the time to look for a job.

He came down to the States to interview in late March. Knowing that he was on a budget, and the hotels in the city were running about a hundred dollars a night, I got Paul a room at a small motel not far from the highway. To be nice, the place was not much to look at, but it wasn't expensive and without a job he had to be careful what he spent. It's amazing to think when I look back, that some of the most impacting moments of both his and my lives happened in that little, rather ratty room.

<u>*PAUL*</u>
February 1998

Early in February I had two very clear experiences involving Alex. Before this, my last conscious memory of him was when I was a child, yet I knew that I had experiences involving him since then.

One night I fell asleep and found myself standing on shipboard. A young child was standing in front of me. His eyes were wide with excitement. He was pointing with his hand and saying, "There's a huge monster through that door."

I looked at the child, paused, then walked over to the door. Everything was white. The walls were white, so were the ceilings and the doors, everything. I opened the door and stepped inside. There were some steps leading down to my left. I saw two very large hairy feet attached to long legs with very knobby knees. The hair on the legs looked like massive hair flakes of oatmeal. A metal section that blocked my view of the rest of the creature from its waist to its head. He must have been well over twelve feet in height. I saw his face. It had human attributes but was not quite human. When his feet moved I heard loud metallic sounds like a large, heavy object would make if it was moved on a ship and caused the metal to buckle from its weight. I sat down quietly. The man, or being, looked at me. He had the most compassionate, tender, loving eyes I had ever seen before. I heard a long, gentle, growling sound. The being leaned forward as if to talk to someone. Suddenly, a man walked briskly over from underneath the conduit the being was leaning over. He appeared to be about six feet in height, had flowing, plumed blond hair, smooth skin, blue eyes and was very handsome. It was Alex.

I felt horribly discombobulated. My mind seemed so open. My emotions were raw. "Do you recognize me?" I asked.

"Yes, I know who you are," Alex said. He did not move his lips or open his mouth. His demeanor was very humble.

"I miss my friends. I could really use a hug," I explained.

Just then the large being with the hairy legs walked over. His eyes were full of kindness. He reached down and gave me a large, gentle hug. I broke into tears. He let me go. Alex then waved for me to follow him.

I followed him over to a door. He motioned for me to walk in.

"Come in and say hello to your little gray friends," he said.

I walked over and looked inside with amazement. There were two gray beings sitting in big soft chairs. One of them I knew was Hetar. To Hetar's right was Michelle. She was also sitting in a big, soft, luxuriant looking chair. Michelle did not appear to be conscious. Her head was tilted to one side. Later I found out she was practicing a particular 'mind' exercise that was a part of her work.

127

Hetar and the other gray laughed uproariously. Then they began to talk a language I did not understand. Moreover, they spoke simultaneously to each other. The one to Hetar's left sounded like a cartoon character with a sing-song, high pitched voice. I could not make out what was going on and it seemed like they were intentionally trying to disorient me.

The next thing I remember was being escorted to the next room by Alex where I observed a man who was about six feet tall and had a muscular build twice as large as any muscle man I had ever seen on television.

"Is this one an alien too?" I asked.

"Yes," replied Alex.

"What do you look like when you don't appear like this?" I asked the man.

He turned to me with a serious look of disbelief on his face.

I held up my hand and said, "Forget it. I don't want to even imagine." I laughed. I knew he was one of the reptilian types who only appeared to be a human. His present appearance was a screen affect.   I watched him work for a few moments.

After a short while, we all went off to do some other things. I found myself doing the mundane task of screwing light bulbs into a bunch of old fashioned looking chandeliers. I woke up the next morning and realized the irony of the imagery being used. The ETs were telling me I had to screw in my light bulbs before my lights could be "turned on."

All that day I felt strangely calm and grateful that my memory was sharpening. I was hopeful that I would remember another experience with such clarity soon.

As my time of surgery approached, it became more and more obvious to me that it would be necessary for Michelle and I to get closer to each other in order to work. This realization was not easy. I knew it would take some time because I would have to heal after surgery, but somehow, over the next few months I would find a way to be with her.

Surgery was once again a bizarre experience. After, it took a good four weeks to be able to walk normally again.

Michelle and I spoke every night on the telephone. During our work, Alex would enter Michelle's body. Michelle would normally black out during these periods but began to have recall of seeing colors, shapes and objects like triangles and circles.

One evening as I lay on my couch Alex began to speak.

"Did you know that when I am here I am also elsewhere?" Alex said.

"No, I didn't," I replied rather shocked.

"Yes. Just one small part of me, one very small part of me, is here when we talk. When I am here, have you wondered where she goes?"

"Yes. Where does she go?" I asked.

"Since you are quick to ponder things, ponder this. Where does her consciousness go? You will be surprised when you figure it out. She may not be as far away as you suspect. I must go now, dear one. Be well. Take care of each other. Be happy. Play with each other. Work is play. The only way this will work is if you play," he said. Then Alex left.

"Good night, Alex. Thank you." As I said this, I felt Alex's energy dissipate and Michelle return.

I listened for a minute and Michelle was silent. Sometimes it would take up to fifteen or twenty seconds for her to take a breath. Sometimes I would call out her name to jolt her into breathing. But that night she breathed on her own.

"So what happened, Mick? Do you remember anything?"

"Yes, I saw more shapes and colors. I felt good but I have no idea where I was," she answered back.

"Alex suggested I think about where you go. He said that I might be surprised and that it isn't as far as we think," I said. Then in a flash, I realized that Michelle went into me! She went into the energy spot in my solar plexus that she had put there during Christmas.

"I've got it!" I shouted.

"What?" asked Michelle.

"You go into me!" I said.

"What? Are you sure?"

"How can I be sure?" I said. "I just felt really strongly that's where you go. Think about it. Doesn't it make sense in some way? I mean it's really weird, but it makes sense. Remember what you put back into me at Christmas?"

"My God, you might be right. I have to think about this. If that's the case, then what does that mean? Does that mean that I merge with you more fully than we thought was happening when we meditated? Oh my God!" Michelle's tone was one of shock now. I could tell from the sound of her voice she was experiencing the same inkling I was.

We agreed that the next time we began working, she would attempt to make some kind of contact with me so we would know if it was true. The next time she was inside me, she tried to stretch out and we both felt something. So, from then on, each time she was in my body and Alex was in hers, she would attempt to reach out. During these events I would feel another person literally inside of myself. I know that I could tell this to people and no one would believe me. But I know it is the truth. It is hard to describe the sensation of having another person inside of your being and you can feel them as they stretch out inside and fill you.

After a while, Michelle would return to her body, then Alex would come through me. We came to call this part of the work 'reversal.'

One evening early in our work I asked him about God. He answered, "The idea of God or the Creator being a single entity is a misnomer. Long ago, in order to grow, Creation broke itself down into many, many parts. All those parts are connected and involved in the creation process. Creation is an ongoing thing and never stops. God is in fact the culmination of all of God's parts. Those parts are in communication with each other and can behave like a large, single consciousness. In fact, in one sense, that is what they are - a large connected consciousness."

Much of the information shook my paradigm to its core.

Alex also taught both of us about the idea of a *"Completer"* and a *"Reflection,"* He explained that in certain instances a being would be developed that was a "Reflection", or holder of power. Another type of being that could be developed was a "Completer," or the one that held the intent to direct the power.

He said, "You, Paul, are a Completer. It is the way you were designed. It is what you are. She, Michelle, is a Reflection. It is the way she was designed, it is what she is in Creation. A Reflection will hold great power, but the power cannot be properly utilized without the intent of the matching Completer. A Completer with the wrong Reflection would only serve to make the Reflection work incorrectly. There are many Completers and Reflections."

"Long ago, when it was decided to break down the units of power in the homeworld, some of the pieces of power broke into two parts, some into four. This was done so that the pieces could come back together again at the appropriate time. Sometimes throughout Creation, a being that split into many parts will come back together again, then perhaps split again. There are people on the Earth who are part of a group being. That is, they are one half, or one quarter, or one eighth of a much larger being. This is one of the reasons why some people will meet each other and feel a strong connection. It is what is going on in the contactee community right now as all the pieces get into place."

I thought for a moment. "So," I explained my understanding of the concept, "a Completer and a Reflection together could represent a whole being or part of a whole being. Would Completers and Reflections who are together be more powerful than if they are alone?" I asked.

"Yes." Alex said quietly.

"Are their others you are working with the way you are working with us, Alex?"

"I don't mean to make this uncomfortable for you and stress your sense of responsibility, but there are very, very few people we are working with in this manner."

I took a deep breath and felt my chest sink into my stomach as the sense of responsibility and the magnitude of what he had just said hit me.

"With that, I think we should call it a night. I dare say you have a lot to think about for now. Good night, dear one." Alex left and Michelle returned quickly after. I spent the next half hour filling Michelle in on what was said and digesting the sense of shock and the weight of responsibility that we felt more than ever resting on our shoulders.

As the nights passed, we learned even more about the ethereal nature of being. Alex explained that eternal beings could split apart and come together over periods of time. That the concept of linear time was not accurate and did not exist in reality. That all times are now. He further explained that many Reflections and Completers had been developed and lived on Earth. These couples needed each other to accomplish their work.

So it went through the month of March. Michelle and I would work with each other and learn from Alex during the evenings. During the day I had a fixed routine. I got up and had breakfast, then went for a long walk at the mall. I was determined to regain my health to the point that I could win the race around the mall against the seventy and eighty year old mall walking veterans.

Every night around 8:00 PM, Michelle or I would call the other and we would begin work. Alex would speak through Michelle for a time, then we would reverse and Alex would speak through me for a while. The information that came through me was not as clear as what came through Michelle. This subject came up in one of the evening sessions.

As soon as we began to speak we felt Alex's presence. We started to meditate and the switch over occurred. Often Alex would wait for me to say hello before saying anything. He preferred to let me feel his presence and the completion of the switch over process as Michelle's consciousness entered my body before he spoke.

"Hello Alex," I said.

"Hello. How are we this evening?" Alex asked.

"Very well, thank you. And you?" I answered.

"Very well, thank you. Do you have questions?" Alex asked.

Often when we started a session Alex would ask me if I had any questions. It allowed me to learn from Alex while Michelle practiced stretching out inside of my body.

"Yes," I said. "When we do our reversal and you come and speak through me, I've noticed that the information and the type of things you speak about are not as clear or dramatic as when you speak through Kris."

Alex asked, "Why do you think that is?"

"I'm not sure. Sometimes I can feel your presence very strongly in me. So much so that it's overwhelming and I almost loose control of all of my normal functions while you take over. I'm just not sure," I explained.

"When we reverse," Alex began, "the process allows me to affect you in a way that changes your energy frequency. The more we do it, the more your frequency changes. What I say to Kris here, I can also say to her when she is home with me. The main purpose is not to teach her anything but to help you to clear. Have you noticed how you understand things better merely by experiencing the energy and the secondary layer of communication that occurs between us?"

"Yes, very much so," I replied.

"Good," Alex said.

As we sat and talked I felt Kris reaching inside of me.

"Alex I think she's almost fully..."

"Stretched out, yes. I can see that," Alex interjected.

I felt Michelle's presence in my body completely fill me so that I could feel her feet in my feet; her hands in my hands; her head in my head. I could feel her body in mine. The feeling was remarkable and close to euphoric. It was unlike any feeling I ever experienced before.

"Alex, this is incredible. I feel so wonderful inside." There was silence at the other end of the phone, but I could almost hear his smile.

After a couple of minutes Alex began to speak. "I have to bring her back now."

"Okay," I said. My body was beginning to feel the strain of the experience.

"What is now done cannot be undone," Alex declared.

"It's okay. She and I trust each other," I said.

"Finally," Alex said with a tone of extreme relief and completion.

I laughed and laughed. I did not expect a reaction like this from him. He was referring to a period of disagreement Michelle and I had gone through in the ET world. As I laughed I felt Michelle slip out of my body and a moment later she breathed and asked me what I was laughing about. I told her and she began to laugh too. It was a wonderful evening. We both felt like something magical had truly happened.

It was during this period that a struggle I was having with my feelings for Michelle finally started to come to a head. For months I kept any feelings beyond that of friendship buried deep inside of me. But what was quite obviously happening was the emergence, or rather re-emergence of feelings that I had for her from childhood.

I knew for some months that Michelle still loved me and was struggling under the most uncomfortable of conditions to respect my wishes to stay just best friends. Indeed, I was afraid that any venturing beyond that might well destroy our friendship.

Still, when we spoke, the memory of our feelings that was imprinted on our being brought us emotionally, mentally and spiritually closer to each other than to any other people we had ever known in this life before. A part of me remembered those old feelings and the magical closeness we had. I remembered our tragic breakup and the years of loneliness that ensued. Deep inside, though I did not want to fully admit it to myself, I knew we were destined to rekindle the relationship we had when we were younger, no matter what.

In late March I packed up my suitcase and headed down to see Michelle again. It would be the first of several trips before I would stay with her in the United States.

The eight hundred mile drive to New Hampshire took about a day. The weather was not too bad and the roads were clear, though snow still covered the countryside. I made arrangements with Michelle to set me up in an inexpensive, weekly rate motel. When I arrived I found the place to be rather campy.

The first night I was there, Michelle and I sat and meditated and could feel Alex approach. The energy was unmistakable and intense. Michelle became groggy and let herself go as I drew her into me. Michelle's body then opened its eyes. It was Alex.

"You did it," he said. The personality was male. The voice had male characteristics. It was bizarre to see this face to face.

"Did what?" I asked.

"You came."

"Yes, of course," I replied.

Alex spoke to me at length. At times I could see his face like a curtain that overlaid Michelle's face. It was incredible. My state of consciousness changed dramatically during my conversations with Alex.

We spoke about everything that had been happening. Alex explained that because I was tired we would not speak long that night and I should get some rest. He said that tomorrow would be a very busy day. Reluctantly, I had to agree and we switched back. Michelle and I spoke for a while and then she went home. I had to do some job searching and she had to go to work the next day.

The next morning I awoke and went into "job find mode." I fired through the day with a fervor. It was productive, yielding several leads. But all day, all I could think about was seeing Michelle that night and beginning our work.

Evening arrived soon enough and Michelle hurried over. When she arrived I could feel her presence before she knocked on the door.

"Hi!" she said in a perky tone.

"Hi." I smiled back. I gave her a big hug and we kissed each other in a friendly way. I could feel this woman was much more than my best friend. She had feelings that penetrated every fiber of my being. Those feelings were beginning to loosen my own.

"How was your day?" she asked. Her eyes penetrated me and we both could feel the energy of the room build as we stood near each other.

"Pretty good," I began. "I got several good leads today. I may have even gotten a job, eh. I was at the job fair and for no reason that I could explain I walked over to a booth and told them what I was looking for and what experience I had and they said they might have something for me. Go figure. They contacted the division who needed someone with my qualifications and I've got an interview on Wednesday."

"You're awesome. You're going to get that job, I can feel it," Michelle replied with confidence and enthusiasm.

We spoke some more as we prepared some tea in the small kitchenette in my suite. A few minutes later we settled down to work.

Michelle closed her eyes and we both focused our attention. The energy in the room changed dramatically as Alex's presence approached. A moment later I felt Michelle's presence slip into my own through the top of my head, then her body gasped and her eyes opened. Alex was now in her body.

"Hello, dear one. How are you?" he asked, with a smile.

"Fine. Eager to begin whatever it is we will begin now," I replied.

"Perhaps we will begin tonight by just talking. How was your job search today?" Alex asked.

I was surprised by the nonchalance of his question, but answered anyway.

"Excellent," he replied. "Perhaps it won't be long before you have a job and can move down here."

"Perhaps," I said with a smile.

"You write your own reality you know. If you want it you will have it. If you don't, you will not. Do what you enjoy. For only when you do what you enjoy will your work be productive."

"What do you mean? I write my own reality?" I asked.

"You write your own reality. What you wish for is what you will get if you truly want it. Not necessarily what you think you want, but what you truly want in your heart. As I told you before, some people are here on Earth to be part of the Earth. You are here, like Kristance, to fulfill a mission. How could we deny you what you want when so much is asked from you? This will become clearer to you as your work progresses. I must go now. There is someone else who wishes to speak with you. Good night, dear one."

"Who wishes to speak to me Alex?" I asked rather confused.

"You will see," he said, then smiled and closed his eyes.

I felt Michelle's presence leave through the crown of my head so I focused my attention in such a way to facilitate her movement. This was one of my 'tools' that Alex had taught me about. I have several internal tools that can be used to affect changes in my consciousness and Michelle's consciousness. I was learning how important these tools were and how everybody had certain internal tools like this.

Michelle's body gasped and she opened her eyes.

"How do you feel?" I asked.

"Kind of shaky. A little dizzy too. I think I'm okay, give me a minute," she replied.

We paused for a minute. "Better now?" I asked.

"Yes better."

"What did you see?" I inquired.

"I saw shapes and colors again. I could see Alex too, but I couldn't see the room around us clear at all. But I could make out Alex's body and face like it was a movie being projected on a veil in front of my own body," she said with amazement. "Oh, Rove is here," Michelle said, interrupting herself.

"Rove? Rovere? He's here?" I asked. I had heard about the being named Rovere from Alex several times over the last few weeks. I had been informed that I would probably meet him this week, but didn't expect it to happen so quickly.

"Yeah. He says hello," she said.

"Hello Rove," I said. I didn't know where in the room Rove was, but I sensed a strong presence by the door and assumed it was likely to be him.

"He says he wants to talk to you. Do you want to talk to Rove?" Michelle asked.

"Sure," I said with trepidation, not knowing what to expect.

"Oh I don't know, my body is really shaky. Oh, okay." Michelle paused for a moment then blurted, "Rove isn't like the others he's..." and her voice trailed off as her eyes suddenly closed and her body slipped out of consciousness.

A moment later Michelle's eyes opened wide. Her body stood up and there stood an extremely male looking individual.

"You don't look so bad," said a very male sounding, accented voice. "Alex said you didn't look too good, but you don't look so bad."

Rove walked over and put his hand on my face. "This is not like you to be so serious. This is not like you."

I sat starring in shock. How could an accent like this come out of Michelle's body? How could her voice become so male? How could she walk around like man and exude male energy in a heartbeat? This was amazing.

"I know you," I said, pointing to Rove. "I remember you! I saw you in a experience once!"

Rove walked around. He was talking and gesticulating very colorfully as he spoke. "Of course you do. We've known each other since you were little. Your memory just sucks."

I was aghast. This personality was not like Alex's at all. This was the persona of a rapscallion of some kind. He was not just funny, he was hilarious and outrageous. We spoke at length about relaxing and not taking some things so seriously as to paralyze my perceptions and ability to function around Alex or himself.

Suddenly Rove told me to stand up.

"Come on, stand up, I have to walk you through your cobwebs. You asked me to do this for you when we were on shipboard. You don't remember, but I do."

"I asked you to do what?" I asked.

"Walk you through your cobwebs so you would be sure how you feel," Rove reiterated.

"But I know how I feel," I said.

"Oh ya? How do you feel?" Rove asked.

"I feel good. This is amazing."

"No. How do you feel about her?" he referred to Michelle. "Do you love her?"

"She is my best friend. I care about her a great deal," I said. "So I guess I love her."

"You told me you could never love again," Rove said.

"No, I don't think I can. I don't want to fall in love again."

"But she's your best friend?" he asked.

"Yes," I responded.

"You care about her?" Rove asked.

"Yes," I replied.

"You drove all the way down here to see her?"

"Yes."

"You're looking for a job so you can move down here and be with her?"

"Yes."

"You sold your house?" Rove pressed on.

"Yes," I answered. I was beginning to feel pain inside.

"But you don't love her?" Rove asked.

"No, I mean yes. I mean. She's my best friend. I respect her. She's still technically married for Chrissakes. Can't we wait for her to sort things out before we deal with this issue. Don't we have time to let that happen if it's going to happen on its own. If it's meant to happen it will. Is there a hurry or something?" I asked in a tone of anxiety and hurt.

"No, there's no hurry. I'm just helping you see how you're feeling," Rove responded.

"But I know how I feel," I said.

"Oh really? You just said that you didn't love her, then you said you did. So which is it?" he asked.

I was feeling like the eggshell of denial around me was cracking. This was becoming a most unpleasant experience.

"Think about it, you sold your house. You have no job now. You're looking for a job down here in another country so you can be with her and work with her. She's your best friend. You're giving up everything where you live so you can come to this place to be with her. But you say you don't love her."

"Maybe I do, eh?"

"Do you think?" asked Rove in a sarcastic tone.

"Yes. I mean no. I mean. Dear God, look what I'm doing! I wouldn't do this for a woman if I didn't love her? But I was hoping love would grow naturally over time that we spent together, then I would love her."

"You already do. You asshole! You're just too pig headed to admit it to yourself," Rove interjected.

His words cut into me. "Oh my God! You're right! I do love her!" I said. In a brilliant quick moment my defenses collapsed and I could see the wall of denial tumble in front of me. My emotions cleared and I realized what I was staring at. It was true. I loved her.

"But you said you could never love again. Oh no, Rove. Not me. I'll never fall in love again. No, no. Not me," he mocked me then smiled and gave me a hug.

"You know on shipboard when you remember things, the two of you are very different with each other. You're a lot closer." He smiled and gave me another hug. "You're a lucky bastard, you know that?" Rove said then laughed. "Rove has to leave now. I better sit down or her body will get hurt when I leave." Rove sat down on the bed. He closed his eyes. A moment later Michelle opened her eyes and I was relieved to see it was really her. She sat up and looked at me.

"What happened?" she asked. "You look in shock."

"Rove walked me through my cobwebs."

"Oh God, I hate it when they do that with me. Are you alright?" Michelle asked.

"Yeah. Just give me a hug," I said. I held her the same way I always did in my arms. But my heart was different now. I realized I had been denying some obvious feelings I had been experiencing for some time.

"Do you want to talk about it?" she asked. She had no idea exactly what just happened.

"No. It's okay. I'll be fine. I'm just a bit tired now. Let's have some tea. I think I'll have a beer."

So we sat and talked for a while until Michelle had to leave and go home for the night. I went to bed and slept restlessly.

The next day I went for a successful job interview. It was a busy day but still all I could think about was seeing Michelle that night. Everything was so new, so incredible, and so different now that I was no longer denying my true feelings.

That night I waited for Michelle to arrive. I pondered many things, but could not possibly imagine what was about to occur. When she arrived we sat down for a cup of tea.

"How was your day?" Michelle asked.

"Good. My interview went well. The fellow is sending me to a third interview with the manager of their technical services out on the coast. I might be working by the ocean!"

"So cool," Michelle replied.

"Can you imagine. I never thought in my wildest dreams I would ever live or work near the ocean again. I miss the ocean," I said.

"I think Alex is here. Do you want to start?" Michelle asked.

"Yes. Let's do it," I replied.

Michelle closed her eyes and I closed mine and we both concentrated. Alex's huge presence entered the room. I felt Michelle's consciousness enter me through the top of my head then I opened my eyes to see Alex removing Michelle's glasses. It was amazing to both of us how Alex could see without Michelle's eyeglasses. Even more amazing was that when she returned she could often see clearly through her eyes for a few minutes until they finally went blurry again.

Alex smiled sweetly then said, "Hello, dear one. How are you?"

"Well, thank you. And you?" I asked.

"Quite well, thank you," Alex replied. "I'm sorry about tonight but we have a great deal of work to get through and not much time. Do you understand?"

"Yes. I think," I said a little confused.

"It will become clear to you shortly. I am very sorry dear one. Rove wishes to speak with you." Then Alex closed his eyes and when they opened again Rovere was in Michelle's body.

"Go ahead and say it. You've been thinking it all day," Rove said.

"No. I won't say that." I knew what he was talking about. I had said nothing to Michelle but all day I kept thinking what an asshole Rove had been for walking me through such pain the night before.

"Go ahead, say it," Rove pressed. "Go ahead. Call Rove an asshole. Go on, say it."

"Okay fine! You're an asshole. It really hurt though I understand why you did it."

"But Rove's still an asshole," Rove pressed.

"Yes. You're an asshole. Do you know how hard it is for me to say that to someone like you?"

"Good. Maybe my little brother is turning into a man now, eh?" Rove said.

"What do you mean? I'm already a man," I protested.

"We'll see," said Rove. "Hey. Alex wants to speak with you."

All of a sudden there was another switch and Alex was back. I was getting confused, unable to understand what the fast switching was all about.

"Dear one," Alex began, "I am attempting to arrange for you to meet with someone else. One you've known for a long time. Would you like to speak with Hetar?"

"Yes, very much please." I had been anxious to speak with Hetar. I had very clear memories of him and had wanted to speak with him about several memories from my youth where I saw him just before going on the side mission.

"I'll go see what I can arrange. He may be busy now and not able to come," Alex said.

"Please forgive me, but I have to go to the bathroom. I'm very sorry but all of this excitement," I said reluctantly.

"Please. Go ahead." Alex chuckled. "I will speak with you later."

I rushed into the bathroom and emerged a very short time later to see Michelle's body sitting in a chair at the table. It was not Alex, nor was it Rove. I concluded it must be Hetar. I held out my hands offering a hug and it was accepted. The eyes were stern. The energy incredible.

I sat down at the table. "Hetar?" I asked.

They shook their head indicating a "no".

"Alex?" I asked.

Again they shook their head.

"Not Rove?" I said.

Once again they shook their head indicating "no".

I had a hunch and took a deep breath. "Molanie?"

She nodded her head indicating "yes". My eyes widened. I took several gasps of air. I remembered Molanie as being in charge of everything. She was a woman I remembered calling mother; a woman who commanded respect from everyone not by authority, but by being. Her energy was even more intense than that of Alex.

"I'm sorry. You've caught me off guard. I didn't expect you," I stammered awkwardly.

Molanie looked at me, reached over and took my hand, then turned it palm facing up. With her other hand she pointed with her index finger into the middle of my palm and said, "Everything right there. Just one small spot. Everything right there."

"What do you mean?" I asked completely confused.

She reiterated, pointing to the palm of my hand. "Everything right there. Just one small spot. Everything."

I looked at her in amazement. Her eyes were incredible. The room seemed completely different because of the intensity and nature of the energy that was now in it.

"Everything right there?" I asked.

"Just one small spot," she responded. The implications of her words combined with the secondary layer of communication she projected created in me a reaction that was beyond description. When she said "everything", she meant "EVERYTHING". I realized the magnitude and importance of her message. Nothing else that was said that night came close.

As the week went on I intermittently felt an overwhelming, powerful feeling on the top of my head, then turned around to see that Rove was in Michelle's body again. As the shock of the new situation sunk in, we realized at Michelle's understandable insistence, that we had to start exercising new protocols concerning when people came and went with the beings we were working with. In retrospect, I suspect that Rovere was pushing us to do this.

"I feel like I'm being hijacked all the time!" Michelle complained. "It gives me no time to prepare if I'm going into you and I can suddenly wake up in my body with no recollection of anything happening."

So over the next while we set out and began to practice some guidelines. Whoever was going to speak to us had to ask first. We then decided if the time was appropriate and we could do it. We found the ET's were willing to visit as much as we were capable of handling when we were together. Our body's became strained from the process and we found we had to say no in certain situations.

Through the week, I learned many things from Rove. Michelle told me how Rove would do outrageous things like pretend to be the Virgin Mary. I recalled to Michelle how when I was eight years old I had an abduction event. I saw three angelic looking beings descend on a cloud out of the sky above me, followed by thirty minutes of missing time. For over thirty years I thought I had a vision of the Virgin Mary. This was all I told her. No details.

Later on, I was talking to Rove and it hit me. I pointed my finger and said, "You! You were the one on the cloud when I was small!"

Rove looked at me, smiled, then winked.

"You mischievous s.o.b.," I accused.

"You remember the woman you saw on the ship that time?" he asked. "The one who asked you if you wanted to help the babies in the room?"

I never told Michelle about the details of this experience. Rove was giving me confirmation.

"Yes, she was very stern with me," I replied. The woman was tall, blond and beautiful and spoke very sternly to me about the seriousness of her question.

"Bitch, you called her," he said and laughed.

"How can you call her that?" I asked in shock.

"I didn't. You did. That's what you told me on board years ago. You just don't remember telling me."

I was speechless. Rove seemed to break all the rules. His language was crass, even vulgar at times. He would teach me with compassion but could also be so forward it was painful. It hurt when he asked me difficult questions about how I felt about things.

Both he and Alex helped me recover my memory of certain ET events and clarified questions regarding things about which I had partial and cloudy memory.

Many of my ET events involved partial memories where things were out of context. Some events had left me feeling scared, confused, hurt and angry.

For instance, the earlier event where I was on my bike at the school yard. I was abducted and Alex stood over me to calm me. I was rolled up onto my left side then something was inserted into my body that was horribly painful and I became upset and started to yell for them to stop. Alex ordered in a quick sharp tone, "Knock it out! Knock it out!" For years I thought that Alex had been referring to me as "it" when he was commanding them to knock it out. I believed he had no compassion for my pain because he allowed them to carelessly insert a large device inside my body without any forethought as to the suffering that it might cause me.

When I asked him about this he explained the following: "Many of the instruments that are used are 'alive' in that they are similar to what Earthers call artificially intelligent, but in a much more sophisticated way. The device we were using had gone bad and had inserted itself much farther into your body than it was supposed to, thinking that you were a full sized adult. I was one of the first in the group to notice your pain and ordered other attendants there to knock 'it' - the device- out of you."

I sat their thinking quietly to myself, "How could you live with me thinking that I thought you did this on purpose all these years without explaining it to me?" I didn't voice the words.

He said, "You know it there." Meaning, I knew it when I was with Alex in the world where he was from, but did not know here on Earth because my memory was taken away from me when I returned from my experiences. He said this as I finished formulating the thought without me saying a word. He was telepathically reading me.

Often I would be in conversation with one of the ET's through Michelle and there would be normal conversation going on while simultaneously a secondary layer of communication would be occurring telepathically. I would be verbally speaking to an ET while experiencing the communication of concepts in the form of energy directly into my mind. Sometimes these concepts supported or expanded on the words the ET spoke. Other times they could be completely different than the topic verbally being expressed.

I realized as first Alex, Rovere, Molanie, then even Hetar, came through Michelle's body to have conversations with me, that these were not evil aliens bent on overtaking the planet and hurting people. They were here to help. Indeed, if what they were telling me was true, they were investing tremendous resources helping people in the contactee community to realize who they really are and what jobs they have to do.

According to the ET's, many of us within the contactee community are in fact ET's ourselves who chose to take on human form at this particular point in the Earth's history in order to experience and aid in a unique period of time. This part of the contactee community the ETs refer to as the "work force." One of the dilemmas the ETs currently have is that many who came to work are not working. They simply did not wake up. Often this is because they became too involved with money, physical possessions and earthly distractions.

The enormity and consistency of the ET message was mind boggling. When I coupled this with my own memory of these beings who were regularly telling me things through Michelle about events in my life that she could never have known about, I was utterly convinced of the reality of what Michelle and I were experiencing. I came to the conclusion that either Michelle was more psychic than Edgar Cayce with an IQ exceeding 2000 and we were both stark raving mad, or it was real. The latter conclusion seemed, and still appears to be, the most logical.

The week came to an end and I had to return to Toronto. Michelle and I both agreed that I would return in a couple of weeks so that I could continue pursuing a job, and so that we could continue our work. Alex warned us that when we were apart we would experience a longing. We didn't grasp the depth of his statement at the time.

Up to this point what the ETs seemed to be talking to us about was seeing ourselves the way we are and helping us to understand why they chose this form of contact. They also spent time explaining some of the ET memories we had from the past. They guided us to work together and impressed on us the importance of what we were going to do. They reaffirmed the sense we both felt that we had a mission that was planned before we were even born.

On my return to Toronto, I rushed around trying to get as much organized as possible. I found that there was only so much I could do until I ran out of options. Michelle and I spoke several times a day, every day.

I wanted to spend a few more days down at the lake, so I planned on an evening when I could go down to watch. I called Michelle that day and told her of my plans, and asked her to keep me in her thoughts and meditations.

That afternoon I went down and watched from about 4:00 PM on. The afternoon was full of activity. I watched small bright gold orbs appear and disappear. Some moved around while others appeared out on the open water where they stood motionless.

I was amazed to see a small, round, white dot of light fly across the sky. It was joined by a second one and they flew off in an erratic pattern. I swung my scope over to get a closer look but they were gone. Then my head jerked straight up in a sudden involuntary reaction. High above me was a black, triangular shaped craft that moved in an absolutely straight line at high speed.

Some months before, Michelle said she asked one of the gray's she knew from her experiences, Jobie, to show himself to me. She asked that he give me some warning first, and that he fly directly over my head. He said he would try. Now, here my head had jerked up for no reason I could understand, and a flying triangle zipped directly overhead. I realized it must have been Jobie.

As the sun was going down, and the dusk rose, I watched out over the open water and noticed that a series of lights had grown quite tall all of a sudden.

I swung my viewing scope over and looked. The series of lights that grew from the water must have been between seventy to a hundred feet tall. I watched as the lights shrunk down to dots on the water, then a few minutes later, grew to an incredible height again. I sat watching in awe and realized that I was having not just an emotional, but a spiritual reaction as well. These were not just ET projected images or craft, these were some type of living beings. I felt it so incredibly strong.

Later that night I telephoned Michelle. After some time, Alex asked to speak to us and we did a switch over.

"Did you see the light that was standing all by itself?" Alex asked.

"Yes. There was one way out on the lake by itself, far to the left of the five that I saw grow. How did you know that?" I asked. I had not told Michelle anything about that lone light.

"It was me," he replied.

"You were there?" I asked with surprise.

"For a time, yes. For a time I stood behind you with my hands on your shoulders as we both watched those that appeared on the lake."

"You were the presence I felt behind me at one point then?" I asked.

"Yes," Alex replied. I also had not told Michelle about the strong presence I felt behind me at the lake that evening and this was another confirmation for me that Alex was truly speaking through Michelle.

"What were those lights, Alex? What were they that they would grow like that? They felt like they were alive," I said.

"Indeed. Alive. Not just pretty lights on the water. What you saw were the Standing Ones," Alex said.

"The Standing Ones? What are those?" I asked.

"In your physical universe, and this is just your physical universe, are beings that hold the physical matter that you see together. They are called the Standing Ones. They do not move linearly, but can move in other ways."

"What do you mean, Alex?" I asked.

"The Standing Ones are a type of being that appear, when viewed from your reality, to be immobile. But from where they are, they can appear at any place in time and space. What we sense and see in this reality may be an actual Standing One, or a reflection of one. They have limited ability to move in human reality, but can move. They hold physical reality in your physical universe together. There is a Standing One that holds the rocks together, one that holds the trees together, and so on. It is more complex than that, but do you get the general idea?"

I was both baffled and almost speechless. "I get the general idea. There is a lot to think about here. Things are far more complex than I thought," I said.

"Indeed. So much for you to learn. So many layers. The physical world, different dimensions, realms, timelines. All overlapping and occurring at the same time and different times. Some timelines running at different speeds than others," Alex explained in a tone of gentle understanding.

Our conversation ended and Michelle and I spoke for a while about what Alex had just explained. Soon we hung up our phones and called it a night.

The remainder of the evening I looked at the photograph of my nephew. I kept it framed by my computer. I had the photo scanned and on the second scan some dirt had formed in the dark area of the photo. I looked carefully at the original photo and determined it was either dirt or an image that appeared on the second output by some unknown force or intelligence. Strangely, it formed a pattern. It looked like a being, one that wore a robe. It had big eyes like a gray, but was not a gray. The head was oval shaped and the chin was not pointed.

I looked and looked, then it hit me like a ton of bricks, it was an exact replica of the beings I had seen the night the fifteen lights appeared across the lake. Alex was not kidding me about these beings. Moreover, there was some type of connection I had with them that I did not as yet understand. It was something to do with the Mother Earth, not just ETs. Yet the ETs knew about these beings. I started to understand with my heart and not just my head that the ET phenomenon was much more complex than I had previously comprehended.

The next time I spoke to Alex about this he reiterated for me that there were so many levels involved. There were different timelines, realms and dimensions. I already knew there were different types of beings, some that were in bodies, some that were bodiless, and some that had a form created by themselves for temporary interaction with us.

For example: Alex had been working with me at night over a period of several weeks. When he did, I began to wake in the middle of the night and be half asleep. He had explained that this was the state that was the most conducive for our work and for me to remember the experience.

When I half woke up, I was feeling clear but not quite myself. My bedroom seemed quite dark, but there was a brilliant white bluish light over my head. It was incredibly bright, yet it did not hurt my eyes. It looked exactly like a light I had seen over the lake before. Even though it was different from lights from a craft, I thought that maybe I was about to be picked up.

The next day I asked Alex if it was a Rye-hun craft or if it was him.

"It was me," he responded in a quiet, gentle voice.

On another occasion I was standing in what seemed like an earth house. There were a number of humans there, there was a man who appeared about fifty years old, slender, with blue eyes. He was standing in front of me. I knew it was Alex, yet he looked a bit different than I had seen him before. It was an incredibly clear experience. People spoke without moving their lips. Molanie was there as well. She was stunningly beautiful. Her dark hair hung down from her statuesque seven and a half foot body. Her energy was incredible.

Alex sat on a couch in the middle of the room with his eyes closed as though he was concentrating on something. He only opened his eyes wide at times to look directly at someone who was looking at him. It was then I realized he could take on any form he wanted to. I thought about it. I had seen him in four different forms so far. As pure light, as a man in his fifties with short hair, a man in his thirties with shoulder length flowing blond hair, and a man in his thirties with plumed blond hair and a more narrow and angelic looking face. Michelle further verified my experiences for me when she explained that she had seen him in these forms as well.

Alex explained to me that where they were from, they exchanged bodies and were not attached to their bodies or their physical image the way Earthers were. He explained that his people who worked on Earth actually lived in a world that his people maintained around the Earth and existed in a different type of reality or a different phased existence. He also mentioned that the Rye-hun could bring their technology partially to his world. It occurred to me that Alex's world could be the root of the Aboriginal belief in the *Sky World*.

Time passed and I had been away from Michelle for two weeks, yet circumstances prevented me from going back to New Hampshire at that time as we had planned. We both decided it would be wisest for me to stay another week in Canada while some business that I was arranging solidified. I had been feeling out of sorts and not quite myself for some time. I had tried to keep myself busy through the day dealing with my business arrangements and other logistics necessary for me to move to the United States but it was difficult to concentrate.

On the Friday night of the end of the second week away from Michelle, I found myself lying on my couch. I was in a terrible state. I was unable to move properly and my chest was in deep pain. I struggled to walk to my bedroom and almost collapsed in the process. I virtually crawled back to my living room sofa where I lay down and sobbed. I picked up the telephone and called Michelle and was amazed to find that she was in no better condition.

Our need to be with each other was not just emotionally devastating, it was physically destroying us. It was utterly horrid being away from each other. I couldn't stand to be so far away from her. I realized more than ever I could not live without her.

"Hi," I heard Michelle say in a tone indicating she knew it was me.

"Hi. Are you in as bad a shape as I am? You sound horrible," I said.

"Worse," she replied.

We called on Rove to try and understand what we were doing wrong. I was at a loss to know how to resolve things. I asked Rove what to do between my tears.

Rove responded by sending some energy at me that didn't do much of anything.

"There. Did that help?" Rove asked.

"No," I said. Clenching my chest as I spoke.

"Rove is no substitute," Rove said.

"So what do we do. Please, give us a hint. I can hardly walk. I feel like I'm going to die without Michelle around. My body feels physically sick," I explained through a sick, raspy voice.

"I think you should come down here as soon as you can," Rove said.

"Drive down. Rove, I can hardly walk!" I protested.

"If you decide you are coming down, I guarantee you will be able to drive and you will be okay until you get here. Looks like the two of you can't be apart," Rove said.

"I won't crash the car or anything?" I asked in a disbelieving tone. I was in serious physical distress.

"No," Rove said emphatically.

"Maybe you're right. I know if I stay here I feel like I'm going to die. Please. I want to speak to her," I said.

"Okay, hang on. Let's switch," Rove said, and was gone.

A moment later Michelle was back in her body.

"I'm coming down, Mick!" I said decidedly.

"But I thought you had to..." she started.

"I'm coming down," I interrupted. "We're going to both get sicker or die if I don't. Obviously I can't live without you and you can't live without me or we wouldn't be going through what we're going through. I love you and I coming down. I'm leaving in the morning."

"I love you," Michelle replied.

"I love you, too. I've got to get packed. I'll see you tomorrow night. I'm on my way. I'm coming. I love you. You gonna be okay?" I asked.

"Now I am, yes," she replied.

We said good night and both hung up the phone. I felt my chest had already loosened a bit. I hobbled to the bedroom and began to pack. I felt the determination rise inside of me. I was a man on a mission. My love needed me and now I could do something about it. Be damned with my planning! I would merely finish whatever I had to from New Hampshire on the phone. I felt stupid for being so set in how I was going to do things.

I did not sleep well during that night. I was up early the next day and I drove with determination and a fire in my heart. I remembered what it was like when Michelle and I were split up in the ET world. I remembered the horrible period of the side mission and coming out of it only to find my memory of my love had faded from my heart. I remembered the years of healing and finding her again through the most incredible and painful period of my life. Now I had found her. I would move Heaven and Earth to be with her. I felt like my life was not worth living without her. She was my best friend, my first love, and I was determined now, that she would be my last love. I would not let her go ever again.

I arrived the next night to find Michelle and her parents in the apartment. She had rearranged furniture with them all day. I remember walking in to find a different looking apartment than the one I had seen before. She was in the bathroom when I arrived, getting ready to see me. I spoke with her mother who I got along with quite well. As we spoke about family matters, Michelle's mother expressed her concerns about what was going on with George.

I reassured her. I explained that I was a black belt and that I would let no harm come to Michelle. I told Mrs. LaVigne that I cared for her daughter a great deal and that she was my best friend. I would protect her. Michelle's mother felt more at ease and we spoke of more general things.

I began to become anxious waiting for Michelle after she did not emerge from the bathroom for a good five minutes, but finally she appeared, radiant and smiling. She looked so glad to see me. I knew I felt so glad to see her. I gave her a huge hug. Her mother looked and smiled. She knew there was more going on than met the eye. She could see how important each of us was to the other.

We spent the next five days dealing with setting up Michelle's safety, and her situation began to settle down. George realized he was fighting a loosing battle and that he needed to deal with some serious issues. It was a difficult time for all of us. Michelle and I knew throughout this, that regardless of what madness and problems were thrown at us, we would end up together.

At the end of a very busy and stressful week I returned to Toronto. Michelle and I decided I would return in a week for an extended visit. There was no question in our minds we wanted to be together forever. We would find a way do it.

MICHELLE
Connected to Paul

It would be lacking for me to write about the conversations Paul had with Alex, Rovere and the others while I was in his body practicing melding with him, even though at times I could hear what was being said and could actually see out of Paul's eyes. Most often, I would not hear or see what was going in the early sessions. It wasn't until Paul and I were able to put in hours of intense practice that I could see more clearly and hear words spoken to him with accuracy. Even at the time of this writing, there are still times when the clarity of sound and vision fades while I am inside of Paul, but the feelings are always very strong and very real. So rather than trying to recap conversation bits I recall from these experiences, I will try and relate to you how it feels to go through the experience of sharing someone's body with them.

Though the transfers are taking place much smoother these days, probably due to the fact that I don't resist them anymore, the sensations are pretty much the same. It will usually start with Paul and I either asking or being asked if we are ready to start the process. Then, whichever being who wants to enter me will envelop me. I will feel them over me as if they were a blanket over a bed or a melted piece of cheese over toast. Then one of two things will happen. The most typical is that Paul will reach forward with his energy and activate a "tool" of sorts that comes from his soul but appears to manifest itself from the top of his head. This tool will find me, grab me and hold on to me. At the same time I will concentrate on him and on being with him. This creates a 'flying' sensation in me. It frees me from my body so that he can draw me into him. Next, he does the actual drawing in of my being via this tool.

Sometimes, if I concentrate very strongly on him, it is like I push my way in and his tool draws me quite a bit faster. Other times, if I am taken out, or leave my body too quickly, I might find myself floating in a milky void. Sometimes during those times I can feel Paul looking for me. I can direct my focus to him and soon his tool will find me and draw me into him.

On fewer occasions one of the ETs - most often Rovere - will somehow grab hold of my being and put me into Paul. This is usually done very quickly causing a jolt of energy to flash through both Paul's and my being. Sometimes this jolt of energy is exhilarating. Sometimes it's frustrating.

Once I'm inside of Paul, my first sensation is an intense feeling of being home. It is a very comfortable, rested feeling. The closest thing I can think of to describe it is that feeling you get when you have been on the road a long time, you get home, exhausted and ready for bed, then you climb under YOUR blankets in YOUR bed in YOUR room and cuddle up and go to sleep. That warm feeling of comfort you get just as you close your eyes to sleep is the same kind of feeling. Actually it is remarkably similar with one exception. When I am inside of Paul, I can feel him all around me. I feel his being, his soul, his energy. It is as if his being is now not only merged into a joining with mine, it is like he and I melt together and we are no longer two people in one body, but we are one person in one eternity.

When I first become aware that I am inside of Paul, I have no visual perceptions. Sometimes I will experience colors or sounds, and see shapes. Still, for the most part, all is warm and peacefully dark. I know when I feel him around me that I am in place and ready to start to work.

I will my mind to expand. I do this by visualizing that I am very small, but I'm growing. I visualize Paul's body as a kind of empty glove and my mind a hand that fits perfectly into that glove. I concentrate on filling every inch of the glove.

At first, the effort needed to do this was tremendous, but it became easier the more I worked at it and we connected. I know when I'm working correctly because I start to feel a wonderful euphoric state as I continue to work. Then, as I keep reaching and spreading out, the shapes and colors I see will sometimes come into focus and I will begin to see what Paul is looking at.

I know this sounds amazing. I began to wonder if it were true myself. Paul and I tested it several times. One time was when he was on the road home to Canada on one of his many trips back and forth before he came to stay. He had become extremely tired and he stopped to rest half way home at a little hotel in New York state. Once he had something to eat, he went back to his room and called me.

While we were on the phone, we decided to test our abilities. We asked Alex to come so that I could enter Paul and see if I could tell him about the hotel room. Alex was amiable and agreed. We accomplished the transfer and I worked hard to expand inside of Paul to the point where I could see out of his eyes. As I worked to expand, Paul took special care to stare at unique objects in the room. He said nothing to Alex about what he looked at.

I told Paul from inside his head that I saw things and was ready to return to my body so I could tell him. To my surprise, he heard my "voice" inside of his head and asked Alex if I could return.

When I returned to my own body I was able to describe to Paul, with some detail, not only the room's colors but also the texture and pattern of the room's curtains, the shape and color of the lamp and the general theme of the painting on the wall. The colors in the painting were very dark, and it wasn't as clear to me as the other objects he looked at.

Soon Paul and I learned that if the object he was looking at was brightly lit it was easier for me to see. The same seemed true about sound. If it were loud, it was easier for me to hear.

The fact that Paul could hear me when I thought things to him from inside his body was important to me. It meant several things. First, it meant that I had some control over things. I could say to Paul, "Please tell Rove I am ready to go home and want my body back now." I could also add to conversations and remind Paul about things when he was otherwise so involved that he had forgotten what we set out to do.

This happened once in a while when we started talking to beings such as the "little people". It seemed that they would sidetrack conversations, often in the most fascinating directions. Paul, who was more physically connected to the awe of the experience would easily get sidetracked and distracted by the wonder, but I would be able to remind him that we had a specific purpose in mind. The process, to this day, is still refining itself as we practice more, but all in all, it's become just about our most useful tool.

Usually when Paul and I unite in the same body, we strive to achieve a state of "awake" or "becoming". What I mean by that is a state where we are aware of things beyond what one normally is aware of in life. We strive to be conscious of ourselves and our united self and of all the energy of the universe. We try to contemplate what it means to know that all times are now and we create our own reality. When we are working really hard and we are sharp and have our timing right, Paul and I can fit together perfectly like the two sides of a zipper. We unite and zip together so perfectly that the being we were before we were split into a "Completer" and a "Reflection" becomes again. We become a greater consciousness.

Amazingly, when Paul and I "zip" together, there is no division between who he is and his personal experiences and who I am and my personal experiences. The emotions created by this melding are so impossible to comprehend in total, and the being we become so incredibly light in nature, that when we separate again to our own personalities we often hold each other for some time after and cry.

You would think that with the ability to do what we were doing it would be hard to want to do anything else. I mean, when you can achieve the states we have, it's really hard to think of walking the dog and washing the dishes. But somehow these things do not affect us in that way.

I know I can say with some confidence that if we were independently wealthy and didn't have to have Earth jobs, Paul and I would spend just about every minute we could exploring our spiritual work, enjoying our children as they grow and teaching others about the wonders we discovered.

Nevertheless, it is not likely that I would spend hours and hours in his body with him - though sometimes I wish I could - mostly because of the stress it puts on both our systems. When I'm in his body with him for a very long time, I start to feel disoriented and will develop a pulling feeling back to my own body. Sometimes I will start to feel very tired and it will be hard to maintain my focus, then my mind will drift. Besides, it is a totally different feeling of "togetherness" than Paul and I have in a physical situation where we can touch each other's skin and look at each other's faces. Both types are important.

Over time, Paul learned he could enter my body too, though not to the degree I enter his. During meditations, at first with Alex's help, then later on our own, Paul learned to reach inside of my being and anchor himself there. When he does this, he is not fully separated from his body like I am when I enter him, but rather, he is aware of where his own body is and can feel it, but he is also aware of where my body is and can feel it. It is more like having one mind in two bodies than two minds in one body.

It is a very intimate experience that can spark strong creative and emotional energy in both of us. It is a very necessary link we have established to feel each other when our daily jobs take us in directions away from one another.

Before we met face to face in this Earth-life, both Paul and I were always physically ill. It seemed there was not a germ out there that didn't have our name on it. We went from one cold to the next. Sinus and respiratory problems were a way of life for us. A month could not go by for either of us without having to have some kind of virus or infection that needed a prescription for antibiotics or decongestants. My condition was so bad that my doctor had me on a maintenance dose of antibiotics for months at a time. Even that didn't help. As soon as I was off the medication, the sinus infections, ear aches, head colds and fevers returned.

Amazing though it sounds, it is true that since December of 1997 to the day of this writing, Paul and I have had only one cold each. I have not taken an antibiotic for over a year. I have not missed even one day of work due to illness and neither has Paul.

To some people, this doesn't sound extraordinary, but you must remember, before Paul and I physically touched here on Earth we were both so sick that he missed hours of work a month due to illness and I couldn't hold a job outside of my house at all.

Considering the pain and actual physical sickness we suffered when we were physically away from each other, I am convinced that all those years I spent terribly ill to the point of disability were due not to an actual physical source, but rather, they were due to my separation from my Completer. I was sick from not having Paul physically close to me. Likewise, he was sick because I was not close to him. This was happening before we even knew the other one existed in this reality and it ended when we first touched at Logan Airport back in December of 1997. We know from experience that maintaining our good physical health is dependant on being together.

My new found health was a good thing for many reasons. In the spring of 1998 it was fortunate that I didn't get sick, because I could not afford to. I had a household to support that included three children.

<u>MICHELLE</u>
Per Chance to Dream

That fact that Paul and I have such a strong bond also makes it easy for us to work together in the ET environment. Most often we are asked to do things as a team. Sometimes these things are as simple as teaching a class or playing with children. Other times they can be more complex, like when we are asked to deal with difficult individuals or calm down someone who is being disruptive. The most striking and awesome job Paul and I are asked to do on a regular basis is something we call *"dream work."*

Dream work, put simply, is the act of giving someone else a particular vivid dream in the hope of suggesting an action or behavior from them. It sounds simple but it's quite a bit more complex than that.

Both good and evil cannot really make anyone do anything. They can only make suggestions. Once in a while, a being like Alex will want to make a very impacting possitive suggestion to someone. Often these suggestions are intended to be life changing, I dare say world changing.

Recently, Paul and I did some dream work with Alex. This is what we recall: There were several events that happened one night. It started when Paul and I were taken from our home and brought onto Hetar's ship. Once there, we met with Alex. He told us that we had dream work to do. He left the room and reappeared. He now looked like a very tall young man with plumed yellow hair and a long angelic face. He was wearing an all white cloak that had a golden sash across the chest. He was almost glowing with energy.

Hetar's people provided us transportation to where we were going. We arrived at a large upstairs bedroom in someone's home. The first thing we both noticed was the man in the bed. He was an older man with a white mustache. He was sleeping alone.

I positioned myself along side of the bed, and Paul stood by the head of the bed. Alex stood at the foot of the bed. Then Alex asked if we were ready to began. We both nodded and so Alex began.

First, he woke the man and spoke to the man in a language that was completely foreign to Paul and me. The man opened his eyes and was totally amazed by the vision of Alex standing at the foot of his bed. The man started to get up.

Alex looked at me. I knew what I had to do. Using the empathic skill I have learned from the ETs, I thought to the man the intense feeling that he did not want to move and he was safe. He calmed back down and did not get up.

Alex spoke some more to the man. Though we could not understand the exact words, both Paul and I knew he was telling the man that the decision the man was about to make was going to be important and that he should be aware of the ramifications. It was also clear that the man didn't care about any ramifications. He didn't take the vision of Alex seriously. Alex then suggested that the man was taking a path that was going to cause suffering and destruction and that there was payment for such things.

Still the man didn't seem to care.

So Alex looked at Paul and said, "Show him the tunnel".

Paul swallowed hard, braced himself, then put his face in front of the man. Both of Paul's hands were at the sides of the man's head.

The man started to moan and writhe as if he were in great pain as Paul projected into the man's mind a vision of what he could expect if he continued on his current course.

The vision shook the man terribly. When Paul stopped the man raised his hands up as if praying to Alex. Even though we couldn't understand a literal word of what he said, both Paul and I knew that he was going to rethink his decisions.

On that same night we visited three men, and ran through more or less the same scenario. The fourth person we visited was different though.

The last place we went was in a big city. It looked to be just about dawn when we got there. The place we were going was an upper story of a big high-rise building. I saw the outside of the building as we approached it.

We appeared inside the building in a room where children were sleeping. Alex was there, Paul was there and a few moments after we arrived, three or four of the smaller grays materialized in the room as well.

The room was clean and lit well enough by the breaking morning light that I could see very well. There was a crib and three mattresses on the floor in the room. There were no bed frames. This seemed by choice, as it was obvious that the people who lived there could easily afford beds if they wanted them.

There were three children sleeping on the mattress. The oldest was a boy who looked about ten or so. It was clear they were from oriental decent, but judging by the position of the sun and daylight it was likely we were in North America.

There was a small baby in the crib. It was a sad sight to see. The infant was wrapped in some strange equipment that I didn't recognized that had some kind of monitor attached to it that was humming quietly. The baby looked thin and sickly.

A small dog came into the room. Oddly enough, it didn't bark. Paul picked up the animal and stroked it. Alex motioned to one of the Rye-hun. The Rye-hun nodded and took out a control wand, tapped the eldest boy with it, then woke him up. The boy seemed to be in a trance. The grays helped him get up then directed him to sit by the wall where he could see everything.

One gray said to him, "We are going to help you."

The little grays then went to the crib and started to examine and work on the infant.

Alex looked at me and smiled. "Go give their father a wake up call."

"What form should I be in?" I asked. It seems that they could make me look different to others around me in these events.

"Look like one of them," Alex said and pointed to the grays.

I agreed, then left to look for the parent's room. I didn't make a conscious decision to make myself look like a Rye-hun. If I recall correctly, I simply just assumed I did, and I did.

I almost walked into a closet and bathroom before I found the parent's room. As a mom, I was surprised to find that they slept with their door closed with such a sick infant down the hall.

I entered their room and saw that just like in the other room, their mattress was on the floor, though their dressers and wardrobe were beautiful and obviously expensive. Like the children, the parents also appeared to be of oriental decent.

I took a breath and smiled. Doing this kind of work always appeals to the mischievous little kid side of me. I took one final look, then climbed onto the bed and straddled the man as I might straddle a horse.

He woke with a start. I knew he could not move and that his wife would not stir. It was just the way it worked. His eyes practically bulged out of his head as he stared at me. I knew he was seeing big, black, almond shaped lenses on a Rye-hun face rather than me.

I looked with fierce intensity at him for a moment. All the while I projected the thought to him, "Yes, I am real." Then said with both my thoughts and my voice, "Only through love changes come."

I climbed off of him and hurried out of the room. I knew once he got over the shock he would likely follow me. He did.

I had just enough time to get back to the children's room. I noticed all the Rye-hun were already gone. I turned to face the door just as the father came bolting into the room. His face was white with shock. His eyes were wide with disbelief. Alex raised his hand and we were back on shipboard.

I asked Alex, " Will he remember?"

Alex replied, "Whatever he does not recall, his son will. The child saw the whole thing."

Then Paul asked, "Will he come on line now?" Meaning will the man realize that he is having experiences and do the work he needs to do to discover what they are and what his role is in the phenomenon.

Alex said, "One would hope so. Now that his baby is healed, how can he stay in denial?"

To this day, Paul and I do not know who this man and his children are, but whoever they are they must have a very important role in this mission Earth for Alex and the Rye-hun to go through such trouble to make him realize his experiences. Maybe he will even read this and contact us. Stranger things have happened.

Dream work can take many forms. The two examples above are the most common by far.

<u>*PAUL*</u>
May 1998

In the beginning of May I came down for an extended visit with Michelle. I made arrangements to survive on money I had saved and we found ourselves playing the reverse roles of man and woman. During the day Michelle went to work and I stayed home and looked after the children, who I quickly grew to love. Michelle had never been in a position before of being the "breadwinner" in the family and I had never before been a "house husband." It became a valuable learning experience for both of us.

Over the next few months, we learned many beautiful and wonderful things. We learned more about our mission and what we were to do for not only ourselves, but the contactee community at large. We learned that Michelle could teach me about the stars and I could teach her about the Earth.

Rovere told us this was one of the reasons we were split up the way we were, so that when we were reunited we could combine our shared knowledge of two places as a Completer and a Reflection to produce a rare and wonderful experience of being that could be used for the purposes of both worlds and shared with those who had ears to hear.

We also knew, more than ever before, that we had always loved each other since we were young children. We knew we were meant to be together as one being, one soul, soul mates in the truest sense of the word. The woman of my dreams— literally my dreams— had entered my life in the most magical way any human being could ever have imagined. I began the process of open Earth based contact with the beings I had interacted with all my life and I had also found my other half. For the first time in my life I was truly fulfilled and truly happy.

Nevertheless, our challenges before we would finally be together were just beginning. I was having trouble getting the necessary documentation together to stay beyond three months in the country. We both knew that we would eventually marry each other and we began to realize we might want to move our plans forward. Her divorce would not be completed until the beginning of July. I had to leave at the end of July and would not likely be readmitted to the country until the next year. This in itself would traumatize all of us, especially the children. I developed strong feelings for them and I knew they loved me and looked to me for support and stability in what was a very rocky period in their lives. Leaving them like that was not an acceptable option. We both knew what we had to do, and after twenty years of being apart, I started to make plans for some very special romance.

On one level, over the next several months, Michelle and I walked a razor's edge. In the middle of preparing for a work-visa, we found out that the total number of visas had already been handed out and there would be no more issued until September at the very earliest. Meanwhile, I was in the country on a ninety day visa waiver from Canada. My relationship with the children was growing everyday and the thought of leaving them and Michelle was heartbreaking.

Michelle and I both knew where we wanted to go. We wanted to be together. We wanted to be married to one another. As the weeks passed, we waited for her divorce to become final.

In late June we went to a musical concert where a band called "YES" was playing. I had secretly emailed Jon Anderson —the lead singer of the band and Michelle's favorite performer— some weeks earlier asking if I could pass him a note before the concert so that he might say something while on stage and I could propose marriage to Michelle.

At the concert I passed my note along with some traditionally bound feathers through security to him. Mr. Anderson walked on stage with the feathers and in the middle of the concert stopped and wished Michelle and I luck on our upcoming marriage.

Michelle turned to me and said, "You didn't!"

I turned to her and said, "I did." Then I pulled out a diamond ring and asked her, "Will you marry me?"

It was wonderful. Though I got a bit nervous because she waited a good two minutes or more in all the excitement to tell me, "Yes, I'll marry you." It was a night we both will remember the rest of our lives.

To our dismay there were some problems and Michelle's divorce got delayed. This caused some hard nights of worrying for both of us. It was not until July 22 it became final. I had until July 29th before I had to leave the country. We needed the divorce certificate from the court before we could get a marriage license, and there would be a three day wait after that was issued before we could get married. We were running out of time. It was not until the afternoon of July 24th that we got the divorce certificate. From there we walked directly over to City Hall where we got our marriage certificate. It was Friday the 24th.

On the following Monday, July 27th, we got married. Our families came from Canada and Massachusetts. We had a small wedding held in a local park. Afterwards, we went out to a nice restaurant to have dinner. It all went well and Michelle and I are a living testament to the fact that you can put a nice wedding together in under forty-eight hours.

The next day we drove up to the *Immigration and Naturalization Service* to file the paperwork. We had everything but two vital pieces of paper. So we headed out to get those. The next day we returned with the documentation, but now the INS safe would not open and the papers we needed were filed in that safe. Michelle and I both felt a huge dark presence pass over the office as if retreating just before the safe finally started to work correctly and opened.

At last we got the paperwork submitted and had to drive down to yet another INS office in Boston, Massachusetts. The New Hampshire office didn't have the proper equipment for the next step in the process.

In Boston, I was issued the remaining paperwork. Finally, all the paperwork was done and I wouldn't have to leave my new family. It was 4:35pm on July 29th, exactly ninety days after I had entered the United States and the last day before my visa waiver ran out.

We felt that we had done the impossible. It is hard to describe the relief I experienced knowing that I would not have to leave the children or my new wife who was literally my soul.

All that while that we were dealing with these everyday human issues —or 3D reality issues as we often called them— the most amazing things were happening on another front. As Michelle and I joined together, we opened up a world of magic. We began to discover *The Voices of the Earth.*

<u>Paul</u>
The Voices of the Earth

After I got settled in with Michelle in New Hampshire, I began to practice playing my water drum again. My water drum was made by Tom, the medicine man from the Wahta reserve. He had done his best to teach me a few songs. It was my first medicine tool.

On one particular evening, I went outside after the children went to bed to play it. A rain storm just passed and there was a magical feeling in the air. As I began to play I looked up and a lightning bolt branched out into a couple of dozen forks directly above my head. I became somewhat excited and ran inside to tell Michelle. We didn't know whether it was coincidence or not, but I felt charged up. Michelle told me she felt a little left out and wanted to join in.

I began to play my drum and we both began to meditate in the living room. As I played, I sang softly. Michelle's eyes began to close and her body began to waiver. All of a sudden one of the children called out. I walked down to their bedroom to see what was the matter. After tending to the children I turned around to find Michelle's body staggering down the hall. I knew something was wrong and hurried to grab her.

Something wasn't right at all. She was not herself and indeed, did not appear to be Michelle. Still, it wasn't Alex, Rovere or any other being we had met previously.

"Michelle? Michelle, are you okay?" I asked.

She said nothing and looked at me with frightened eyes. She appeared to be disoriented and her motor control was poor to say the least. I guided her into the bedroom and sat her down. I was quickly beginning to realize that it was definitely not Michelle I was speaking to, nor was it an ET. Whoever this was appeared surprised, shocked and frightened at what they were experiencing.

I looked calmly at the person in her and said, "It's okay. You're safe. You're only going to be here for a short time.

"Can you speak?" I asked.

The being mouthed some words and appeared to have a great deal of difficulty articulating anything at all.

"Keep trying," I said. "Repeat what you just said please. I saw your mouth move but could not make out any of the words."

"Wh - er? Where? Where am I?" they asked. Their voice and presence appeared to be male.

"New Hampshire. Merrimack, New Hampshire," I replied.

"H-w? How?" they asked.

"We prayed to the Earth and asked her for help. It appears she sent you. My name is Paul. What is your name?" I asked.

Slowly the person lifted there hand so that their palm was facing me then they fell back on the bed and went unconscious. A moment later Michelle's eyes opened and her body sprang up on the bed. It was Rovere.

"What the heck are you two doing? Did you call up some poor Native or one of the ancient ones?" he asked in a half scolding tone.

"All I did was play my drum," I explained.

I looked at Rove and saw the playful expression in his eyes. I began to understand that he knew exactly what was going on and was just teasing us. He explained nothing further, and after making sure that we were okay he left and we switched Michelle back into her body.

"Did you see anything?" I asked.

"No. I completely blacked out. What happened? Michelle replied.

"I'm not entirely sure," I began. "I was playing the drum, your eyes closed, then the kids called. Then I saw you staggering down the hall. What do you remember?"

"I was listening to you play the drum and the sound of the rhythm drew me into a deep state. My God, I'm a sucker for the effects of music. The next thing I remember is waking up on the bed," Michelle explained. "Dear God, I'm hungry. cereal, I've got to have cereal right now!" She said in a near panic. "I can't explain it. Out of the way." Michelle then hurried out to the kitchen and practically inhaled a bowl of cereal and milk.

We talked some more and then called it a night, but not before agreeing that we would try it again as soon as we had a chance. We were both very tired.

It was a few days before we had a chance to play the drum again. We waited until the evening when the children were in bed. Just in case something happened again, Michelle was sitting in a chair where her body would be safe. I was kneeling in front of her playing the drum. Michelle's eyes closed slowly after a few minutes or so and she sat motionless. I continued playing the drum and singing quietly. Slowly Michelle's eyes opened, but it was not Michelle. The shape of her eyes was different and the person behind them struggled to speak.

"Ppppaaaul," he said, pointing his finger at me.

"Yes, Paul!" I said. I pointed to myself.

"Where?" the being asked.

"New Hampshire," I replied.

They nodded their head as though they understood something.

"When?" They asked.

I told them the exact date, day and the time.

"Is it your time and date as well?" I asked.

They nodded their head again. "Yes."

"Good. Good!" I said with excitement.

"Why?" he asked. "Why?" He shook his head in wonder and disbelief.

"We asked the Earth for help and she sent you. We need your help. We need to know what the Earth needs. We are star people, born into this life to help with the prophecy. We need you to teach us. You speak to the Earth and know what she needs," I explained.

We exchanged some more sketchy dialog. The person in Michelle's body said very little. It was clear that whoever I was speaking to was being extremely cautious. They appeared to be overwhelmed by the experience, yet still possessed the ability to absorb the shock of having their consciousness transferred to another location and speak coherently with me. Nevertheless, they clearly were struggling to make sense of it.

After a short while, they appeared to become groggy. Just before their eyes closed they said, "Uma Hawkna Kautchura." Then they were gone. Michelle returned and we struggled for the next few days to find the word "kautchura" in any aboriginal language we could get information on. But after many dead ends our search ended in vane.

A few days later, just after 9:00 PM, I went outside with Michelle to put down some tobacco, pray and play our water drum. As we played the drum we gave thanks to the Creator, the Earth, our guides and teachers. We prayed for strength and guidance from the Earth. The wind began to blow quite strong. Next we put down some tobacco and I began to play the drum. Michelle went into a trance. Her body walked forward and bumped into me, as if drawn by the drum beat.

Her body opened its eyes and I could tell it was the same person as before. The shape of the eyes was the same, as was the energy. He looked into the wind and smiled. Then he opened his hands and said, "Wind!" The wind picked up to a fierce howl about twice the intensity it was blowing before he arrived. I held up my right hand.

"Ooooooh," I said. I looked over. The person in Michelle was smiling.

I asked, "Uma? Uma Hawkna? Kautchura?" I pronounced the words I suspected were a name I had heard the last time from this person.

He turned around and looked at the town from the hill where we stood. I pointed and said "Merrimack. Merrimack, New Hampshire." I waved my hand across the landscape.

The person we called Uma turned to me and asked with a strained voice, "Paul?"

"Yes, Paul," I said. "We didn't forget about you. Our teacher told us to call you on the new moon. We're sorry we called you sooner. Can we please call you on the new moon?"

Uma smiled. Closed his eyes and said, "Wind." Then he grabbed my right hand, pulled it out so that my palm was facing up, and with his right hand in a fist, slapped his fist into my palm. He said it again, "Wind." Then he let his head fall back and he was gone. Michelle returned to consciousness a few seconds later.

She said she saw patterns and heard a voice tell her to remember the patterns because they were important. We went inside and she drew them while I recounted what happened on my end. I was in a state of shock and exhilaration.

On May 23rd, Michelle and I went canoeing. We paddled down a small river system that ran behind the place where I stored my canoe. I heard there was a lake down the river, and so we went to explore.

After struggling up some fast moving water, we soon navigated the twists and turns with smooth agility.

On arriving at the lake we paddled through some wind and explored along the shoreline. We found a beautiful little campsite on an island that was covered on one side by marsh. We docked the canoe and stepped ashore. Michelle was exceedingly pleased with herself that she did not fall into the water in the process. We pulled the canoe up on shore and climbed a small incline to a flat area on top of the island that seemed like a perfect place to pitch a tent. We split up to do some exploring.

On my return to the top of the hill I found Michelle had already started to meditate and work on generating energy. I joined her and took out some tobacco to put down. As we meditated I felt a presence approach. My state began to change and I felt waves of deep emotion. I felt like I was going to collapse on my knees. The feelings and sensations became overwhelming and finally I did fall to my knees. I felt as though someone else had joined me inside myself.

"Who was this?" I thought. I felt my body moving on its own and turned around to look at Michelle.

Then the labored words, "Who, who are you?" came out of my mouth as I looked at Michelle.

"Kristance.

My body did not respond. I felt someone looking out of my eyes, wide with wonder. Eventually a voice came out of me, "Kris." Then, whoever was inside of me felt the tobacco in my hand. I found myself looking at the sun, then at my watch to determine direction. I knew it was the person we called Uma. He was looking for the east.

Then my body knelt down and cleared an area of pine needles from the forest floor to form a small circle. Uma then put a small bundle of tobacco in the middle. He took Michelle's hand and put it into the tobacco so that she would put some down as well. After, he rubbed her hand in the dirt, followed by his own. He then directed Michelle's hand to her face, and rubbed dirt on her face. Again he followed by rubbing dirt on his face, or rather, my face. Then Uma rubbed his hand on Michelle's hand. Next Uma knelt down by the small fire pit he had just created and prayed. Michelle joined him briefly. As she did, I felt Uma gradually leave my body. Then Michelle walked around to my left. I felt like I was in shock from enduring such deep emotions.

I looked up. "Rove?" I asked. It did not look like Michelle.

"Ya," he replied. "Cute trick."

"I didn't expect him to come through my body," I said to Rove.

"Oh no?" Rove asked with playful sarcasm.

I was on the verge of tears.

"It's a shock to your body, ah?" said Rove. "Look behind you. The Earth has left something for you. She gathered them up while you were busy."

I turned around. Directly behind me was a small bundle of twenty or thirty sticks that were approximately three to five inches in length. They had not been there before!

"You figure out what to do with them. Here, give her back to me now." This was a phrase Rove would use when he wanted me to send Michelle back to her body. A moment later Michelle was back.

"Wow!" Michelle said. "We have the coolest job in the world!"

"Don't we?" I responded rhetorically.

"Look, Rove showed me where the Earth left us a gift." I pointed to the sticks and said, "Rove said we should figure out what to do with them." I knew what to do, I could feel it. We gathered the sticks and made a small wood teepee with them in preparation for a fire.

A moment later the wind, which had been blowing all day, calmed.

I had forgotten to bring matches or a lighter. I didn't anticipate we would burn anything that day, so we offered what we had to the Mother Earth and explained that we did not have matches, that we loved her, and that we gave thanks for bringing all that she had to us.

Michelle and I stood facing each other with our palms almost touching. I began to sing a song of thanks that I simply made up on the spot. Michelle's eyes closed and I could see she was falling into an altered state once again. Soon, Uma appeared, this time in Michelle's body.

Uma motioned to me with two fingers to his head. I knew he was asking how we could have both been in the same body at the same time.

"You saw out of my eyes a minute ago, yes?" I said to him.
He nodded in the affirmative and struggled to say, "K... K... Kris"

"Yes," I said, "Kristance."

Uma nodded and smiled.

I knew he didn't have much time so I tried to explain as quickly as I could that I was designed differently. When people came into me, they joined me. However when people went into Michelle, she would first come into me, then the visitor would go into Michelle's body.

"The Earth left a gift for us," I said.

Uma turned around and looked. I pointed to the small fire pit and said, "We prepared a fire but we have no matches or a lighter to start it with."

Uma picked up a stick from the small fire pit and put it in my palm, then closed my hand over the stick. He smiled and said, "The Earth is in agreement. That is good."

I looked and could feel Uma's words. I felt a great wave of emotion.

"White Eagle," Uma said.

"White Eagle?" I said with excitement. Uma was finally telling us his name. "White Eagle!" I said again.

White Eagle nodded and smiled. He trusted us enough to tell us his name. I gave him a huge hug and burst into tears, then stood back to look him in the eyes.

White Eagle then took his right hand, and with his palm open, slapped himself on the chest, smiled broadly and said, "Ed."

"Ed," I said. Tears of joy rolled down my face. Then, without warning Michelle's body went limp. A moment later she was back.

We spoke with excitement for a while about Ed White Eagle and the cautious, but humble, manner in which he introduced himself to us. We were overjoyed. We had a new friend and teacher. Soon Rove came into Michelle and spoke to both of us. He would not give us any answers. He just said, "This is yours to figure out." Then he was gone. Michelle and I talked for a bit before we settled down. Then we walked down to the water and launched the canoe to continue on our day's paddle.

The next Sunday, Michelle and I went out to do our spiritual work. We travelled about the countryside and got lost. We felt the presence of Molanie. She asked to speak to us. We both agreed and she came in through Michelle. Michelle entered me so that we both could hear Molanie speak.

Molanie guided us to a rock quarry that had a pathway to a waterfall. Michelle knew of the rock quarry but not the particular path we took. Along the way both Michelle and I were amazed that we somehow ended up back in Milford, NH, since we were going in the opposite direction and were well north of Milford when Molanie appeared. This had happened once before with Rovere. He guided us through a short cut by the beach. Later we went down the same road only to find out that the road led to a different place than the first time when we were with him. His short cut took over thirty minutes off our drive and took us to the main route through the area. But when we took it again, it lead to a dead-end by the ocean.

When we arrived at the quarry, Molanie gave us instructions on how to get to the place she thought would be good for us to work. We switched back over and Michelle entered her body once again. Then we got our things out of the car and walked up the path Molanie had instructed us to take.

Eventually we arrived at a beautiful waterfall and found a campsite at the top of the falls. The area was resplendent with beautiful old carved rock and deciduous forest. We gathered some sticks and two small pieces of birch bark from a tree so we could start a fire.

We built up the fire pit with sticks. One of the sticks had fallen on Michelle's head as we were gathering wood. We set this piece aside, then we laid down some tobacco on top of the small fire teepee we built.

We both started to meditate. Michelle stood on the west side of the fire, while I stood on the east side of the fire.

I looked at Michelle and said, "Let's start."

She looked back and said, "Okay. I'll work on my state."

As I watched, Michelle appeared to become groggy and meditative. I began to play the water drum. I could see Michelle's body moving differently and the energy changed between us. I saw her walk towards the fire. The last time Ed had shown up he walked toward the sound of the drum. I moved so that if he did it again Michelle's body wouldn't walk into the fire.

As the energy changed I saw her eyes open. It was not Michelle. It was Ed White Eagle.

"Pau..." Ed mouthed my name again.

"Yes, it's me. Hi Ed," I responded.

He looked at the fire and at the sun, then got down on his knees facing east. I walked around to the other side of the fire pit to watch. Ed looked at the fire pit and at some of the old charred wood from long ago and proceeded to pull some of it out. I pulled some out as well. We did this without disturbing the small teepee of wood that Michelle and I had built.

After he prayed, Ed stood up and said, "Star People."

"Yes," I said. "We were born here. Made by the Rye-hun. They told me you've seen them. The small ones with big eyes, Rye-hun."

Ed looked at me and put his hand about waist level and said, "Mooshees?"

"Mooshees?" I said with a smile. "They are Rye-hun, pronounced Rye-hhhhuhhhhn," I told him, emphasizing the nasal sound at the end of the 'huh.'

Then I looked at him and said, "Important, we don't remember everything here. We remember everything when we are home." I pointed at the sky as I said this. "Here, because we are in the dream, we don't remember everything about the prophecy."

"Star people forget?" he said, then grabbed my right hand and pointed, directing me to walk to the water.

We walked out onto a small rock outcropping and Ed stuck his hand in the water. He directed me to do the same.

"Feel," he said. "Water remembers. Water will protect Star People."

I repeated what he said.

"Rocks remember everything. If you want to remember something, ask a rock," Ed said. Then he turned around to look at the shore and said, "The creepers and the bugs remember. They live in the ground and talk to the Earth."

White Eagle turned around and put his hand up in the air and said, "Wind." The wind suddenly picked up. Before there had not even been a breeze.

I could feel Michelle inside of me. We both stood in awe. "How do you bring the wind and calm it down?"

He grabbed my hand and put his finger to his mouth indicating I should be quiet. "Listen," he said.

I listened. Then the wind settled. Ed held up my hand and I said, "Wind."

Ed looked at me and indicated with his hands that there were two of us, Michelle and I, in my body. He did this as though asking a question.

I nodded yes.

"Both of you must have a clear heart."

I raised my hand a certain way. Ed mimicked the way I had done it and said, "No, like this." He pushed his upward and at an angle and forcefully said, "Wind."

The wind started to blow again.

After the wind settled we tried it again. As though sensing we were trying to direct the wind, which is exactly how we felt at that moment, Ed said firmly, "The wind is a brother, not a servant."

I nodded my head. I could feel Michelle working inside me, listening to Ed. We attempted to work in consensus. We pushed my hand forward and said, "Wind." Suddenly the wind picked up.

"Wind is learning to trust you," Ed said. "I've talked to wind for many years. Hmm, can't talk good here. Easier to move though." He felt his neck. "Young skin," he said and smiled. Then he moved both arms and legs up and down. "Ah! No pain." He smiled like a kid.

We walked back up to the fire pit. Ed stomped his feet on the ground while he walked. "Solid Earth," he said. I stomped around with him. We talked a bit, then walked down to the water one more time. After returning, Ed looked at me and said, "Find a place where the Earth is porous. A place where there are ants. Go there three times. Then tell me." Then, suddenly, he looked across the water. I looked and could feel it was one of the team, probably Rovere.

"Can you see that?" I asked Ed.

Without answering, Ed closed his eyes and Michelle's body went limp. She collapsed into my arms. A few seconds later she was conscious in her own body again. We looked at each other with a look of amazement. We hugged each other. After a while Michelle and I headed back.

 Molanie joined us on the way. When we arrived at the apartment we sat in our parked car and talked. Molanie surprised us by tapping me on the head with some kind of energy. When she did, Michelle and I felt melded smoothly as one being. She did this without warning and it took us both totally by surprise. The effect of melding was strange. Our state of being changed dramatically. We sat experiencing the state for some time. Rovere arrived and he and Molanie switched over.

"She wants you to experience this state for a while," he said. Rovere tapped us on the head twice in two different spots on our forehead.

Suddenly we remembered who we were as a single being. Michelle and I melded as one, a whole being long ago. We were the being we were before we split. The feeling is hard to describe in words. It was an incredible experience. We walked back into the apartment and into the bedroom. Rovere apologized, saying that he had to bring us back now. Then he pulled Michelle away from me and out of my body.

The state had been so intense and so real it created a sensation of being emotionally and spiritually ripped in half when he took her away. We both fell into each others arms, crying. It took some time before we could function normally again.

<u>*Paul*</u>

Making the Rain Rattle

"This is the spot," White Eagle declared with sure authority. He spread his arms wide over the clearing in the rock quarry.

"Take three leaves from a tree here. Boil up sugar and water into a paste, then dip both sides of each leaf into the paste one time on each side. Come early in the morning. Pray to the east, to the rising sun. Clear yourselves. Then place the leaves facing east and west, not north and south. Make an offering to the ants. Tell them you need their help. Then go dance around that rock over there," he pointed to a large embedded rock not far from us. "Dance around it five times, counter-clockwise in larger and larger circles. Then go sit on the high ground over there and wait to see if eagles come." He was very specific about each step in the process. His explanation of exactly how to do each step was very detailed.

Suddenly he looked up and said, "Look, eagles."

I looked up. "Aren't those hawks?" I asked.

"No," he replied, "hawks have tail feathers like this." He motioned with his hands, spreading all his fingers wide. "Eagles have feathers like this." He pointed all the fingers on one hand straight.

I looked up. White Eagle raised his hand, the wind started to blow. "Wind," he said. Then he turned to me and I could see he was leaving Michelle's body as he appeared dizzy and his eyes closed.

Michelle soon reappeared. We walked over to the ant hill. I began to feel dizzy and then Michelle soon followed. Something was happening. I felt Michelle move into me, then her body opened its eyes.

"Hah! It worked!" White Eagle exclaimed.

"How did you do that?" I asked.

"I prayed to Grandfather to bring me back," he replied.

White Eagle then went on to question us about everything he had told us. He listened and corrected any mistakes we made. He had us repeat his instructions over again until we had them straight in our heads and could explain them to him correctly.

Soon White Eagle left and Rove appeared. Rove, Michelle and I discussed what happened. I listened for Michelle's voice inside of me, then voiced the questions she thought to me. Sometimes Rove would telepathically hear Michelle and answer the question as she was communicating it to me before I spoke out loud.

Rove left after a few minutes and Michelle was back in her body. We went over White Eagle's instructions and made sure it was clear in our heads.

Michelle and I planned to rest the next evening, so we took the children over to the local park where they could play a while. We were not there long before Rove showed up. He told Michelle and I that he had something important to talk about.

"White Eagle is not doing too well," Rove said.

"What do you mean?" Michelle and I both asked simultaneously.

Rove began a long explanation. "He hasn't eaten or drank in days. All he does is fast and pray to see you again. He told his son what's been happening and his son thinks he's crazy. His son is looking around for a nursing home to put him in."

Rove went on to explain that in White Eagle's culture death did not mean the same thing as it did the average person. Rove said, "He is lying down to let himself die. He is not afraid of death and he thinks if he leaves his body he will be able to enter Michelle's body permanently so he can teach you both. He knows that because she goes inside of you, he is not killing her, thus he believes that taking over her body like that would be okay. But it's not, is it?" Rove almost smiled. "He believes his spirit will be able to stay here with you and work, but it will not work out the way he thinks. He will not be able to do it because there is still some work he has to do on his soul."

"Can we speak to him?" we asked.

"What are you going to say to him?" Rove asked.

Together we thought about much of what Rove said and we came to a consensus. Then Rove brought White Eagle to us. Michelle's body went limp, then her head raised. White Eagle was there. He looked around trying to determine where he was.

"Ed," I said. White Eagle looked at me.

"How are you?" I asked.

He looked at me and nodded.

"Rove, tells me you haven't been eating or drinking. You need to eat and drink. We need you alive."

"But I could stay in spirit and teach you. Star people need help," he said.

"You think you can come and take over Michelle's body. It will not be allowed. She and I have work to do. We need you to teach us. You must teach us this way, when we call," I said.

"But my spirit could be here," he said pointing at the sky, "and come and teach you."

We could hear Rove asking to speak with him. "Watch closely," I said. I raised my hand to my temple and closed my eyes. I felt Rove enter me and join with Michelle and me. We opened our eyes. It was clear that Rove was in control.

White Eagle then stood up on his feet. He looked bewildered. "You are the Traveller!" He got on his knees. "Oh! You are the Traveller!" Ed then stood up and started looking around like he was lost.

Rove smiled and said, "Take a deep breath. Sit down."

"Sit down! How can I sit down?" White Eagle exclaimed. "You are the Traveller." After a moment, White Eagle brought himself to sit. Clearly he was in an excited and overwhelmed state.

White Eagle's eyes opened wide. "You are the Traveller!" He exclaimed yet again as if he couldn't make himself believe it. "You are the Traveller! How can this be? How can you do this?"

Rove raised his right hand, snapped his fingers and said, "Magic," then smiled at White Eagle who looked back in astonishment. Rove held up three fingers and indicated with his hand that three beings were now in my body.

"The Elder Brother, the Younger Brother, and the Spider Woman? Do you fight over the Spider Woman?" Ed asked. It was as if he were trying to fit what was going on into his paradigm.

"No," Rove replied.

"How?" asked White Eagle.

"Love," Rove responded.

Then Rove started to speak. "You have to stay in your body. You have to live. This is all planned. It's part of the prophecy. You remember this plan when you are home with the Mooshee's but you forget when you are here. You cannot die. You have to stay alive so you can teach these two," he said as he pointed to my body.

"You think your spirit can stay but it cannot. Listen very closely. You have some work on your spirit you must do first before you would be able to do that."

"But my son will put me in a nursing home. I will die there anyway," Ed said in an incredulous tone.

"I will take care of your son," Rove said. "Did you think maybe he is jealous because his is the son and not the grandson of White Eagle?" Rove had explained earlier that certain medicine people passed the messages and knowledge from grandfather to grandson and that the middle generation was skipped when passing down the knowledge of old medicine.

"Your son will be fine. He will not put you in a nursing home. Get up and eat some food when you return. Go about your business. It will be fine." Rove paused then stared at White Eagle. "So, what are you going to do?"

"I will think about this. If the Traveller tells me to live I will think about this," he said. Then White Eagle was gone and Rove was in Michelle's body.

"What face did you show him Rove? He looked like he was going to faint when you went in me?" I asked.

"I showed him a face so that there would be no question in his mind as to who I was," answered Rove.

"You said he remembered when he was home with the Mooshee's. He was one of the aboriginals who sat in the circle with me on shipboard wasn't he?" I asked.

I had an experience several months earlier where I was sitting in a circle with some aboriginal people in a room that was all white. I was in a heightened state of awareness and felt intense energy in the room. There was a woman next to me who spoke with broken English in a thick Native accent. She said, "You are like an orange that peels itself."

Later, when I asked Alex about the experience he responded by explaining it was a compliment. That you peel an orange to get to the sweet bits. It was an allegory she was using to discribe my efforts at self discovery.

I asked again, "Was he one of the Native Americans I sat with on shipboard?"

Rove responded to my question with a question. "What do you think? You think that he is here because he is a stranger? You think this is all accident? Boy, are you stupid. If she was not in there with you I would slap you!" He smiled coyly at me, then he left. But not before reassuring us that Ed would be eating steak by tomorrow night. Michelle and I were both relieved. Rove also said that thunderstorms were coming that night and they would be very intense. He said we should wait until after the next full moon before returning to the ants.

The next day Ed showed up briefly. He said he had to tell us something important. Ed told us it was important to plant wheat, tobacco and corn as soon as possible. We explained we had found a plant related to the tobacco plant, but we couldn't get actual tobacco seeds. We didn't know if that was acceptable.

"Plant it," Ed said sternly.

"Rove, the Traveller, told us to wait until after the full moon to see the ants because of the storms," we explained. We had been having a lot of terrible thunder storms— many more than usual for the time of year.

"The storms will keep coming until you plant. Powerful medicine has been started," White Eagle said. He was adamant.

He agreed that we should wait until after the next full moon to start again with the ants. We were both disheartened. But we knew we would wait until the next full moon as White Eagle instructed.

When the next full moon arrived, White Eagle once again went over the instructions of what to do with the ants, we gathered three leaves and went home. We boiled up some sugar water and dipped the leaves as White Eagle had instructed. We stuck the works in the fridge, fixed a cup of tea and drank it as we talked about the days events. Then we went to bed. It was late.

The next day we got up before 5:30 AM and headed over to see the ants. When we arrived the sun was just getting up. The summer solstice was only a couple of weeks away and it was beginning to be light by around five 5:00 AM.

Following White Eagle's instructions, we found our ant hills, made note of the naturally occurring rocks in the area, built a small fire, burned some sweetgrass and prayed to the east. Next we layed down our leaves. A large ant came over to one of the leaves immediately. He appeared out of nowhere it seemed.

"That looks like a good sign, eh?" I mused.

We watched as the large ant walked over the leaf and began to harvest the sugar off of it. After a minute we walked down to the area we decided to dance in and began our dancing. We danced and sang. Afterwards, we walked down to the open area where the car was parked and stood to watch for birds, like White Eagle had instructed.

We felt a large presence circle us then stand in front of us. I looked around. Up in the sky behind us was a huge arrow shaped cloud pointing to the south.

"Look!" I said. "Rove is painting clouds again."

"What do you think it means?" Michelle asked. She paused a moment then said, "I just heard Rove say 'isn't it obvious?', maybe we should just look in the direction of the arrow." The second we turned and looked in that direction, a group of blue jays flew straight for us from some trees in front of us. We watched as they flew around a large tree then over to where we were standing, then they flew around us. They vanished down the road between the trees where we layed the leaf offerings for the ants. Then, we both realized simultaneously that we felt it was time to go. So we left.

We repeated the ceremony each morning for the next three days. Then we rested for three days. In the evening of the seventh day, as per White Eagle's instructions, we went to begin collecting rocks.

When we arrived, we called Rovere and asked if he would bring Ed to teach us the next step. Only a few moments later White Eagle arrived.

He walked over to where we had offered the leaves to the ants days before. "Here, look here," Ed began. "See these rocks here on the other side of the hills from the ant holes?"

"Yes," I replied.

"This is where rocks will be that the ants brought up, on the other side of the little hills from their holes. Look, here's one, take this one."

I picked up the small rock White Eagle pointed to.

"Here is another one here, and there too," he said.

We continued to pick them up as he directed. "There's a lot more holes here than there were a few days ago," we remarked as one.

"Yes, your offering of leaves nourished them. Now they are working hard for you. Here, look inside this hole." White Eagle pointed into a small ant hole and chuckled. We looked down into the hole and saw several ants working on moving a rock that was many times their combined size.

"Wow. They really are moving rocks up." I said.

"Of course." White Eagle looked surprised, "You don't believe?"

"Yes. I do. I mean we do. We can see with our own eyes now," I spoke our combined words.

After we knew what to look for, Michelle returned to her own body and we finished looking for rocks for that day. We made sure to take a close look so that we didn't miss any gifts from the "bug people." We placed the rocks in a medicine pouch that White Eagle had shown us how to make a few days before.

On the eighth day we arrived once again to collect more rocks. Much to Michelle's and my surprise there were a number of new little rocks strewn about the area that were not there the day before. We collected up our rocks. We were careful to only take rocks that were not there the day before. We didn't have any idea if there were a certain number or type of rock we were suppose to be looking for, so we didn't bother to count them. We simply collected the rocks that appeared to be recently put there. We repeated the same process for the ninth day then went home.

A few days later we were speaking to White Eagle when he said, "If you did everything right and the ants were willing to help you, you have one hundred and four rocks."

Michelle and I quickly tipped out our medicine pouch of rocks and counted them. Yes! White Eagle was right. We had one hundred and four rocks.

"Good," he said.

" How did you know?" I asked.

"That's how many you're supposed to have. Fifty two each." he state.

"Fifty two each?" Michelle and I asked with surprise.

"Yes. That's the way it is."

I know that Michelle was amazed by all this. The number of rocks that Ed White Eagle said we would need in order to make our rattle was identical to what the old man in the desert who "summoned" her with a rattle had told her were in his rattle. Could the ants we just asked for rocks for our rattle be the same as the creepers and crawlers that the man in the desert spoke of? The man in the desert told Michelle he had fifty-two stones in his rattle. And without counting at all, White Eagle was so sure we had exactly one hundred and four rocks in our medicine pouch, and he was right.

White Eagle told us the next step in building the rattle. We had to find a piece of wood. It had to be a piece that was about the thickness of a man's wrist and long enough that we could cut it a length equal to the distance from our elbow to our wrist.

"Look for a piece of wood that talks to you," he said. White Eagle said that he once looked for several years to find a piece of wood that spoke to him. "Somehow," he said if only to give us hope, "I think that Star People will find one sooner."

Michelle and I chuckled. We figured he was probably right. Knowing Rovere and his playful nature, we would probably find one sooner rather than later. Sure enough, after only a few days of searching I thought I had found a piece of wood from a fallen tree that was perfect. Michelle and I went to collect it. As we were walking out of the forest — which we didn't know at the time would end up being our backyard— Michelle stopped, looked at the ground and picked up a piece of dead wood that was a perfect fit for all of our criteria.

"I just stopped for some reason. I heard a voice in my head say, 'pick me up.' So I did," she said.

I looked at her, then at the wood that appeared to be some type of pine. For some reason I could not explain I had the overwhelming feeling she was right, and so we had found our piece of wood that "talked" to us for our rain rattle.

White Eagle instructed us to strip the bark off the wood and cut it to the correct length, then we cut a small section off to plug the bottom later on. Next we wrapped a long piece of rope around the length of the wood so that it would not split. Then I began the arduous task of hollowing out the wood. White Eagle said I could not use power tools and had to do everything by hand. I used an auger, a wood chisel and a hammer. It took about two days to hollow out. Then I fashioned a plug to fit into the top of the rattle to seal it up with after all was done.

White Eagle was impressed with my work and I felt good. Next, I sanded down the wood and treated it with linseed oil. We glued on the bottom cover and let it dry for two days. Following that, we carved the symbols for our spirit names on the rattle. One represented myself, the other Michelle, and the third Rove, who White Eagle to this day refers to as the Traveller. After carving the symbols, I painted them with our colors. Rovere insisted his be painted white. My symbol I painted blue and Michelle's purple.

All the while that we were doing this, we were on the look out for feathers. We had to find some feathers. We couldn't buy them. The way we found them just blew me and Michelle away.

Michelle and I had been keeping our eyes open for weeks for some large feathers. We were having no luck at all. One day Rove was in Michelle's body and he and I were driving to go somewhere.

"Did you check out that duck pond over there for feathers yet?" Rove asked.

Taking his hint, I pulled a U-turn and drove into a large parking lot by a college that bordered on the duck pond.

"Perhaps you should go right," Rove said.

But the duck pond was to the left. I ignored Rove's suggestion and turned left. I drove a short distance but could not find a place to park.

"Maybe we should go down here," I said and pointed to the right.

"You mean the way I said to go originally?" Rove interjected.

As I drove in the direction Rove originally suggested, I saw that there was only one parking space left. It was by the road and quite some distance from the duck pond. I pulled the car in and got ready for a walk to the pond. When I did, I could not believe my eyes. Directly in front of the car were four pristine large goose wing feathers.

I broke into laughter and then I hurried to gather up the feathers. When I returned to the car, I was greeted by a rather smug looking being. "Now do you believe Rove?" Rovere stated with a tone of justice.

We learned from White Eagle how to bundle the feathers with other smaller feathers. It is a very beautiful art. This gave us four bundles of feathers. Three of the bundles we used for the rain rattle. The fourth and most beautiful of the bundles we saved for our next adventure that was unfolding just as we were finishing the rattle.

We varnished the rain rattle which took about a week of varnishing, sanding and re-varnishing. We put in the rocks the ants had given us, attached the feathers, then plugged the rattle and glued it firmly shut. One final coat of varnish on the plug and we had our first hand made medicine tool.

From start to finish it took us approximately two months to construct our rain rattle. It looked beautiful. We had to be very careful not to shake it until the rattle was fully dried or else the rocks could stick to the inner traces of glue and varnish, so we had to wait another two days. Once again, following White Eagle's instructions, we drove down to see the ants who had given us the rocks to show them the rattle and shake it for them. White Eagle said we would not know what the rattle would bring until we shook it. To this day we are constantly amazed at what happens when we do.

Paul
In Hollis Forest

The whole time we were working on making our rain rattle I searched around the countryside for small forested areas where we could work in private. I found a small town forest about thirty minutes from where we lived. There was an energy to it and I was drawn to the place. I took Michelle there one Saturday morning.

It was a very beautiful forest. There were a lot of glacial boulders, heavy green moss and a pleasant little stream that flowed down a hillside. Some of the trees were very old and large. There were old town walls made of stones like you see so often in New England running along both sides of the main path and in and out of the surrounding woods.

We went there that morning because White Eagle asked us to find a private place where we could do a specific task he asked us to do. After showing Michelle around a bit of the forest, we asked Rove to get White Eagle. White Eagle was soon in Michelle's body and she and I were sharing my "container".

"What a beautiful place you've found," White Eagle said after a short pause. He turned his head suddenly. "Hey! There are little people here. Look, over there."

I whirled my head around and saw a blur move behind some bushes. I looked back at White Eagle with wide eyes.

"What the heck was that?" I asked with surprise that bordered on shock.

White Eagle laughed and pointed again. "Little people. This is a place of the little people." He must have thought my reaction was amusing. White Eagle laughed.

I heard some bushes rustle behind me and I whirled around again only to find nothing, not even an animal there.

"They like to play with you. Maybe they like you?" White Eagle said.

Inside me, I could feel Michelle was all excited, but eventually, together, we managed to calm down. We talked to White Eagle about our original reasons for visiting. Without notice, in the middle of our conversation, Rove took over Michelle's body and White Eagle was gone.

"Sorry about that," Rove said, "His daughter-in-law is trying to wake him up to eat some lunch. I had to send him back."

"What's this about little people here, Rove?" I questioned. I had never told Rove about the little man I saw on the Wahta reserve. "You mean they're here too?" I asked with surprise.

"This is a nice place, huh? Maybe you should bring the children here sometime and let them play in the water," Rove said rather than answer my question.

"Why bring the children?" Michelle asked through my voice.

"Little people like children. Maybe you should talk to them. Why don't you try." With that Rove left. A brief second later, Michelle opened her eyes, she was once again in her own body.

"Did you hear that, Mick?" I asked.

"Yes. What do they mean, little people?" she asked with a nervous tone.

I began to explain rather hesitantly. "You remember I told you about what I saw on the Wahta reserve? The little man by the river. I've seen one of these beings with my own eyes. I don't like the idea either. It's definitely 'out there.' But I saw it with my own eyes. Tom told me about several reports from people on the reserve who had seen them too. Should we try and talk to them?"

"Oookay," she replied. It was obvious she would have preferred to get in the car and go home.

I focused my intent to make contact with whatever "little people" were, and Michelle opened up her being. When we open up and apply intent like this, both of us can elevate our psychic levels in ways neither of us can do alone.

Michelle said she heard a voice and began to relay what it was telling her. Then, whoever or whatever was speaking to her got the better of her. She continued to talk, but it wasn't her voice at all.

"Come back tonight. You can see us better when it's dark. Come back when it's dark," the voice from her body said. A moment later she was back.

"They want us to come back tonight, I guess," Michelle said.

"Okay. Geez. What's going to happen. I guess we'll see, eh?" I said. I was almost at a loss for words.

Evening came and one thing led to another. There were a lot of issues around our daily, typical human life that got in the way and we never made it to the forest. We missed the next night as well. Two days after our meeting in the forest Molanie came to see us.

"It's come to my attention that the little people invited you to visit them. Correct?" Molanie inquired.

"Yes," I replied.

"When was this?" Molanie asked.

"Two day's ago," I answered hesitantly.

"And have you gone to see them yet?" she asked.

"No, we were busy. We were hoping to…" both Michelle and I tried to explain as a team.

"Busy," Molanie interrupted. "You know, they are quite put out that you didn't show up. Did you think it was an open invitation?"

"Oh dear," we said. We both realized there was a problem.

"So when are you going to go see them?" Molanie asked.

"Tonight. We'll make the time. We'll go tonight," I promised.

"Good. I'll let them know. Just a word of caution, precious. Be careful whom you think you're talking to and under no circumstance, none, dare take anything that is offered to you tonight. Even if it is the most wonderful magic you could ever ask for," Molanie explained.

We both nodded our understanding. Her warning made me more than a bit nervous about going back to the forest.

"Would you please tell them we're sorry. We really didn't mean to insult them," I implored her.

"I will. Let me see what I can do to appease them. After all, they are MY little people," she said in a matter of fact way, yet stressing the word "my".

We must have looked rather confused.

"Are you nervous?" Molanie asked.

"Yes," we said in tandem.

"Good," she replied. Then she closed her eyes and was gone.

We quickly made arrangements to free up our evening. Then after dinner, we headed over to the forest and waited for night to fall. We brought tobacco. I wished we had brought finger and toenail clippings as well. Tom told me that the little people liked nail clippings. They ground them down to use in medicines that they made.

We arrived just as it was getting dark. We walked in through the bush and over to our favorite rock. As we sat, Rovere called to us and asked to speak. A moment later he was there.

"Are you ready?" Rove asked.

"Yes. We've heard rustling and seen moving blurs, but nothing definite yet," Michelle and I said speaking with one voice from my body.

"Tubee!" Rove called out. "Tubee. Yes, Rove loves you. Come on, Tubee!"

"Tubee?" I thought.

Just then we noticed several very strange, very large lights come out of the darkness.

"Strange fireflies," Michelle said through my voice.

"What color are fireflies?" Rove asked.

"Green," I replied.

"What color are those?" Rove continued.

"They're orange! They're spinning!" Michelle and I both said with surprise.

"Bye," Rove said and then he was gone.

"Hello, dear one," came a voice from Michelle's body. I thought it was Molanie. "I see the little people are coming out to see you. Are you ready to apologize?"

"Yes mother. Can you ask them if we can speak to them please?" I asked.

"Ask them yourself," she said. There was some more light talk that was almost idle chit-chat.

"Tell me, do I feel like Molanie to you?" she said as she held out her hand.

I reached over and felt nothing similar to Molanie's presence or energy at all. "No. No you don't," I replied.

"Ha ha ha ha ha ha!" A wild cackle came out of Michelle's mouth. "You don't know nothing! You think you are so smart, but you can't even tell when we are here!"

I put my head in my hands, humiliated.

"We're very sorry about the other night. We had every intention of coming back but one thing led to another. We had to get things organized with the children. Then we had shopping to get done. Then it was time for bed. We're sorry," I attempted to explained.

"We made dinner for you. We all came to the Edge to see you and you didn't show up," exclaimed the high pitched voice. I could not make it out to be male or female.

"We're truly sorry. We didn't mean to offend you," we apologized again.

"You are sorry? Are you sure?" the little person asked in a belligerent tone.

"Yes. We didn't mean to offend you," we assured them.

As we spoke, orange lights moved around us. At times I would see one move slowly, then speed up to a blur and disappear. I knew they were not fireflies I was seeing.

"You think you are so brave and strong. You are the children of Alex and Molanie, yet you did not know? How could you not know?" The little being paused. "Did you know there are bears in these woods?" the little person asked.

"Are there? I've seen bear before. I've had one walk into my camp," I said. I doubted there were bears in that patch of forest.

"They do not scare you?" the person asked tauntingly.

"No," I said.

"What about wolves? There are wolves here too," they chortled.

"I am a wolf. Hasn't Rovere told you?" I answered.

"You are a wolf? There are wolves here, and they are bigger than you," the little person said.

"Then we would all be friends," I said.

"Friends. Hmmm. Okay. We can be friends. What do you want from us?" the little voice asked.

"To be friends. To share in information and knowledge," I answered honestly.

"What do you know that we would want?" the voice asked. "You see the lights from those things down there?" The little person pointed to a passing car in the distance. "Those lights make the trees sick. We work hard to make the trees healthy. The plants get hurt too.

"People hurt many things that we try to keep healthy. They cut down trees and throw garbage around. They drive through here on noisy things that disturb the forest. We don't like them and the trees don't either," the person said.

I tried to explain, "You know what is going to happen soon. You know about the prophecy concerning the Earth. You know what we have to do. We have to understand the planet and its needs. You and your people understand the planet very well. We need your help to understand her as well as you do. Clearly your people are important in what is going to happen in the near future."

"Yes. Do you have salt?" the being asked.

"No, but I have tobacco. We brought some as a gift. I understand you like hard salt. What about loose salt?" I asked.

"No. We need lick salt." The little person grabbed a leaf from a tree. "Here, would you like this? It is magic!"

"Thank you, no. Not this time. Maybe next time." I remembered Molanie's warning.

"Are you sure? It is magic," the little person said again.

"Thank you very much, but not this time. Maybe next time," I answered politely.

"You have to go. We will follow you down when you leave.

The next time Michelle's body opened its eyes, it appeared as if Molanie was in her. "Everything alright now?" she asked.

"Is it really you, mother?" I asked. Only half believing.

"More apprehensive are we? Here," she said. She reached out with her hand. I reached back and opened up to her. I could clearly feel Molanie's incredible energy.

"Satisfied, dear one?" Molanie asked. She knew I could feel her.

"Yes, thank you." I sighed with relief.

"You should think about leaving soon. The bugs are getting quite bad. I believe the little people are going to follow you down the hill on your way out of the forest. Good night child," she said, then closed her eyes. A moment later Michelle was back in her body. She had no idea about the little person, but had a vague memory of feeling Molanie nearby.

Michelle and I decided to wait just a little while longer so Michelle could get a sense of the magic in the forest. I took out my water drum and began to play. When I did, the little people lights seemed to be dancing to the music around us. It was a truly magical night.

It was getting late, so we gathered up our things and walked down the hill. By now it was very dark out, but we barely needed our flashlights because so many little orange lights followed us. They darted around then disappeared into the darkness before our eyes. At times the little lights hovered and spun. It was remarkable.

At the bottom of the hill, just before we reached the road, Michelle froze with fear and surprise. "What's that?" was all she managed to say.

Sometimes, when we were working, Michelle would stay in an ultra-sensitive state for hours. During those times she saw things that others would not see. Often these images scared or at least startled her. It was not that they were something new to her. She explained to me that for as long as she could remember she could see people who had passed away from this life and see events that happened in the past. Sometimes these images were vague and misty. Sometimes they were separate from her as if she were watching a movie. Still other times they would be as vivid as if they were solid and real in front of her. In this forest, she generally saw things very solid and lifelike.

I later found out that this night she was seeing people on the hillside in the woods. Not little people like we had seen with White Eagle, but human people. She said they were obviously victims of some kind of battle, yet they didn't seem to be doing anything but standing there. Even though I clearly sensed that they meant no harm, Michelle became frightened of them and suggested that we hurry to the car.

I understood she was feeling uneasy. We hurried out of the woods. As we approached the gate that led out of the forest limits, Michelle stopped again.

I felt an intense energy mass in front of me. That energy mass appeared to Michelle to be a large electric blue, transparent blob. It was standing in front of us, between us and the gate. She said that it was waving what looked like arms wildly back and forth. I could feel Rovere nearby, so I knew we were safe. Still it was clear that it bothered Michelle to see this thing blocking our exit out of the woods and the relative safety of our car. I reached forward with my hand and got a sense of a very strong presence. "I can feel something, but I can't see it. What do you see?" I asked.

"It's a large blue thing. It looks like it's waving its arms at us," Michelle said.

"I don't know about you but I feel like I've had enough for tonight. How about you?" I asked. Molanie had told us it was time to go, and it was obvious Michelle was shaken up. I just wanted to get her home.

"Yes." She was more than happy to call it quits for the night. The horror of the people on the hillside was the final straw for her.

We made it to the car and drove home. It took some time to unwind before we were ready for bed. Neither Michelle nor I slept well that night. Something was wrong. I couldn't figure out what it was, but something was truly bothering me.

Over the next two days, Molanie, Rovere and others explained to us some things about the little people and the Hollis forest. They told us that particular part of the forest has something very special in it called an Edge.

Edges, we were told, were inter-dimensional doorways between our Earth and other places. Most of these places were worlds around our world. Some were other places all together. We learned that there are many different kinds of Edges that lead to many different kinds of places. In the Hollis forest, there is an Edge that leads to the place where the little people live. They can come through the Edge, but it's seldom that a human can go through to their side, though it has happened, we were told.

It was explained to us that the Earth itself doesn't have a voice, but there are many kinds of beings that create a voice for her. We were told the little people were part of that voice and we had much to learn from them. With that in mind, a few days later we returned to the forest.

Michelle
Seeing Little People

It was dark in the forest outside of Hollis, NH. The ground was muddy. Water ran across the path at several places on the hill we climbed making it a tricky hike for a city girl like me. The air was thick with the smell of the spring grass. The trees were still and silent, and I was scared. I'm not generally a "scaredy-cat", but then again, I'm not generally walking through the forest in the middle of the night. At least I wasn't alone. Paul was with me.

He led me to a patch of rocks about twenty feet or so off the trail. He was excited by the intense energy that was flowing like music around us. I was excited by the adrenaline that was pumping through my body at the thought of all the fury things that come out in the forest at night, the least of which were bears. I was sure that at any moment I was going to turn around to find I was about to become a midnight snack for some rather unfriendly cousin of Yogi. Actually, it was more likely we were going to become a midnight snack for the million mosquitoes that were hovering near, just waiting for our deet to wear off.

When we approached the large rock in the center of the forest where we liked to sit, Paul asked, "Do you feel it? Do you sense anything? Do you feel them?"

I didn't answer right away. I wasn't sure if I was feeling anything other than nerves. Paul shut off the flashlights and there we sat in the dark, in the forest. surrounded by the most unusual energy I had ever experienced to that date.

The forest at night was like being on another planet. The sounds, the smells, the feelings were all so different to me. It took some time to settle. After a short while, my eyes began to adjust and I got over the fear of bears and skunks and was able to relax. Once I did, I could feel what Paul was sensing. There was something, or rather, someone nearby. Soon I was aware that there were people everywhere around me. I could feel them looking at us. It was a clear, sharp feeling.

We had been asked to go to the forest by Molanie. She told us that the "little people" of the forest were upset that we didn't show up after we talked to one of them two days before. Despite the excitement, I had been reluctant to go. It's not every day that someone tells you that not only the legends about little folk who live in the forest are true, but that they want to physically meet you. This was something that was sure to shake my paradigm beyond a comfortable level, if true. Little people less than a foot tall living in the woods was something I couldn't bring myself to believe.

So, there we were, Paul and I, Completer and Reflection, Batman and Robin, sitting on a cold damp rock, in the middle of the forest, in the pitch black darkness, feeling the eyes of a hundred beings on us. What now?

It seemed like the thing to do would be to communicate with them. We were not exactly sure how to do that. First we called out to them, greeting them with "hello's" and "promises not to hurt them". We followed these with "projections" of our thoughts of the same themes.

Paul began to play his water drum and sing. I joined in quietly. Soon the whole feeling of the forest changed. The eyes we felt watching us were coming closer. Within a few seconds time the forest came alive with balls of orange light. Dozens and dozens of orange lights filled the forest in front of us. They appeared a few at a time, then more until they were everywhere we looked. Most of them were at least two inches across, many were even bigger. They were intensely bright and orange. They danced around us—spinning, hovering and darting about. A few even came to us and landed on our shoulders, then darted away. They were not bugs or fireflies. They were far too large and they moved in what was obviously an intelligent manner. Besides, they were bright auburn orange. All the fireflies I've ever seen around here are much smaller and yellow-green in color.

We watched this light show with amazement. It was as if each light were alive and trying to talk to us. Paul suggested we open up to them and see if we could communicate with them. So we tried. Paul played his drum again, and I allowed myself to slip into a deep meditative state. Soon I was no longer aware. When I returned to consciousness, Paul told me what happened. Someone had spoken through my body.

He said it was one of the little people. The being explained that they decided at that time to appear in their "light" form. The being said that they lived in a place that is in another dimension. They said they crossed a doorway they called an Edge to get to us.

As Paul was telling me all this, I found myself fighting to believe him. My paradigm was being asked to bend beyond the point of breaking. It was much easier to think I was crazy and digressed into some delusion of being a "little forest folk" than to face the truth that they actually existed and one had been in my body. But as he spoke, his eyes were so wide with amazement that I knew something extraordinary had happened. He told me how the being made light appear. And how it called to the orange lights and they came closer.

I wanted to believe it, but it was just too much to comprehend. I found myself thinking, "Well this forest has strange fireflies and we are just so worked up we are imagining it." At this point, my body was filled with a strange feeling, and a chill ran up the back of my neck.

Then Paul said, "There is one on your shoulder."

I turned to see a bright ball of light on my shoulder. I could clearly see that there was nothing in the light at all. There was no firefly connected to the light. There was nothing at all on my shoulder except this ball of light about the size of a ping-pong ball.

I heard a voice from the ball speak to me. It was very quiet and to be honest I can't say it was an audible sound and not just in my head, but the voice said, "Look behind you."

I did. Behind me I saw something that to this day I still feel amazed by. I saw, standing by a bright orange light that hovered low to the ground that lit up a two foot area, a small bearded man. He stood only eight or nine inches tall. He was wearing green overall type pants and a light colored shirt. He had on a hat that was rolled at the brim as if its cloth was pinned up. He smiled at me and his eyes seemed to twinkle in the orange glow. Then he turned, and in a sprint so fast my eyes could barely follow him, he darted off into the darkness and was gone.

I sat there totally dumbfounded for a long moment. If I didn't see it with my own eyes I would never have believed it. Since then, I have seen them in this physical form at least three more times. Each time it takes me totally by surprise and reminds me that the little people are real physical beings, not just spirits or pretty lights in the night.

Paul
Lois

It took several days for Michelle to be ready to return to the forest after what she saw there. It was a hard time for me because I was experiencing a very strong desire to return there as soon as possible. I felt at peace in that little stretch of the woods, so much so that I would often walk there in the mornings when Michelle was at work. But there was more. Something about the little person I talked to was so familiar to me. The whole feeling that came with their presence was so comfortable to me that I found while we were away, I longed to get back and experience it again. It felt like home.

When Michelle and I returned to the forest, I was a bit concerned because of what she had seen just a few nights before. But I knew there was no malice in whatever those spirits were. We had only walked in about fifteen feet when I heard a high pitched sound come from Michelle. I whirled around.

"Hello, big people," the person inside her said as they marched past me. "Big bodies. Follow me."

I walked behind the being and up into the forest. The being inside of Michelle gave me a tour of some huge old trees and areas where the forest had been damaged. They also pointed out some things I had not seen before. I was familiar with the patch of forest we were in, but Michelle was not. It was clear that whoever was in her body knew the forest well. They knew it well enough to be able to just walk straight to things I didn't even know were there and that were not obvious at first glance.

One of these things was a circular "power ring" from a tree root that grew out of the ground. It was about a foot and a half wide. Tom from the Wahta reserve told me about such things and how medicine people harness their power by obtaining the root in a specific way.

After the tour, we settled down on a big rock. "Somebody is here who want's to talk to you," the little person said and before I could ask who, there was a switch over.

"Hello," the new being said.

"Hello," I replied with a smile. "I hope it's not too forward, but I could not tell with the others. You seem to be female.

"Yes, I am," she said, then started to talk about things.

What I heard next blew me away. The little person told me she was named Lois and she used to know me. She said they all use to know me before this life as "Little Andrew". She said that in that life, I was her brother. The story she told to me while we sat on that rock was amazing.

She said The Traveller had brought me to the place of the little people many years ago, before my current human life. I was a young spirit who needed to learn from them. I guess I didn't always pay attention to my lessons because at the young age of

468 years, I was run over by a tractor as I attempted to prevent it from destroying a part of the Edge. She said that was back in 1952.

I learned from her that their people live two thousand to three thousand of our years. They communicate both verbally and telepathically. They have a tremendous sense of play and can be quite mischievous. Their reason for crossing the Edge is to cultivate and harvest plants that live on this side of the Edge. They consider themselves the keepers of the forest and the Earth's gardeners.

As Lois spoke, my heart weighed heavy. Was this real? Was I really a little person in a former life? I remembered dreams I had as a young child — dreams of huge giants that towered over me as I hid with others my size in the grass. All the years that I spent in the woods and felt the presence of happy, bright spirits near me began to make sense. "You're people have always been around, always been near me, haven't they?" I asked.

"Yes. Why do you think you always found wood? We would bring it out for you, Twigman." replied Lois. As she said this she smiled and spoke sweetly. I looked back and returned the smile.

I remembered many a time when I would be out gathering wood on a canoe trip and heard or saw wood falling out of the trees near me. I attributed it to some natural phenomenon, only to have two or three more pieces of wood fall down around me at the same time. I felt the spirits of the forest near me, but did not know what they were. Now, not only did I know they were actually spirits, I realized they were the little people I had learned about from the Mohawk.

I spoke with Lois some more then she said, "Someone is here who wants to speak with you."

"Who is it?" I asked.

"You'll see." Then she closed her eyes and left.

A moment later Michelle's eyes opened and another little person was staring at me. I should mention that all the time this was going on, orange spinning lights were flying around us.

"It's good to see you again, I know you don't know me, but I know you," sang the little person as they spoke.

"Why are you singing your words?" I asked.

"A long time ago, you told me never to speak to you again, so that's why I'm singing," they answered in a singsong voice.

I laughed, then asked, "Did we not get along? Is that why I asked you not to speak to me again?"

"Oh no. We got along quite well. But you always thought I had a big mouth, so you told me never to speak to you again, because you said I would change your focus," they sang their answer.

"Change my focus?" I asked.

"If you knew what was here, then you would want to live here, and it would change your focus, that's what you told me," they continued.

"What's here?" I asked.

"I can't tell you that. You'll have to find out on your own and I have to go now."

"You can't tell me?"

They reached over and looked at me with eyes that expressed the affection of someone who had not seen an old friend for many years. I hugged them, then they left.

Lois reappeared a moment later and said, "It's getting late now and the bugs are getting bad. We can't keep them away from you for much longer."

I had been so caught up in conversation I failed to notice that swarms of mosquitoes hovered in small clouds about four or five feet away. I found it odd that no bugs were flying around either of our bodies.

"Okay," I said.

"I will walk down with you. The others will follow us out," she said.

We got up and walked down the pathway out of the forest. As we walked the little orange lights followed us down the path. Lois and I spoke some more. When we neared my car I told her about how my journey had started with the death of my nephew.

"I know what it's like to loose someone close. I lost a brother once," she said. She was referring to me.

I felt a deep pain in my heart and reached over to hug her. She hugged me in a way that brought tears to my eyes.

Michelle returned to her body a moment later. Across the road at the edge of the forest an orange light appeared. We both looked over and watched as it flew off into the forest. We looked behind us where we had just walked and watched as several orange lights that had followed us down the pathway flew back into the forest.

"Wow, my body feels terrible," Michelle said.

I was emotionally shaken but managed to ask, "What's wrong?"

"I don't know. I feel all shaky. Hang on, Rove's here," Michelle said.

She closed her eyes and a moment later Rove was in her body.

"The little people have a pretty high frequency, you know?" he said with his accented voice. "It's affected her body. Here, Rove will buffer. Her body will get used to it the more they come through her, but it will take some time."

"Will she be alright?" I asked. I was very concerned.

"Yes, she'll be okay. But you should both go home and get some rest."

After a minute Rove left and Michelle was back. We drove home. Michelle was very tired and worn out. I was emotionally shaken and my body felt different somehow. That night I did not sleep well at all. I tossed and turned. I felt a longing to talk with the little people and a feeling of missing them that was disproportionate to the data I had. By that I mean, I had only spoken to them a few times, yet some type of memory had been triggered in me. There was something very, very familiar abut them.

As I lie in bed, Michelle slept soundly, I looked outside and noticed several tiny orange balls of light resting on the branches of a bush beyond our window. I got out of bed and walked to the window for a closer look. Sure enough there were several little balls of orange light sitting on the branches of the bush.

"A trick of light." I thought. Then I looked down into the bush. There, inside the base of the bush at ground level, was a brilliant ball of orange light approximately six inches across that stayed there for as long as I was watched. After a time I went back to bed and lay down. I was emotionally pained and in a state of longing that I could not understand.   Somehow, through the night I must have fallen asleep because at one point I opened my eyes and it was daylight. I got up and walked over to the window and looked at the bushes. Nothing was there from the night before.

A few days later we returned to the forest in the early evening with our two youngest children. It was getting dark so we turned on our flashlights and marched along the path through the forest to the large rock we normally sat on. We brought some hard salt and our fourth set of ceremonially wrapped feathers that — with the help of the children— placed in the crook of a tree as a gift for the little people.

"I can feel one of them here now," Michelle said. "Ready?"

"Okay," I answered.

"Catch me," she said, then closed her eyes.

When Michelle's eyes opened next it was quite remarkable. The shape of her eyes had changed so that the outsides came to a sharp point. Her voice was high pitched and whoever this little person was he or she was very, very vibrant.

"You came back," the little being said.

"Yes, Rove suggested we bring the children. He said you are quite fond of children," I explained.

"Yes, we love children. They are still innocent and haven't become dull like big people get. Look, here comes everyone now," the little person said.

I turned around to look and watched as several dozen little orange spinning lights flew out of what seemed like nowhere in the forest and began to circle us. Without warning there was a huge, brilliant flash of orange light directly in front of my face. Everyone saw it.

"Wow!" I exclaimed. "That's incredible! Who was that?"

The person in Michelle's body just looked at me and smiled. We all watched as the little orange lights flew around us like a small air show. Some of them flew in an up and down pattern like a sine wave, others flew for a bit then hovered, then moved on. Some flew slowly then sped up very quickly, got very bright then disappeared into thin air.

None of the lights were green like fireflies. They were brilliant orange. They stayed bright for several minutes at a time. Some were many times larger than a firefly could ever physically be. We all watched in amazement.

After a while the little person in Michelle's body said, "I think you should go now. It's late and the children look like they'd be more comfortable back home."

"Yes, I think you're right," I replied.

"Thank you for showing them to us," the little person said and smiled.

"Our pleasure," I said.

When we walked out of the forest, we let our children lead us with the flashlights. For weeks afterwards the children talked about the lights of the little people. Though our youngest discovered he was not fond of the darkness of the forest, he did find the orange lights very fascinating.

Michelle and I met the little people many times after that. We had to work hard to establish protocol with them at first so that they would ask before jumping into Michelle's body. But with persistence and the help of Molanie, we soon got everyone's "ducks in a row", so to speak. Eventually, Michelle's body became acclimatized to their frequency so that she did not get ill after her body hosted them. Sometimes upwards of a dozen of them would come through in a single session. We found keeping the number of them that she hosted to one or two helped a great deal.

The knowledge the little people have shared with us has become invaluable to Michelle and me. Their friendship and sense of play is incredible. Everything is fun to them. More than once, one of them has scolded me in a playful fashion for being far too serious. Alex and Molanie have both told us over and over to make sure and play, that work is play. It seems the little people have made it a way of life.

<u>*Michelle*</u>
Little People, Little Problems

Even though Paul seemed to be in heaven with the little people, our interactions with them caused all kinds of annoying problems for me. First and most annoying was that I couldn't step five feet into just about any forested area for weeks without having my body highjacked. It was as if they just couldn't understand that they had to ask first. At one point one of them even ended up arguing with Paul after the being highjacked me. Paul told him he should ask, it was the way we do it. The little person insisted that I was some kind of bipedal telephone and if this is what I do, then why not use me to do it!

It got so bad some times that I would be walking with Paul in the woods and the next thing I knew I was somewhere totally different. Often the little people would strain my body to its limits. They are very lively and move through the forest quickly at root level. When they are in my body it seems that many of them just don't seem to understand that things are different when you are a "big people". Paul has told me that many a day he had a hard time keeping up with them as they ran through the trees, over rocks and around bushes. Though they run with an agility that I just do not possess myself, they run without much regard to the effects of their jaunts on me. On more than one occasion I returned to my body to find scratches, bruises and swollen knees.

It is not that the little people are the only ones who do things like this. Sometimes another being will enter my body and do things I would not, or could not do myself. This is one of the things that always amazes Paul and me when it happens. For example, one time when Paul and I were in Paul's body and White Eagle was in my body, we were driving down the road and passed a large overturned birch tree. We had been looking for a birch root for some time for a project we were working on. We just couldn't pass up such a good opportunity to get a root.

Paul pulled the car over. While he was opening the trunk to get out an ax, White Eagle, who had forgotten he was in the body of a five foot-four inch woman and remembered being his six foot-six inch large strong self, walked up to the tree roots. He found one that was about four and a half inches thick, then as we looked on with amazement, he grabbed the chosen root, twisted once and then ripped it off the tree!

He turned to Paul and I, freshly ripped root in hand, and said, "Here. This should do the trick."

Paul and I were astounded! How could he do that? There is no way Paul could have pulled the root off, never mind me. Paul looked at White Eagle and playfully said, "You know Ed, you're some gal!"

Ed remembered where he was, blushed then laughed.

Later, after White Eagle was gone home, Paul and I returned to the same tree and tried to break a root off ourselves. Regardless of how much effort we put into it, neither of us could break off anything near the size Ed did.

Ed also showed Paul and I how to do all kinds of Native crafts. He showed us how to bind feathers, make dreamcatchers and even cook Hopi flat bread. These were all things I did not know how to do, nor could I have done them so quickly as Ed did. When he did things like this you could see the years of experience in the way he moved my hands.

So it was not unusual to hear about, or see people doing things in my body that were impossible for me to do. Still, the fact that the little people never asked bothered me.

It is hard to tell how many little people Paul and I have talked to since we first encountered them. They very seldom will tell us their name. They seldom project a feeling of being male or female and they all seem to have the same high pitched voice when they speak through me.

Another little problem I had with these forest folk is that their sense of humor and my own didn't always see eye to eye. You see, they love to play practical jokes and it seems I have been the target of many hours of entertainment for them. This was especially true when we first met them before we got them to respect our rules of contact. It was not uncommon for them to find ways to separate Paul and I when we were in the woods — particularly if it were dark. Then, once he was a distance away, they did things to scare me. I would be standing there, waiting for Paul and trying not to panic when a branch would — for no apparent reason— swing out of the forest edge and whack me on the backside. Or the tops of the trees would shake, causing it to rain pine needles and acorns on my head. Sometimes they would make a strange animal noise or call out my name. But their favorite would be what I call hide and seek.

I would be standing on the path in an open area waiting for Paul to return and suddenly I would see a just a glimpse of little person standing by the edge of the woods then they would dart off. If I went over closer to get a better look, inevitably a tree branch would swing out and snap my bottom or a stick would come out of no where and snag my back pack. When I turned, I would see yet another glimpse of one of them and the process would start all over again.

Sometimes I would get close to one and a puff of strange smelling dust would fill my nose and they would be gone. Later I found out that they were giving me some kind of herbal medicine at those times. It was considered by them to be a "wedding present". I considered it annoying. Hetar considered it dangerous. He was very upset that they were messing with my biological systems and wasn't happy again until he finished analyzing exactly what it was they were blowing in my face.

Once Paul and I were walking on a wide clear path in the Hollis forest and I was complaining to him about what they just did to me and how it frightened me. He said that he wished they would do something like that to him, because they more or less left him alone physically. Just as he said that, a branch came out of no where and tangled itself in his backpack. Then moments later, as we walked off the path into the forest proper, the tree tops rattled and big sticks came raining down around us. Not one stick hit us.

Every time I talked about it, Paul assured me that the little people were not doing anything harmful and were just a bit over zealous in their play. Still, it bothered me how they would find ways to split us up. I became afraid that with the ease they could take over my body and how quickly they could move through the woods when they did, that I would black out and find myself lost in the deep woods without a clue to which way was home. That, coupled with the ease at which they seemed able to draw Paul away from me, made me more and more reluctant to go into the woods.

Finally, after some discussion, Paul and I told the little people that we were not going to be able to work with them until they promised to abide by some simple rules. First and foremost, they had to ask, not just take over.

At first it was difficult to get them to follow the rules, simply because it seemed there were so many of them and no matter where we went, we ran into a new group of them. Nevertheless, they all seemed to fall into place rather quickly after we spoke to Molanie about it and asked her to have a word with them.

Over time, I came to trust them and even love them. Now they no longer scare me. As a matter of fact, when Paul and I were planning our "modern" wedding, we talked to Ed White Eagle about the way his people got married. He told us about baskets and dolls. Paul gathered bull rush reeds and then White Eagle wove a beautiful little basket using nothing but the bullrushes. He lined it with sweetgrass and sage. Then he made a lid and gave it to us as a wedding gift. He showed us how to make "promise dolls" and Paul and I made our promises to each other standing on the same exact boulder we were sitting on when we first met the little people. It was a magical ceremony. There were dancing little people lights everywhere and it seemed like the forest was alive and watching as we exchanged our dolls and promises. Later on when we got married in the "legal" sense, we used the vows and words from this special bonding in our ceremony.

Once in a while when we go to a forest where we have never been before, we still may encounter little people who don't know about our ground rules or who have to be reminded. We are glad they always listen after being informed of the rules.

Paul and I have learned many things from these unusually, happy little people. If I would have to choose the most important thing I have learned from them, it is probably the thing that bothered me the most in the beginning. That is, their sense of play.

<u>*Paul*</u>
Wannalancette

In the Hollis forest where Michelle and I met the little people, we also ran into a very old and powerful spirit.

One evening after talking to the little people, Michelle and I were walking out of the forest down the pathway that lead to the road. I felt a large number of presences lining the path to the left of us. Michelle told me she was spectrally seeing a great many Native looking individuals. She seemed very shaken and scared. Later she told me it was because she saw them as they looked at the time of their deaths— beaten, slashed, and covered in blood. By the edge of the forest we both stopped. I could sense a large presence directly in front of us.

"What is that, Mick?" I asked.

"I see that large, blue blob again. It looks like it's waving its arms or something," Michelle answered.

This was the second time we were in the forest and this blob like being stood in front of us, blocking our path to the car. This time I decided not to just pass by. This time I felt we needed to investigate.

I walked over and reached out with my hands to feel the energy more clearly.

"I don't sense anything malicious in it. What do you think?" I asked.

"I don't know." She still seemed shaken up a bit. "I'm not sure I want to open up to something like this. Even if it is trying to communicate."

I opened my senses. "Oh, wait a minute, I can feel Rove nearby." His presence was strong. I felt safe. Michelle must have felt him too.

"Okay let's try it," she said. "But, if it's something not so nice what do we do?"

I said, "I just heard Rove say it was okay. Alright, let's try it."

Michelle closed her eyes and I could feel her enter through the top of my head. A moment later I heard a deep raspy voice coming out of her body.

"Who? Who are you? What are you doing here?" the person asked.

I walked forward and looked at them as best I could in the dark forest. There was just enough light to make out the outline of Michelle's body and face.

"My name here is Paul. My name in the stars is Andrew," I said.

"Andrew? Little Andrew?" the person asked.

"Little Andrew. That's what the little people said I used to be called, little Andrew," I said.

"Little Andrew! Little Andrew. It's you. You've come back like you said you would. I've waited. I waited like I promised. Little Andrew, it's good to see you!" the person said in a tone of excitement.

"Who are you?" I asked. "You seem to know me, but I have to tell you that I do not remember very much of anything about the time I was little Andrew."

"You said you would not remember when you came back. That is expected. It is I, Wannalancette. I am Sachem of the Pennacook. Chief of the Pawtuckaway," the person said.

"Wanna-who?" I asked.

"Wannalancette. Little Andrew, you helped me so much. I could not forget you," he said.

"You're telling me you knew me. How long ago was that?" I asked.

"Oh, I don't know," he replied.

"What about a date? Do you know a date, the number of the year when you last were alive?" I asked.

There was a moment's silence. "I do not know if it was my last year, but I remember 1 - 7 - 6 - 8. Yes, one, seven, six, eight." He pronounced each number individually.

"1768? You've been dead over two hundred years! You're telling me you've been waiting all this time just to speak to me?" I asked.

"Little Andrew helped me and my people so much. I owe much to little Andrew. You helped Wannalancette. You told me not to fight. You said they would kill us anyway, that we should not fight. That it was wrong to kill. You were right," Wannalancette said.

"Not to fight. I told you not to fight, and you died?" I said. Shock ran through me when I made the connection between what he just said and the condition of the spirits Michelle said she saw on the hill.

"You said if we fought them, we would loose and they would kill us anyway. If we killed, we would have to come back and would not be free. Oh, little Andrew, it's good to see you again."

I stood looking at the man. Even though his presence was very strong, he seemed to be having trouble speaking. He had a thick Native accent and the way his head moved, it looked like he was having trouble seeing out of Michelle's eyes. Nevertheless, all the time he spoke, his tone of voice was very excited.

I did not understand what was going on or what he was talking about. What did he mean, I told him not to fight? Why would I do that? Why should anyone stand there and be killed.

"How were you killed Wannalancette?" I asked.

"Not me. My people. All the Pennacook. The last of my people were killed by Mohawk. They killed them here in this place, then let me live to shame me."

I stood in shock. "All your people, and they left you alive?" I asked.

"To shame me. Many of us died when they first came. My father made peace with them. He said we must make peace with the English. Little Andrew told me the same thing. Many of us died from sickness when they came."

"You're talking about the white man?" I asked.

"Yes. When they came, many of my people became sick and died. Later they put us on the Wickasee and many died there. Some of us were able to leave and come to this place to hide. But they found us here, the Mohawk, and they killed us all," he said.

"Why? Why did another tribe kill you?" I asked.

"They listened to the French. The Mohawk traded with the French. The French and the English did not get along. The Pawtuckaway were friends of the English.

"Friends of the English?"

"Yes. We made peace with them. They said we had to be Christian, so many of us pretended to be Christian to be at peace. But we still lived like Pennacook," he said.

"You pretended to be Christian?" I repeated with surprise. "Why?"

"Yes. Even I pretended to be Christian. They kept telling us if we were truly their friends we must not be like savages and must be like Christians. To keep peace we pretended to be Christian. When we were with them we were Christian, but when we left their English homes and went into the forest we would live as Pennacook again. We could not let them see us like this or they would not trust us," he explained.

"So you gave up your way of life to be at peace with them," I said.

"No, we only pretended. We did not give up being Pennacook. We would never give up our way of life. We only pretended. But it was hard."

"Excuse me, this is all so much." I was reeling trying to make sense of everything. "Why did you stay here? Why did you wait for little Andrew to return?"

"Little Andrew did so much to help me. You asked me to remember five things for you. Oh, I cannot remember them now but I will. I promise. It has been a long time but I will remember them," he said. "There is a voice. It says I must go."

I knew the voice was Rovere. "Good bye Wannalancette," I said. I looked at him in consternation not knowing what to say or do next. Finally I said, "Thank you."

He reached over and grabbed my arms then pulled me over to hug me.

"Thank you, little Andrew. Thank you." Then he closed his eyes and was gone. A moment later, Michelle's eyes opened and she looked at me. I could barely make out the whites of her eyes in the darkness.

"Wow! What was that all about? He seemed to know you," Michelle said.

"He knew someone named little Andrew. I don't know, I mean, this is something else. Can you feel all the presences around here? Look up here." I pointed to a small hill to the side of the path.

"Oooooh," gasped Michelle.

"What, what is it?" I asked.

"Can't you see them?" Michelle asked.

"No, but I can sure feel them. I sense no maliciousness, but the energy is very high isn't it?" I said.

I walked over to the base of the hill. I felt the presences approach me. They came in groups of twos and threes, as they seemed to walk right through me.

"Watch out!" Michelle shouted.

"You don't have to be afraid, Michelle. They're just spirits, and they are our friends." I said.

"I know, it's just," and her voice faded.

I stood there for a few minutes as the seemingly unending number of people walked through me. It felt like it was a form of greeting.

Over the next few weeks we spoke to Wannalancette on and off. He began to recall some of the five things that he said little Andrew asked him to remember. It is not yet time to share some of the things, but the first thing he remembered was about my current life.

Wannalancette said that little Andrew asked him to tell me that there would be a delay in the paperwork from the "magistrates". He said that it would shorten the period for the other papers to be done and that I had to prepare everything ahead of time, because there would be no time after.

Michelle and I pondered on the meaning of these words. We figured that there might be a problem with the paperwork that would have to be filed for Immigration and Naturalization so that I could stay in the United States. He said I had to make sure to have all the paperwork done ahead of time. "A head of what time?" I wondered.

At the time, Michelle's divorce was just becoming finalized in the Supreme Court and the amount of paperwork to be processed was enormous. Along with the mounds of INS applications that had to be correctly filled out it was almost overwhelming for the two of us. We had been putting off doing some of the INS paper work because we figured it would be easier to do once her divorce was final. Besides, we wanted to take one issue at a time.

Based on the court date of the divorce, we believed we had plenty of time. Erring on the side of caution, we decided to take Wannalancette's warning seriously and did the paperwork necessary for INS even though we had to leave some sections of it open until we got "last minute" information.

Several days after Wannalancette told us about the paperwork, Michelle got a call from her lawyer. There was a problem. In the process of changing over the computer system at the lawyer's office, a terrible mistake happened and all of Michelle's records were destroyed. All of the information and paperwork had to be recreated from scratch. The hearing date had to be delayed and the time for filing for a new hearing date in a safe time frame had passed. She could not get another hearing date until the end of July. After that we only had forty-eight hours to go to the INS to get everything else done.

There was no way either Michelle or I could have ever known about the delay. Wannalancette's prediction proved to be accurate and true. That meant that there was the possibility that little Andrew was a reality and somehow he knew the future as well. We were both surprised and stunned by the confirmation.

In the weeks and months that followed we spoke to Wannalancette and began to learn about the Pennacook people and some of their beliefs. For instance, as we walked along Wickasee Island where many Pennacook people had died, Wannalancette pointed to where a tree had been cut down.

"Look, they cut down the trees. That is no good. A tree is planted over those who die so that their soul may travel up its trunk and find its way to the sky with the Creator. Every time a person dies you plant a tree.

Wannalancette pointed to another large tree. "See the faces in the tree, those are the souls of the people who died under the tree that are making their way to the Creator."

I looked at the tree and was amazed. I could clearly see several areas in the trunk where there were formations that looked very much like the faces of people. The gentle beauty of aboriginal beliefs struck me once again.

Michelle and I went to the local library and did some research into the history of the Pennacook and found out that Wannalancette really did exist. Indeed, at the entrance to Wickasee island is a plaque bearing his name.

The history books tell of Wannalancette leaving the area with his people and going north. Later, when he returned alone, history records he said his people were safe in Canada. This is far different from the story Wannalancette told us of what happened. After all, what Chief would ever leave his people?

The story Wannalancette told was about the ways the Pawtuckaway people were killed by sickness and genocide at the hands of Europeans and other Natives. The final destruction of Wannalancette's people took place in the very same small forest in Hollis where we met him. But more than stories of death, Wannalancette taught us stories of life.

In the time since we have met him, he has taught us how to build everything from shelters to children's toys from bullrush reeds. He showed us how to make medicines from leaves that grow on the forest floor. He told stories of how his people lived, what they believed and how they survived and maintained peace for countless generations.

Our contact with Wannalancette continues, as does his teaching. So far he has revealed to us three of the five secrets he holds for Little Andrew. Each has turned out to be of incredible value to us. When it is time, he will remember the last two secrets.

Wannalancette has since been joined by many of the Pennacook people, including his father Passaconaway. Passaconaway is a man recorded in historical documents by the English settlers as having magical powers of the supernatural; a man, who we are told, once went to the water's edge and called out to the fish, "My people are hungry! Please brother fish, feed us!" and the fish, themselves, jumped from the water onto the land.

The tiny stretch of forest in Hollis, New Hampshire is filling with the spirits of aboriginals who once lived on Turtle Island. They say they have come back to wait for the time of tuning. They have been told that once the younger brother (modern man) is corrected by the mother, he will be more humble and will be willing to learn the wisdom of his elder brother (the aboriginals). At that time, they tell us they will be given new bodies so they may walk among the younger brother and teach them. This is foretold in the prophecy's of many Native peoples. In their new bodies, the Elder Brother will join with the true Younger Brother and together they will turn a page in a much larger prophecy that will bring us from the prophecy's edge.

<u>Michelle</u>
Voices of the sky

Our odyssey continues. Over the last while, Paul and I have learned more about the Earth than I ever thought I would know. We have seen and spoken to all manner of beings — beings I never would have believed in if I didn't see them with my own eyes. We've seen beings that could best be labeled sasquatch, little people, tree people, and at the time of this writing we have a multi-dimensional Edge in our backyard, courtesy of Rovere. The forest behind our home is occupied by a very large tribe of passed away Natives, lead by Passaconaway. This weekend, we have to finish building our wigwam because the Native spirits would like a place to meet with us and teach us but don't like to enter our "English house."

All the while that these amazing Earth theme events are going on, *the Voices of the Sky* continue. Rovere, Hetar, Alex, Molanie and many more beings who live in the stars come to visit us on a regular basis. We also are "gathered" by them to visit with them in their own environment where we can talk to them physically face to face.

They talk to us and teach. Some of the things they teach us are very hard to imagine and fit into our paradigm. We question things, explore their total meanings in both our own lives and the universe. This challenges us to grow and expand our consciousness.

The Voices of the Sky tell us we are on the edge of an amazing prophecy that will give birth to a new Earth. They also said that Paul and I are not unique. Countless people across the world are being asked to find their *Completers* and *Reflections*, wake up and get to work.

To these people, their message is simple, be true to your inner self and the special things that move your soul closer to Creation. It is a lesson that is easier said than done. Paul and I found that a road map would have been a lot of help on our own journey. Then it occurred to us, by keeping records and accounts of all that has happened on our own journey as we did, we have created a road map of sorts that others could use to help them on their way. We have the resources and the knowledge needed to get this road map into the hands of those who may benefit from it.

Maybe this was the point of all the difficulties we faced and all the wonder we discovered? Maybe it is the reason why the *Voices of the Earth* and the *Voices of the Sky* have blessed us with their company and teachings.

Regardless of the reason, Paul and I are both honored that we were chosen to bring their words to you. It is worth every sleepless night, every tear we cried and every seemingly endless hour of anguish we endured.

The anguish and tears did end and they were replaced with a joy that we had not known before. Remember this when your journey seems too hard to face. A great

Teacher of ours, Yasui, once told us, "When a darkness falls, the path you chose in the light and in better times remains the same even though you cannot see it in the darkness. But if you remain on the same path that you've chosen in light, it will become light again soon."

As Alex would say, "Be good to each other."

For more information on Sweetgrass Press Titles and Authors
Check our our website at:
http://www.sweetgrasspress.com

Email: info@sweetgrasspress.com

Sweetgrass Press also recommends the following websites:

Voices of the Earth
http://www.earthvoices.org

&

The Electric Wigwam
http://www.electricwigwam.com

For more information on Paul and Michelle Wedel visit

http://www.sweetgrasspress/wedelbio.html

or

http://www.sweetgrasspress/prophecysedge.html

You can write to Paul and Michelle:

Michelle LaVigne Wedel & Paul Wedel
C/O Sweetgrass Press
P.O. Box 1862
Merrimack, NH 03054

Email to:

paulwedel@sweetgrasspress.com
michellewedel@sweetgrasspress.com

www.ingramcontent.com/pod-product-compliance
Lightning Source LLC
Chambersburg PA
CBHW022147050726
47590CB00002B/593